INVENTING AMERICAN MODERNISM

JOSEPH HUDNUT,

WALTER GROPIUS,

AND THE

BAUHAUS LEGACY

AT HARVARD

INVENTING

AMERICAN

MODERNISM

JILL PEARLMAN

UNIVERSITY OF VIRGINIA PRESS
Charlottesville and London

University of Virginia Press

© 2007 by the Rector and Visitors of the University of Virginia

All rights reserved

Printed in the United States of America on acid-free paper

First published 2007

9 8 7 6 5 4 3 2 1

LIBRARY OF CONGRESS CATALOGING-IN-PUBLICATION DATA

Pearlman, Jill E., 1954–
Inventing American modernism: Joseph Hudnut, Walter Gropius, and
the Bauhaus legacy at Harvard / Jill Pearlman.
p.   cm.
Includes bibliographical references and index.
ISBN-13: 978-0-8139-2602-5 (cloth: alk. paper)
1. Hudnut, Joseph, 1886–1968. 2. Harvard University.
Graduate School of Design. 3. Gropius, Walter, 1883–1969.
4. Modern movement (Architecture)—United States. I. Title.
NA2304.H37P43 2007
720.9—dc22
2006028539

This book is published in association with the Center for American Places,
Santa Fe, New Mexico, and Staunton, Virginia (www.americanplaces.org).

FOR PAUL, CLARE, AND SAM

CONTENTS

Acknowledgments   ix

Introduction   1

1 Hudnut: A Brief Memoir, Long Past Due   11

2 Modern Movements in the Ivy   50

3 Modernism Triumphant   85

4 Trumpet Blasts   123

5 Conflicting Views of House and Town   155

6 The Battle over Basic Design   200

Notes   239

Index   271

ACKNOWLEDGMENTS

During the long course of writing this book, many people gave me crucial assistance. The Graham Foundation for Advanced Studies in the Fine Arts provided a grant essential for the writing of the book. The Bowdoin College Faculty Resources Fund gave me a generous subvention for the images reproduced here. For their never-ending support and wise counsel over many years, I am deeply grateful to Neil Harris and Katherine Taylor of the University of Chicago, and to Sally Promey of the University of Maryland. I thank the incomparable Mary Daniels, Special Collections Librarian at Harvard's Frances Loeb Library, for her enormous help and friendship over the years, and for opening many doors for me along the way.

I am also grateful to the archivists and librarians at Harvard's Pusey Archives and Houghton Library; the University Archives and Columbiana Library as well as the Avery Archive at Columbia University. I also thank Cynthia Field of the Smithsonian Institution; Tony Wrenn, former archivist at the American Institute of Architects; Leslie Edwards at the Cranbrook Archives; and Bridget Gillies of the University of East Anglia. I am indebted, too, to the librarians and archivists at the Archives of American Art; Auburn University Special Collections; Bentley Historical Library at the University of Michigan; the George Arents Research Library at Syracuse University; the Smithsonian Institution Archives; University of Virginia, Manuscripts and Archives; and Yale University, Manuscripts and Archives.

For their careful reading of my manuscript and their invaluable suggestions, I thank Kathleen James-Chakraborty, University of California, Berkeley, and Joan Ockman, Columbia University, both of whom made this a better book. At Bowdoin College, Nancy Grant came to my rescue a number of times and, with Ruth Maschino, has set me on the road to technological proficiency. Rosie Armstrong has helped me in countless ways, with the administrative tasks that come with putting a book together and by weighing in with needed opinions when I no longer had any. The staff at the University of Virginia Press could not have been more helpful as I prepared this manuscript for publication. I am particularly grateful to the Director of the Press, Penny Kaiserlian, and to Ellen Satrom, managing editor. Susan Brady read the book with great care, and I am indebted to her for her suggestions and comments.

I had the great fortune to interview several alumni and teachers from the Hudnut/Gropius era at Harvard's GSD. I am especially grateful to the late G. Holmes Perkins for an extremely informative and lengthy conversation. Many thanks, too, to Richard Filipowski for his time and for the photographs and papers that he shared with me from the early 1950s. The late Willo von Moltke, Henry Cobb, Martin Meyerson, William Lyman, John Kausal, Frederic Day Jr., and John Black all received me warmly in their homes to talk about their educations in modern architecture, while I met with Jean-Paul Carlhian and John Harkness at their offices, now long ago, as I first began this project. Thanks also to Elizabeth Deviney, who spoke to me about Hudnut in his final years, and to Christiane C. Collins, for sharing with me her expertise on Werner Hegemann.

I owe my parents more than I can say. I regret that my father did not live to see this book finished, not least of all because he personally would have ensured that it quickly went into a second printing. Clare and Sam, who grew up with this project, have made every day lively and full of joy. Finally, my greatest debt is to Paul, not only for his patient and thoughtful criticism of every chapter, but for companionship beyond my wildest dreams.

INVENTING AMERICAN MODERNISM

INTRODUCTION

From the late 1930s to the early 1950s, the Harvard University Graduate School of Design (GSD) played a critical part in shaping the course of modern architecture and the modern city. Architects, planners, teachers, and students from all over the world turned to the newly formed GSD, with its celebrated faculty and curriculum, for the path to modern design. Prominent graduates and teachers—including Walter Gropius, Marcel Breuer, I. M. Pei, Paul Rudolph, Hugh Stubbins, Edward Larrabee Barnes, Philip Johnson, Henry N. Cobb, Ulrich Franzen, and members of TAC (The Architects Collaborative)—also helped spread the GSD's modern gospel in the postwar era through their many prestigious commissions and through teaching in architecture schools across the United States. The GSD was so successful in disseminating its brand of modern architecture and urbanism in an era of unprecedented building that it is no exaggeration to say that the school transformed the physical landscape worldwide.

The importance of the GSD in this era is widely recognized, though historians and critics have mostly remarked on only a small part of its history. Publications that discuss the Harvard School in its modernist era share a common argument—that Bauhaus founder Walter Gropius transformed Harvard's old Beaux-Arts School of Architecture into a "Harvard-Bauhaus," a radically new school with a single outlook. I begin with a different premise in this book, that Gropius by no means transformed Harvard's program alone and that the GSD was not merely an offshoot of the Bauhaus. Though the charismatic Gropius and his

1

ideas came to dominate the GSD and, ultimately, American architectural education and practice, the School's modern history was far more complex and rich than an exclusive focus on Gropius and Bauhaus objectives would suggest. In making this argument, my book unravels the story of the Bauhaus legacy in the United States and sets the history of modern architecture and urbanism in a new light.

The central figure in my book is Joseph Hudnut. Though Hudnut has gotten mostly passing mention in histories of modern architecture, he was the founder of the GSD in 1936 and, until the early 1950s, a major player in making it the world's premier school of modern architecture. Hudnut's progressive educational views and the unlikely path that he followed to modernism had been shaped by a few different experiences: his "civic design" work in the early 1920s with the German city planner Werner Hegemann; his sustained interest in the history of architecture; and his engagement with the democratic educational philosophy of John Dewey. Hudnut also owed a debt to the Americanized Beaux-Arts architectural system in which he had gotten his own education, despite the fact that he devoted much effort to overhauling what he considered its myriad shortcomings.

For a brief moment during the 1930s, many regarded Hudnut as a hugely important figure in the architectural world, a guiding light in the quest to invent an American modernism in the fields of architecture and city design. In these Depression years, with building at a standstill, progressive-minded architects and planners turned to the schools of architecture for new ideas and advancement in their fields. Hudnut was the only educator situated in a lofty post—first at Columbia and then Harvard—to bring modern design and new teaching methods to the students. When the time came in 1935 for Harvard to hire a new dean to overhaul, modernize, and lead its three different Schools of Architecture, City Planning, and Landscape Architecture in a new direction, Hudnut was the clear choice. As the departing dean, George Edgell, declared: Hudnut makes all other educators in the field seem "like milksops."[1]

Hudnut's moment in the sun was destined to be short. He was a fuddy-duddy in appearance, a musty figure who clearly lacked the allure of those in the avant-garde, like Le Corbusier or Gropius. Added to this, he was modest and, unlike either Gropius or Corbu, content to direct the show from behind the stage. Gropius himself observed early in their time together that "on account of his modesty, Hudnut is much too much in the shade, and people generally do not know of his rare qualities and strength."[2] Moreover, in the decades that modern architecture and urbanism captured hearts and minds, Hudnut was merely a university administrator. Though he may have wielded power that allowed him to guide key developments in the architectural fields from behind the scenes, what could be duller than a dean? Hudnut had given up designing in the early 1920s and so had no buildings or modern plans of his own to match his pronouncements on modern design and his progressive educational schemes. Besides, Gropius was at Harvard by 1937 to do his own bidding, as was Marcel Breuer, and Mies van der Rohe soon after took up his post in Chicago. There was no longer any need for a middleman like Hudnut to serve as a broker between the modernists, their work, and the students who aspired to practice in a modern vein.

By the end of the 1930s, those inclined toward modern design looked to Gropius for guidance rather than Hudnut. In the years that followed, Gropius continued to sideline Hudnut to the extent that in 1952, when he left the GSD, Gropius got credit in the national press for having been the sole director of the School.[3] At Harvard, the *Crimson* hailed Gropius as the GSD's "spiritual leader": "To the outside world he was the school; to much of the faculty, he, not Dean Joseph Hudnut, set the policy; and to the students, he was the ideal architect, the master mold into which they poured their talents."[4] For more than fifty years, Hudnut had remained on the sideline, and his time at the GSD with Gropius is remembered as the era of the "Harvard-Bauhaus."

Although Hudnut brought Gropius to Harvard and then worked closely with him for several years, Hudnut ultimately tried to prevent the Bauhaus master from dominating the GSD. Challenging the hero of the Bauhaus, of course, did little to endear Hudnut to the many who revered Gropius. But by the early 1940s, Hudnut had understood that his own ideas of modern architecture and modern urbanism differed radically from Gropius's. While Gropius was determined to promote the Bauhaus philosophy at the GSD—especially through the creation of a yearlong Basic Design preliminary course modeled on that of the German school—Hudnut stood firmly against it. Moreover, Hudnut did not think that Gropius had advanced his students beyond the kind of pristine abstract architecture that had dominated the modern movement in the 1920s. Hudnut had greatly admired buildings like those at the Weissenhof Siedlung (1927) or displayed at the International Style exhibition at the Museum of Modern Art (1932). But he also believed that two decades hence, modern architecture should have moved beyond this strident era of design. Finally, Hudnut adamantly opposed the "de-concentrated" functionalist approach to urbanism, akin to the CIAM's 1933 Athens Charter, that Gropius taught his students.

In contrast to Gropius's agenda, Hudnut sought a more responsive modern architecture and urbanism, a humanistic approach to design that expressed "emotional content," as he liked to say—spontaneity, symbolic values, individual concerns—and he embraced the larger, surrounding contexts of design. Pedagogically, Hudnut sought to bring modern architecture and urbanism in tune with those humanistic qualities that had made cities and buildings great in the past, though he had no intention of returning to the Beaux-Arts teaching methods. Hudnut tried, above all, to create strong ties between the education of planners, architects, and landscape architects, preparing them to tackle together the ultimate design problem—the city. Creating an urban pattern that worked to foster social harmony and to satisfy individual needs and the needs of the human spirit in a world increasingly shaped by industrialization, cars, and suburbanization—this was the focus of Hudnut's efforts at Harvard, and it was the reason he had founded the GSD.

Given Hudnut's humanistic approach to education and design, it was perhaps inevitable that Hudnut and Gropius began battling each other for control of the GSD and for the direction of modern architecture and planning in the United States. The two continued to clash throughout their years at Harvard. While Hudnut became a noted and fierce critic of the Bauhaus pedagogy, Gropius dismissed Hudnut's approach to architecture and urbanism by referring to it insultingly as "applied archaeology." Gropius ultimately won their battle, and the result was that he, rather than Hudnut, decided the direction of modernism at Harvard and beyond. If the GSD had followed the path Hudnut had wanted it to take, modern buildings and the modern city might well have been different.

Hudnut's prominent position at Harvard afforded him tremendous opportunity to promote his ideas of modernism both at the School and elsewhere. Yet, he failed to do so. Why he failed, and why Gropius succeeded so well, are questions my book considers. Was Gropius's modernism so compelling, or was he simply the better salesman? Did Hudnut offer a sound argument? Was it even possible to sell the idea of a modernism that openly embraced certain traditional values in the interwar and postwar era? What means did Hudnut and Gropius use to promote their views, especially to students at the GSD? And how did students respond?

While Hudnut and Gropius play the largest parts in my book, the cast of characters also includes others teaching with them at the GSD, Marcel Breuer, Martin Wagner, and Christopher Tunnard, as well several other architects, city planners, and landscape architects, some from abroad and others homegrown. From their posts at the GSD, these modern designers also helped transform teaching and practice in their fields. The most artistically talented of them all, Breuer served as the inspirational tastemaker in the design studios. And while Wagner brought his uncompromising moral conscience to the GSD, particularly in the areas of housing and planning, Tunnard introduced new forms, materials, and methods in landscape architecture, as well the notion of social improvement through landscape design. With the GSD set squarely in the middle of Harvard, the wider social and intellectual tendencies governing the university from the 1930s into the postwar era affected developments at the School and in the architectural fields. In addition, many individuals and groups from within and outside the architectural professions helped determine the direction of the modernist GSD: Harvard's president, James B. Conant; certain powerful alumni and students; and various professional organizations, including the Museum of Modern Art and the short-lived but important American Society of Planners and Architects. In bringing these people and groups into the history of modern architecture, my book fills in a number of gaps and sheds light on important episodes that have gone unnoted.

In addition to holding his post at Harvard, Hudnut played the part of a public intellectual in the Deweyan mold, educating and encouraging citizens outside the university to participate in the architectural and urbanistic matters that affected their lives. I explore in the pages that follow the various ways in which Hudnut brought his expertise to the public realm: he published widely in the professional and architectural presses, lectured frequently in a variety of forums, and headed a number of important modern architectural events and organizations. When Hudnut spoke out on architectural issues, he did so with particular eloquence. As William Wurster once remarked, Hudnut's writing and educational work are "as creative as the work of any contemporary designer."[5]

In the public sphere as at the GSD, Hudnut ultimately advanced a philosophy of architecture that set him apart from the mainstream of modernists. He was among the very first critics of modern architecture (if not the first) from within the circle of modernists in the United States—and a vociferous one at that. And although in 1945 Hudnut coined the term "post-modern" in his essay "The Post-Modern House," he was no architectural postmodernist either.[6] Just as he disdained the sterile modern houses and other stark buildings of the 1940s, he would have despised much of the facile ersatz architecture that began surfacing under the name "postmodernism" three decades later.

Others besides Hudnut began to reassess the direction of modern architecture with a critical eye, especially in the postwar era. After 1945, the consummate insider, historian Sigfried Giedion, a major player in the Congrès internationaux d'Architecture Moderne (CIAM), led the heated debate over monumentality and the need for modernists to design large-scale symbolic buildings.[7] In 1947, Lewis Mumford—never quite an insider—led the way in a second controversial line of reassessment by championing the Bay Area architects for emphasizing the "non-mechanical" elements of design in their work: the quality of the local terrain, the climate, way of life, the individual and commonplace aspects of their own region. Similarly, in England, the "New Empiricism" challenged the purist modern aesthetic, inspired by the work of Swedish architects who had turned to local materials and a homey aesthetic.[8] Several prominent modern architects had also broken away from the mechanistic perfection of their early work. Le Corbusier had first embraced the vernacular as early as 1930 in his unrealized Errazuris House, with its irregular rock-faced lower walls, planned for a site in Chile. Alvar Aalto certainly departed from the rigid international style, and J. J. P. Oud dared to reintroduce decorative elements, symmetry, and hierarchical massing in his Shell Building, begun in 1938 in the Hague. Frank Lloyd Wright, of course, always stood apart from the mainstream of modernists, embracing regional expression in his modern designs, symbolic representation, qualities of the organic, and deep ties to the natural surroundings.

Hudnut's critical reflections included many of these same issues that Giedion, Mumford, and others—Bruno Zevi, for one—had raised, though he did not always agree with them. For example, while he too argued for symbolism in modern architecture as Giedion did, he saw the need for it even at the smallest level and not just in the monumental. And while Hudnut embraced the idea of regionalism in architecture and urbanism, he remained skeptical about the Bay Region style, the "woodshed-and let-your-suspenders-show" domestic architecture that, like the international style, seemed to him lacking in what mattered in a home—the feeling of domesticity.[9] Hudnut weighed in on issues of concern to other critics of modern architecture, but he was also a loner who preferred to make his own nuanced analyses rather than joining a particular side in established debates. One thing clearly set him apart from other critics in the interwar and postwar years: his passionate concern, above all else, for what modernism was doing to the city.

Mine is not the first book on the Hudnut/Gropius years at the GSD. That honor goes to Klaus Herdeg, author of *The Decorated Diagram: Harvard Architecture and the Failure of the Bauhaus Legacy* (1983). Herdeg's is the book of an architect and polemicist, written with a keen eye and intended to sharpen the eyes of other designers. He makes no attempt in his slim volume to offer, in his words, a "minihistory of the Gropius and Breuer years at Harvard and the exploits of their former students."[10] Hudnut does not figure at all in Herdeg's book. A question that the critic Clement Greenberg had put to Herdeg prompted the book: Why are so many new buildings so ugly? As Herdeg realized, many of those "ugly" large-scale urban buildings had been designed by GSD alumni from the Gropius era. His book sets out to find a connection between those buildings and what their architects had learned in school from Gropius. After comparing the content of a few Gropius-era design problems and a series of buildings designed decades later by the likes of Pei, Johnson, and Barnes, among others, Herdeg answered Greenberg's query: the cause of the ugly buildings from the 1970s and 1980s emanates from the "failure" of the Bauhaus legacy. Herdeg's engaging polemic had a didactic purpose: to assure that architects learned to avoid the mistakes of the Gropius-era graduates. Perhaps inadvertently, it also roused the curiosity of historians, like me, to explore the Bauhaus legacy.

In 2002, Anthony Alofsin published a book that surveys a century of architectural education at Harvard, from the 1890s to 1990s. Alofsin's *The Struggle for Modernism: Architecture, Landscape Architecture, and City Planning at Harvard* argues that the history of modernism at Harvard did not begin with the creation of the GSD or the start of the Hudnut/Gropius era but with the opening of its School of Architecture forty years earlier. Alofsin claims that back in 1895, when an Americanized Beaux-Arts system of architectural education was firmly in place there, Harvard began its "struggle toward modernism" by emphasizing collaboration among students in architecture, landscape architecture, and city planning. In the first half of his book, Alofsin attempts to cite instances in which collaboration among students occurred before 1936, while, at the same time, offering details of curricula, student assignments, and course descriptions.[11]

The problem with Alofsin's interpretation is that it places far too much emphasis on the idea of collaboration. On the one hand, there has always has been tremendous common ground—discussion, shared concerns, and even occasional cooperative projects—among the three fields of architecture, landscape architecture, and city planning. On the other hand, it is a stretch to argue, as Alofsin does, that a conscious "philosophy of collaboration" governed the architectural fields at Harvard before 1936.[12] Instead, the common thread running through those four decades at Harvard was the Americanized Beaux-Arts method of architectural education found at all elite universities. It was this method of education that Hudnut decisively overturned, first at Columbia and then at Harvard. Ada Louise Huxtable is much closer to the mark than Alofsin when she writes in her 1969 obituary of Gropius: "Until the '30s, American students had been taught in a reactionary void." Huxtable did not attribute the start of a new era in education to Gropius but claimed that "the credit for breaking the barricades of sterile tradition in this country and opening the frontiers of modern practice must go to another man, Joseph Hudnut."[13]

Alofsin does attempt to give Hudnut his due, and he also tries to explain the ideological differences between him and Gropius, but he does so by returning to the theme of collaboration. The essence of his argument is that Hudnut and Gropius had two different views of what collaboration meant and thus their relationship fell apart. While Hudnut embraced an "American" view, which meant that architects, landscape architects, and city planners should cooperate, Gropius's "European" perspective held that only architects and artists should collaborate, with city planners and landscape architects "irrelevant" to the process.[14] My book tells a different story: it argues that Hudnut and Gropius fought over their differing ideas of a "core" education for modern designers; over the place of history in education, in architecture, and in the city; and over what form modern architecture and the modern city should take. Ultimately, I argue that Hudnut and Gropius fought over the essence of modernism—or how to express the ideas, qualities, and spirit of the technological age in built form. The most important aspect of Hudnut's endeavors—which Alofsin does not mention—was his near-total preoccupation with establishing a modern form of "civic design" at the GSD and in the architectural fields more broadly.[15]

In the pages that follow, I have offered neither a hagiography of Hudnut nor yet another condemnation of Gropius. Gropius's brand of modern architecture and urban design has been roundly criticized for decades. And yet, no one understood better than he that the complexities of the modern world demanded a new role for architects as team players in a socially minded architectural practice. By dint of his powerful personality, Gropius's ideas ultimately carried the day. Nevertheless, my book shows that Hudnut also played a key role in the history of modernism. As an educator and a critic, he tried to advance modern architecture beyond its severe beginnings to a humane and expressive social art. Moreover, in this same dual capacity, he worked tirelessly to create a modern city shaped by humanistic values. Though his own time was not entirely propitious for him, Hudnut clearly deserves a place in history for his part in inventing American modernism.

1 HUDNUT

A Brief Memoir, Long Past Due

I am just now reading the new book on Patrick Geddes . . .

bad writing, but some useful stuff. *Moral,* Vi, write your own

memoirs and get going at it so we will have long and juicy ones.

—JOHN GAUS TO HUDNUT, 1944

A colleague remembered Vi Hudnut as "the least modern individual you could find." He never looked the part of the architectural avant-garde, preferring a crumpled, baggy tweed suit and unstylish glasses to the bow-tie and owl-round black spectacles that Le Corbusier had made the requisite fashion. Small in stature, he was "physically unprepossessing," in the words of another colleague, who also thought him less distinguished in appearance than many of his academic contemporaries, but for his high forehead that made him look intellectual. Walking across the Harvard campus, Hudnut often shuffled and gazed downward, either out of shyness or preoccupation. In the classroom, his lectures were undramatic and informal, and his voice was not always audible. He was said to have had "a small mouth, but an excess of saliva and often appeared to have a cough drop in his mouth, so that occasionally led to problems of delivery." He had no slide operator to advance the slides on screen at a time when professors took pride in how many they could speed through "machine-gun style" in an hour. When he wanted to change a slide, he would journey from up front at the screen to the back of the dark room, stumbling over chairs before pushing through to the next image, and then amble back to the platform. He used no notes and no lectern. Despite his erratic manner, Hudnut managed to express his ideas with elegance and clarity and to demonstrate a "breadth of sensitivity" as he interpreted a period of history and its civic form.[1]

Although many people found Hudnut "shy," "quiet," and "mild-mannered," he was well known for his quick wit and his ironic and

self-deprecating humor. An amusing profile of Hudnut offered up in a Harvard newsletter quoted a colleague who remarked with awe: "See that little man in the brown tweed suit trudging across the Yard? You might not realize it, but ideas are fairly popping in his head." Hudnut's unremarkable presence betrayed the fact that he was determined, "ruthless" some even thought, a "commander without looking like it" with "supreme self-confidence." Though he looked crumpled and diffident, a colleague called him "as much an iconoclast and firebrand as the militants of the 1960s." Another colleague described him as "an idea broker" who "liked larger concepts and imagery to explain them." Because he did not carry on an architectural practice during his Harvard deanship, he was able "to range further and do more of a theoretical kind" of reflecting about the field than most other architecture and planning school deans. He had a "great talent for tact" and, reputedly, for "clever discharge of administrative duties."[2]

An official Harvard photograph of Hudnut, taken in his office in 1946, offers some clue to his preferences in politics and in art. He is pictured next to a photograph of Woodrow Wilson, whom he no doubt admired for his progressive reforms, and a print by Renoir, a more surprising choice for an avowed architectural modernist, though several such prints were among his few effects at his death.[3] Hudnut's friends and colleagues called him "Vi" in honor of a violet fragrance put out by the perfumer Richard Hudnut, who may have been a distant relation. Curiously enough, Dean Hudnut's longtime favorite architect, Eliel Saarinen, designed the Hudnut Building for the perfumer.[4]

A portrait of Gropius at Harvard looks quite different from this one of Hudnut. Gropius is often pictured with his admirers or in the center of a large group of students, bow-tied and fashionably bespectacled, though certainly not following the vogue set by Le Corbusier. Gropius was always in "iron control of himself" and perhaps even in control of the image others held of him. Until you knew him, he might have seemed unapproachable, austere, and cold, but this was far from the case. Those who worked closely with him mentioned his great sense of humor, although he was in no way lighthearted, gregarious, or outgoing. One might have expected him to be a hard-boiled logician, but he was surprisingly sentimental, romantic even, brought up on James Fenimore Cooper stories.[5]

One of his GSD colleagues, G. Holmes Perkins, described Gropius as "a revolutionary figure" and claimed that "you could feel that in the man." He was deeply committed both to his ideas of design, architecture, and teaching and to his students. No one could doubt the profundity of these commitments or that he was, in Perkins's words, "intellectually honest in everything, a completely sincere person."[6] Gropius was remarkably inspirational to numbers of his students, and they spoke reverentially of his "humility in the role of greatness, his anonymity in the role of personal genius, his purpose and positive conviction in a society too given to expediency." Many students found themselves "in awe of the great master who came from Europe to teach us the gospel."[7] Accounts from all stages of Gropius's life describe him as a charismatic spiritual leader—aptly nicknamed "Pius" since his Bauhaus days. Smoking his ever-present cigar, he would talk at length to students in his GSD studio, always with absolute confidence that what he said was the truth, persuasively so.

Walter Gropius with students in Robinson Hall, March 1946. (Courtesy of the Harvard University Archives, call no. UAV 605.1.2, G427)

It is amazing that the very different personalities of Hudnut and Gropius ever found themselves together at the Harvard GSD. Though they were close in age, Hudnut born in 1886 and Gropius in 1883, the paths that led them to this high altar shared little common ground.

Hudnut's Background

Much has been written about Gropius's life and work by historians, former students, acolytes, critics, and Gropius himself. Archives in Germany and the United States hold abundant materials pertaining to Gropius and his legacy, partly due to his own fantastic skills as a publicist, and those of his wife, Ise. Gropius and Ise worked hard throughout their lifetimes to keep the Bauhaus's and Gropius's own legacy alive.[8] It seems quite in character that Hudnut left no record of his journey, no collected papers or memoirs—though he joked about the possibility—no family members to offer recollections, and certainly no disciples. He and his wife, Claire, did not have children, and Hudnut seemed to have lost contact with his two siblings. What remained of his estate after his death in 1968 went to the local taxi driver, a woman who chauffeured the Hudnuts around the small Massachusetts town of Dover, where they lived after his Harvard years. She had no knowledge at all of Hudnut's single-minded devotion to modern architecture and urbanism.[9] Fortunately, Hudnut loved to reminisce, and he did so colorfully in the institutional records that do survive (at Harvard and scattered elsewhere) and in the many articles he wrote for professional journals and popular magazines. It was through this other career of his, as a prolific architectural critic at a time when magazine readership attained new levels, that his quiet voice reached a wide public, from the readers of women's fashion and home magazines to the architectural press. He was a rapid communicator, with a journalistic bent and a penchant for generalized conclusions, not unlike Lewis Mumford.[10]

Hudnut liked to say that his architectural career began at age ten, when he drew up plans and elevations for his family's new house in Big Rapids, Michigan, a lumbering and manufacturing town on the Muskegon River, a world apart from Gropius's Berlin birthplace. In a rather different vein from Gropius, who traced his family's architectural roots to Schinkel, Hudnut had family ties to the building world. His parents, Edward and Jane, co-owned the firm that designed and constructed Big Rapids' principal business buildings and residences, and they owned a local manufactory of building materials. The Hudnuts were among their town's prosperous families, and they sent their son to the exclusive military school nearby. After graduation and an unhappy year studying law, Joseph Hudnut enrolled in the Harvard School of Architecture.[11]

Hudnut proved to be a less than stellar student at Harvard, though it was too soon to blame his dismal performances in the History of the Ancient Styles, Drawing (the Orders), and Freehand Drawing on any modernist leanings.[12] He left Harvard in 1908, and though he planned to return after a short break, twenty-seven years passed before he did so. From Harvard, Hudnut went to Chicago and worked as a draftsman for a small architectural engineering firm in the Monadnock Building, where he impressed his colleagues as "an ingenious sort of a chap, capable of doing anything."[13] Hudnut spent two years in the inspiring environs of the Chicago Loop and then headed to the University of Michigan, where he finished his architectural degree with distinction in 1912.[14] His drawings that remain from his time at Michigan demonstrate his loyalty to the École des Beaux-Arts and to the midwestern regionalism of Frank Lloyd Wright, both held in high regard at the school.[15]

Michigan's architecture program differed at that time from those found at most other universities. The eastern and more elite university programs allied themselves with the Beaux-Arts methods of teaching, while at midwestern universities, schools of architecture generally followed an engineering-based technical approach.[16] Under Emil Lorch, a well-known figure in architectural education before the 1930s, Michigan sought a compromise between the two approaches, emphasizing both the "art" in architecture and practical building construction. Developing students' creative abilities and the artistic aspect of architecture offered the greater challenge in Lorch's compromise pedagogy. Intriguingly, Lorch met this challenge by importing contemporary methods of art education into his teaching. Specifically, Lorch turned to the "theory of Pure Design"—intended for painting and drawing—devised by Denman W. Ross, an aesthetic theorist who taught in Harvard's Department of Fine Arts from 1899 to 1935, and Arthur W. Dow, the painter and teacher.[17]

What makes this so intriguing is the web of connections between Lorch, Ross, Dow, their theory of Pure Design, and Hudnut's career—not just his early years in architecture but his fifteen years with Gropius. Pure Design shared much in common with Gropius's course in Basic Design, the famous first-year preliminary course, or *Vorkurs,* developed at

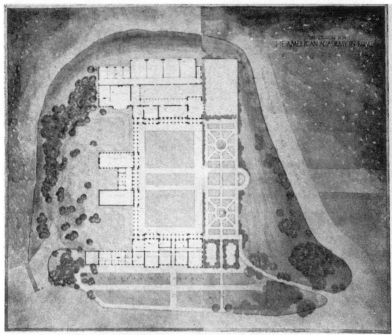

Joseph Hudnut, "Group of Buildings for the American Academy in Rome," 1912, an early drawing in the manner of the École des Beaux-Arts. (A. Alfred Taubman College of Architecture and Urban Planning Publications, box 1, *Department of Architecture, Announcement, 1912,* Bentley Historical Library, University of Michigan)

INVENTING AMERICAN MODERNISM

the Bauhaus some twenty years after the invention of Pure Design that would ultimately trigger the major battle between Hudnut and Gropius at the GSD. Both Basic Design and Pure Design sought to develop their students' creativity and imaginations through exercises in abstraction rather than through the usual slavish copying from historical examples. Ross devised student design exercises much like those Gropius would later use at the Bauhaus and at Harvard, making a quick sketch that denoted growth, or perhaps a repetitive line drawing that suggested rhythmic movement.[18] Gropius, Ross, and Dow all believed that abstraction of the elements of design—dots, shapes, color, lines—in conjunction with principles of balance and rhythm—offered essential training for future designers. Although no direct connection existed between Pure Design and Basic Design, Ross, Dow, and Gropius even spoke of their two approaches similarly, as scientific, objective, and intuitive in nature. In addition, they viewed their respective theories as democratic in character, or conceived to be, in Ross's words, "understood by everybody."[19]

There were, of course, important differences between Pure Design and the Bauhaus approach. While Gropius would offer up Basic Design as the requisite alternative to the historically based design education that he so adamantly rejected, Ross and Dow believed that Pure Design strengthened one's appreciation of the historical styles and even justified their use.[20] Moreover, while Gropius considered abstraction to be the language of modern architecture, Ross and Dow never viewed it as a style at all but as a means of developing one's visual and aesthetic sensibilities. Learning to discriminate in "tones, measures, and shapes of things," they believed, opened the way for genuine appreciation, and on rare occasion, the creation of orderly and beautiful art.[21]

Even before he studied with Lorch at Michigan, Hudnut may have encountered Ross and his theories at Harvard, though he never took a course from him. He also might have encountered Arthur Dow, whose time at Columbia overlapped with Hudnut's student days at that university. There's no mention of either Ross or Dow in any of Hudnut's writings nor any mention of the similarities between Gropius's Basic Design course and his own experience in Pure Design with Emil Lorch.[22] From where he stood during his years with Gropius at Harvard, Hudnut may not have recognized the similarities between Pure Design and Basic Design.

Not insignificantly, along with his architectural studies, Hudnut's literary career also began to flower at Michigan. He authored the libretto for the university's annual opera—cast with an Egyptian king, a professor, and two athletes—served as literary editor of the university's monthly journal, and published his poetry in the yearbook.[23] With a few courses to go in 1912, and no summer classes at Michigan, Hudnut finished his coursework at the University of Pennsylvania, where he met his future wife, Claire Ring. She was a pianist and the daughter of a textile manufacturer.[24]

Emil Lorch described Hudnut at the end of his studies in a way that befitted a successful graduate of Michigan's unique program, as a young architect of "unquestioned artistic taste, real ability in the field of decorative design, a high degree of cultivation," who understood well "the significance of architecture as an art of building rather than a free art of design."[25] With these words, he dispatched Hudnut to a teaching position at Alabama Polytechnic Institute in Auburn. The five-year-old architecture program there, the oldest in the South, brought on the new graduate as its sole faculty member. Hudnut was the master of all subjects in his new job: design, drawing, building materials and specifications, and—the course that he most enjoyed teaching during his four years there—architectural history.[26] Auburn's architecture program resembled those at many other state or midwestern universities early in the century. Unlike the more elite eastern schools—Yale, Harvard, Columbia, or Penn—which looked to the École des Beaux-Arts, it focused largely on the processes of building, engineering, and construction. Its faculty, Hudnut would be the first to admit, was undistinguished.

Along with his teaching in Auburn, Hudnut designed his first two buildings, the President's House, a classical revival mansion that he described as "an echo of Homewood," the century-old Federal-style coun-

Joseph Hudnut, President's House, 1915, Alabama Polytechnic Institute. (Courtesy of Special Collections and Archives, Auburn University Libraries)

INVENTING AMERICAN MODERNISM

try house now on the Johns Hopkins campus. He also designed a large addition to the Methodist church in town, which, he claimed decades later, "got me into trouble, for it established my reputation as a church architect and, to this day, I am called in to give advice about Sunday Schools and Boys' Rooms."[27] Back in his Auburn days, Hudnut looked to his favorite architect, Charles McKim, for inspiration in design, admiring in particular McKim's handling of the classical tradition as a "living thing" adapted artfully to American traditions. Hudnut later likened his enthusiasm for McKim to what "my students now feel for Gropius."[28]

Looking back on his time at Auburn years later, Hudnut recalled that he had been a "romantic and promising architect" who had earnestly tried to recapture the "thought and feeling" that lay behind each of the styles. He had believed unequivocally in "no higher excellence in architecture than the decorum, the conventional choice, the charm and universality" that the historic styles seemed to offer. Beyond practical objectives, Hudnut passed on to his students his belief that "certain ideals of form" result from principles "more or less absolute in nature."[29] In 1916, Hudnut left Auburn to enroll in the master's degree program at Columbia. His two years in that Beaux-Arts program affirmed for him the importance of precedent, architectural history, and the search for beauty derived from universal principles of design.[30] At age thirty-one, a prize-winning student and a believer in the methods and absolute values of the French tradition, he finally finished his formal education.

In the meantime, Gropius had already begun to emerge as one Germany's leading modern architects by 1916. He had completed the acclaimed Werkbund Exhibition Building in Cologne and the Fagus Shoe Last Factory in Alfeld, much lauded for bringing to architecture a remarkable sense of weightlessness and transparency. Gropius's experience working in Peter Behrens's office between 1908 and 1910 has often been cited as having sparked his lifelong interest in industrial building, design, and prefabrication. By the end of his term with Behrens, the entrepreneurial young Gropius had even authored an elaborate proposal to start his own prefabricated housing company in which he laid out ideas that would form the basis of the Bauhaus and, later, his teaching at Harvard.[31]

In addition to his interest in industrial design and prefabrication, another factor was shaping Gropius's approach to design in these early years of his career—his inability to draw. As he lamented in a 1907 letter to his mother: "My absolute inability to bring even the simplest design

Walter Gropius, Fagus Works, 1911–13, Alfeld an der Leine, Germany. (Reprinted with permission from *Architectural Record* 169 [July 1981]: 115)

to paper is casting a shadow on many otherwise beautiful things and often makes me worry about my future profession. . . . In my darkest hour, I had never feared that things could be so hopeless."[32] Gropius soon came to terms with his handicap, deciding that drawing was merely a "support activity" for architecture and that he need not master it after all to achieve success in the field. He drew as little as possible in his years of practice, and when he could, he worked with someone else who took on the task of drawing.[33] In the words of historian Winfried Nerdinger, Gropius's ability to transcend his drawing problem by assuming a "'lordly posture' is characteristic of his entire life; but more significant is an awareness of his own importance, demonstrated even at a young age, that gave Gropius the lifelong air of a missionary."[34]

While Gropius rose above his inability to draw, Hudnut was mastering the art of the *esquisse* and the rendered drawing at Columbia. Like their counterparts at the École in Paris, Hudnut and his fellow students (as well as those at many other American schools of architecture) studied descriptive geometry, architectural history, and the art of drawing with pencil, ink, charcoal, and washes. Not all aspects of the École translated easily into the American programs: the École's centralized structure and its atelier system did not translate, for example. Students in Paris prepared for the École in the studio of a master practitioner and passed rigorous exams in order to enter the school. No such exams existed in American schools, which admitted students through a casual process that, in case of the elite private universities, often involved having the right social connections. American architecture schools, unlike those in France, had been attached to universities since 1868 and were staffed with professional teachers rather than architectural masters.[35]

Nonetheless at Columbia, Harvard, and numerous other schools, the French *esquisse* system formed the heart of architectural education. Student projects began with a *parti,* an unalterable commitment to a design approach in response to a written assignment or program. In as short a time as twelve hours or as much as a few weeks, students developed their *parti* in a sketch, or *esquisse,* always working alone and sequestered from other students. Their efforts culminated in sets of plans, sections, and elevations elaborately drawn according to established conventions. Several of Hudnut's drawings from Columbia, including his English Gothic "Country House," won awards from a jury of New York architects for their commitment, clarity, and drawing skill. Columbia was strong in architectural history as well, and Hudnut seems to have deepened his interest in the subject there.[36] By the time he finished his degree, he had become a favorite son to the extent that within a few years, his teachers would conspire to appoint him to a professorship in the history of architecture.[37]

After graduation, Hudnut opened his own small office in New York in 1917, intending to practice architecture as "a pleasant and gentlemanly vocation." He imagined a career that would afford him "a rich variety of human contacts" and the satisfactions that result from the "competent performance of a craft."[38] But for one encounter, Hudnut's career might well have developed in this direction—from fine schools to a pleasant practice.

Portrait of Joseph Hudnut in his Beaux-Arts days, ca. 1916. (Courtesy of University Archives and Columbiana Library, Columbia University)

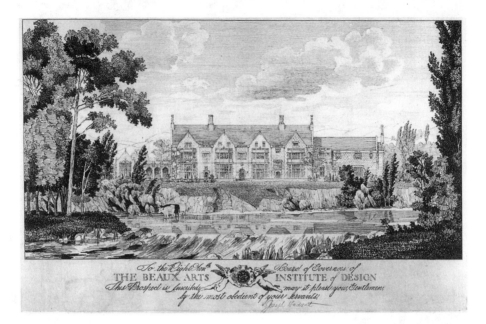

Joseph Hudnut, "Country House," Columbia University student design problem, 1917, submitted to the Beaux-Arts Institute of Design. (Avery Architectural and Fine Arts Library, Columbia University)

Joseph Hudnut, "A Spanish Patio," Columbia University student design problem, 1917. (*Annual of the School of Architecture, Columbia University*, 1918)

Joseph Hudnut, "Plans for a Country House," Columbia University
student design problem, 1917, submitted to the Beaux-Arts Institute of
Design. (Avery Architectural and Fine Arts Library, Columbia University)

Werner Hegemann

The encounter that gave Hudnut's career a distinctive turn occurred right after he left Columbia. Within a few weeks of graduation, Hudnut somehow met the well-known German city planner and theorist Werner Hegemann. Hegemann was then working in Milwaukee with the landscape architect Elbert Peets, under the patronage of the city's German community.[39] He had established a city planning practice there in 1916, when, after he had completed a lecture tour in the United States, World War I broke out and prevented him from traveling home to Germany. "Keenly curious" about the "new art of city planning" and impressed by Hegemann's obvious intellectual breadth and social commitment, and by the small volume of Goethe he always carried in his pocket, Hudnut signed on as his assistant.[40]

Hudnut had learned nothing of city planning while at Harvard, Michigan, and Columbia. His sole venture into planning before meeting Hegemann had been in 1915, when he entered a Chicago City Club design competition for a "neighborhood center," a grouping of public buildings and outdoor spaces aimed at creating a sense of community in a depressed area of Chicago. His proposal for a cluster of Gothic and Tudor structures—a library, theater, and coffeehouse—organized around a common nucleus and surrounded by picturesque spaces and playgrounds, did not win the competition. The idea of enhancing urban life with buildings and spaces intended to foster community spirit did, however, capture Hudnut's interest enough that he published his first article on neighborhood centers and even began (but never finished) a book on the subject.[41]

Werner Hegemann, ca. 1910.
(Courtesy of Eve Hegemann Ladd)

At the time Hudnut met him, Hegemann was well known in the planning community throughout the United States. In 1909 in Boston, he had joined forces with Boston's civic improvement movement "Boston-1915," founded by businessman and reformer Edward Filene. The group included the distinguished American planners John Nolen, Frederick Law Olmsted Jr., and Charles Mulford Robinson, as well as business and civic leaders, who had joined forces to confront the housing and planning problems plaguing the city. Hegemann helped out by organizing a much-publicized city planning exhibition to advance the cause of the movement. Held in the old Museum of Fine Arts and attended by more than two hundred thousand visitors, it was one of the first American city planning exhibitions ever held.[42] Hegemann thereafter returned to Germany for three years and in 1913 found himself once again in the United States, this time at the invitation of the People's Institute, a progressive organization that encouraged intellectuals to engage in public life by bringing them into contact with interested (and nonacademic) audiences.[43] The institute sent Hegemann on tour throughout the United States to persuade chambers of commerce, planners, and city officials of the benefits that came with creating long-range city plans. At the end of his two-year tour, Hegemann prepared city plans for Oakland and Berkeley. The ideas he proposed for these two cities, stressing the importance of culture, aesthetic refinement, and harmony with nature, anticipated the civic design schemes he and Hudnut would realize while working in Wisconsin and Pennsylvania.[44]

When Hudnut joined Hegemann, the planner was in the midst of one of his first design projects, Washington Highlands, a garden suburb in Milwaukee. Here, and again in 1921 in Wyomissing Park near Reading, Pennsylvania, Hudnut helped Hegemann create picturesque residential communities, using the historical styles of architecture common to each region. In both suburbs, Hegemann carefully ordered street systems, public squares, vistas, and extensive parks to accentuate the beauty and irregularity of the natural setting. To ensure the overall aesthetic quality of the projects and the congruity of their architecture and landscape with local traditions, he enforced strict building codes and regulations, much as New Urbanist planners are doing today.[45]

Hudnut worked off and on with Hegemann for four years, until 1921, when the planner returned to Germany. Hudnut did not see him again until he came back to New York once again as a political refugee in 1933. Though their design work together had lasted only a few years, Hudnut described in 1936—at the time of Hegemann's death at the age of fifty-five—how his association with the planner had been "the critical one in my professional life. . . . By this I mean that the view of the world and of the architect's place in it which I formulated at that time has become continuously and definitely more clear to me and has retained to this day the essential character which it then assumed."[46]

What amazed Hudnut in Hegemann's work was his belief that city planning was "the basis of architecture." Hegemann saw the city "not

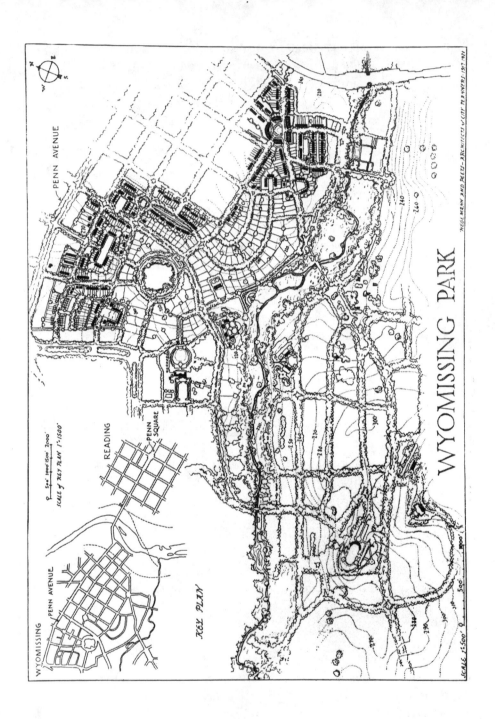

WYOMISSING PARK

PENN AVENUE

KEY PLAN

WYOMISSING

PENN AVENUE

READING

PENN SQUARE

SCALE of KEY PLAN 1":1500'

SCALE 1:500'

HEGEMANN AND PEETS ~ ARCHITECTS & CITY PLANNERS; 1917-1921

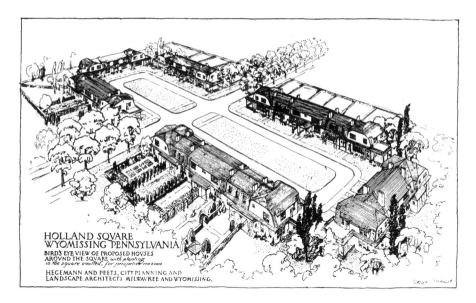

HOLLAND SQVARE
WYOMISSING PENNSYLVANIA
BIRD'S EYE VIEW OF PROPOSED HOVSES
AROVND THE SQVARE with planting
in the square omitted, for perspective reasons
HEGEMANN AND PEETS, CITY PLANNING AND
LANDSCAPE ARCHITECTS MILWAVKEE AND WYOMISSING.

Werner Hegemann with Joseph Hudnut, "Holland Square, Wyomissing, Pennsylvania," 1917–21. (Werner Hegemann and Elbert Peets, *American Vitruvius* [New York: Architectural Book Publishing Co., 1922], 283).

Opposite page: Werner Hegemann with Joseph Hudnut, "Plan of Wyomissing Park, Pennsylvania," 1917–21. (Werner Hegemann and Elbert Peets, *American Vitruvius* [New York: Architectural Book Publishing Co., 1922], 281)

as an arrangement of streets which afford building sites to an architect" nor as "an arrangement of spaces and structures which might assure the architect opportunities for the exploitation of his formal principles." Instead, he regarded it as "a living and growing organism," forever changing and therefore impossible to mold into a predetermined form. Hegemann taught Hudnut that the city's physical pattern—of which streets, parks, waterfronts, and buildings were components—must grow out of the ever-changing "idea-pattern" (shared values, customs, and symbols) that governs the lives of its citizens.[47]

Hegemann's commitment to a "socially integrated" architecture and planning made a deep impression on Hudnut. He recalled that few understood the social aspect of Hegemann's work, least of all his clients.

> If they were manufacturers and built houses for their employees, they were astonished to find that Hegemann gave as much thought to the happiness of the workers as to a proper return on their investments. If they

were "real estate men," they thought it eccentric indeed that the plan for their subdivision should be as closely studied in relation to the life of the community as a whole as it was in relation to the sale of lots. And when, as sometimes happened, Hegemann's client was engaged in building a private house or garden, he, too, was astonished to learn that his architect wished to mitigate the proud insolence which his chateau focused upon its neighbors.[48]

Hegemann further taught Hudnut that architecture and planning should combine both "science" and the "art of expression." While working with Hegemann, Hudnut came to believe that as they applied "science" to the problems of shelter, traffic, or public health, architects and planners must also achieve aesthetic excellence by creating integrated patterns of the city's streets, squares, parks, and buildings. Ultimately, Hudnut came to accept, as Hegemann did, that architecture and planning could succeed only "at those rare moments in which its two objects (service and expression) are seen to be attained as parts of a common process."[49]

Hegemann was unlike any person Hudnut had ever encountered. Hudnut described his "wide perspective . . . consonant to the culture of Germany" before the war, "whose vision of the world embraced the apprehension of a reasonable and humane structure of society."[50] He was a broadly educated man who had studied philosophy, history, political science, sociology, and economics at several different universities—in Berlin, Philadelphia, Strasbourg, and Munich, as well as at the École des Beaux-Arts in Paris—preparing himself for the new field of city planning at a time when no formal course of study existed. Hegemann finished his schooling with a Ph.D. in economics at Munich.[51] By the end of his life, he had written countless articles and numerous books on a variety of subjects, several of them controversial. In 1912, he was prosecuted for publicizing Berlin's miserable housing conditions (with Käthe Kollowitz); he also wrote critical books on Napoleon and on Frederick the Great; and Hitler later publicly burned his *Entlarvte Geschichte* [History Exposed], which was in press when Hegemann left Germany for the United States in 1933.[52] Among his many endeavors, Hegemann made his greatest impact in the field of city planning. One historian has described him as the best known of Germany's young planning commentators and, at the same time, the most admired of North America's scientific planners.[53]

Hegemann drew Hudnut's and Gropius's distant worlds somewhat closer together. He introduced Hudnut (albeit long-distance) to the architectural and urban culture of Germany, and while in Berlin, he promoted American planning accomplishments to German audiences. Hegemann was well known in Germany by 1910 as a tireless promoter of the American park movement for its part in remedying urban congestion and of American-style comprehensive planning, beginning with Burnham's plan for Chicago (though Hegemann disliked the imperial aspect of the City Beautiful).[54] After he had returned home from exile in 1921, Hegemann took on an important role in the German architectural planning community as editor of the *Wasmuths Monatshefte für Baukunst* and *Der Städtebau*. He held this post until he sought political refuge again in the United States in 1933.

Having been absent from Europe in the war years, Hegemann had missed the beginnings of the new architecture in Germany. He did see the modern movement blossom in the 1920s, however, with Hudnut's future colleagues Gropius and Martin Wagner making their significant mark, the latter then director of the central building administration in Berlin (a position for which Hegemann had also been considered).[55] But Hegemann stood apart from the modernist contingent in both his outlook on architecture and urban planning and in his character and personality. As historian Werner Oechslin has written: "Any attempt at an historical account of architecture that takes its orientation from the ideals of the New Architecture . . . will almost be forced to overlook Hegemann. He does not fit nicely into the modernist perspective."[56] Hegemann was far more "impartial," "balanced," "middle-of-the-road," and "in-between," to use Oechslin's words; he viewed the world from "a perspective of exceptional breadth."[57] The historically rooted, detailed commentary on architecture and planning that Hegemann put forth contrasted sharply with the crisp manifestos of the modernists. Not surprisingly, no summary of Hegemann's credo exists.

Hegemann never became a proponent of modern architecture or planning, and though he provided the modernists with an "open forum" in his journals, he occasionally offered sharp criticism of the new architecture and planning.[58] At one point, he challenged the modernists for their superficial fashionableness and ill-conceived social remedies, and he even singled out Martin Wagner for seeking "commissions for a group of extremist architects who were his close friends."[59] Another time, Hegemann reproached the seemingly irreproachable Le Corbusier for his "ghastly" skyscrapers and city planning ideas. Perhaps most irritating to the modernists, Hegemann dared to compare the architectural excesses of academicism to the excesses of modernism.[60] Though Hudnut certainly did not share Hegemann's opinions of modern architecture during the 1920s, decades later he would find himself leveling similar charges against the modernists.

Hegemann certainly had doubts about the modernist approach to urban planning, but he was even more distressed with the existing order of things, which he made clear especially in his *Das steinerne Berlin* (1930). In this book, he argued that Berlin had become the "largest city of housing barracks in the world" because the city's leaders had failed to understand the importance of urban planning.[61] As he wrote, "it is a German illusion to believe in the possibility of creating an intellectual capital as long as the so-called educated people are almost proud of their inadequate understanding of urban planning."[62] Educating citizens about the significance of urban planning had always ranked among Hegemann's highest priorities—and this too he passed on to Hudnut.

Hegemann best described the importance of urban planning in *American Vitruvius: An Architects' Handbook on Civic Art* (1922), written with Elbert Peets during the years that Hudnut worked in his office. Profusely illustrated with planning projects from ancient to modern times (including a few drawings by Hudnut), the book celebrates Vitruvian principles: beauty, commodity, longevity, and the idea that so impressed Hudnut, that "the fundamental unit of design in architecture is not the separate building but the whole city."[63] A primary purpose of Hegemann's book, and later of Hudnut's efforts at Harvard, was to assure that cities were shaped with these ideas in mind and also, as Hegemann phrased it, "to bring out the necessity of extending the architect's sphere of influence" in the city.[64]

Hegemann's book attracted only a small audience in the United States, in part because it challenged the professional interests of the American city planning establishment. At the other extreme, *American Vitruvius* was issued the same year Le Corbusier exhibited his "Ville Contemporaine," with other modern schemes soon after coming to light. The book had only minimal appeal to either of these large groups, the planning establishment or Le Corbusier's supporters. Despite the neglect in its own time, Hegemann's book was reissued in 1988 (and again in 1999) in the cause of postmodern urbanism. In its new preface, Leon Krier argues that with its "emphasis on civic morality, public mores and

Joseph Hudnut, drawing of "View down Lake View Avenue, Wyomissing." (Werner Hegemann and Elbert Peets, *American Vitruvius* [New York: Architectural Book Publishing Co., 1922], 283)

manners," *American Vitruvius* offers a way to confront our dehumanized modern cities. Krier laments that few people looked to Hegemann in the period of postwar rebuilding, and that "soon after 1945, schools and authorities were effectively purged of followers of Hegemann and Peets."[65] While this is largely true, Hudnut is an important exception. He remained a loyal Hegemann disciple, and at a time and place when it was most unfashionable. Hudnut's persistent connection to Hegemann was at the crux of his conflict with Gropius.

Hudnut's Architecture

In April 1919, as Hudnut worked with Hegemann and on his own building designs, the Bauhaus opened its doors in Weimar. There was little immediate notice of the new school in the American press, and Hudnut likely knew nothing of it or its founder for a few more years. Hudnut certainly knew of Walter Gropius by the time that Gropius entered the 1922 Chicago Tribune exhibition. As one who kept up with the current architectural press, Hudnut likely saw the notices of Gropius's work and the Bauhaus that immediately followed. It was Le Corbusier, though, and not Gropius, who made the stronger impression on Hudnut in the mid-1920s. As Hudnut would later describe: "My first interest in modernism arose from an attempt to adapt the traditional church to the needs of my clients. From the problem of the immersion tank disguised as an altar, I escaped through the doorway opened by M. Le Corbusier."[66]

Before making his escape, Hudnut practiced full-time between 1919 and 1923, and he completed his final building in 1926. His designs—churches, houses, and commercial buildings—were unremarkable, especially by Hudnut's own account. When he was not working with Hegemann, Hudnut worked from his office on West Tenth Street, a street he described as "all oriel, finial, and crenellated tower." The office itself, with its marble fireplace and walnut spiral stairway, made the "perfect *mise en scène*" for Hudnut in his Romantic period, and the perfect "trap for sentimental clients." Both office and street, Hudnut later joked, were "more colleagues than accessories."[67]

> We designed and built—the street and I—quite a number of buildings. All were developed from an historical precedent, Gothic or Georgian, and in one instance Greek Revival. Each had its source, as we knew, in an order of thought and feeling forever passed away, but our faith that we could recapture that order and build it into our present scene was absolute and imperative.[68]

Because Hudnut left no papers from his architectural practice, it is impossible to know for certain how many buildings he designed or where, how he got his commissions, or how he ran his practice. It is clear that he worked mostly alone, in partnership only for a short time with his brother-in-law, Carl Montgomery, and that he later took on occasional associates.[69] Hudnut claimed to have designed eighteen churches during his career, largely Baptist and Methodist, despite the fact that he himself was "less than faithful." Most of these churches and his houses—which numbered a "score or more"—could be found within an hour's distance of New York, in New England, or in Virginia. Three of his churches and one house renovation actually found their way into the architectural press, no small feat for a lowly practitioner.[70]

Hudnut later relegated his first churches to his "Early Christian Period," a time when he believed, as 1920s Gothicists did, that he was carrying on the "tradition of Canterbury."[71] Other of his churches drew from Georgian or colonial precedents, occasionally in a somewhat literal way, although Robert A. M. Stern purports to find "hints of a Modernist sensibility" in a few of the churches.[72] No matter what style or type of building he designed, all of Hudnut's architecture shared a penchant for careful detailing, local materials, and fitting into the natural and

Joseph Hudnut, "First Baptist Church, Jamaica, New York," 1923. (*Yearbook of the Architectural League of New York*, 1924)

built surroundings and historical context. When he designed a church in Charlottesville, for example, Hudnut studied Jefferson's sketches and writings and used a local brick similar to one Jefferson had used, along with several Jeffersonian details. For a house set on a wooded Charlottesville site, Hudnut turned to a rough, native stone and irregular Gothic massing (see illustration on page 35). The vertical proportions of this house, its asymmetry, irregular window placement, steep-pitched roof, and overall rustic simplicity carefully echoed the nature of its landscape. His design for a nearby house on an urban street in the same city fit neatly with the surrounding Federal-style houses in its detailing and materials. Hudnut gave it a saltbox form, unusual for Charlottesville, to reflect the slope of its hilly site (see illustration on page 36). Hudnut later reflected ironically about all these buildings that he had "laid upon the patient soil of Virginia." They "wear their counterfeit frills as awkwardly as I and as little deserve an entrée to a polite society."[73]

After just seven years, Hudnut gave up practicing architecture. He was no longer content with the styles, and he was frustrated with his own inability to integrate form with new social uses. While designing churches especially, Hudnut recognized the limitations of approach-

Joseph Hudnut, "First Methodist Episcopal Church, Jamaica, New York, 1926." (Reprinted with permission from *Architectural Record* 60 [July 1926]: 40)

Joseph Hudnut, First Methodist Church, Charlottesville, Virginia, 1923–24. (Courtesy of First Methodist Church, Charlottesville)

ing architecture as he did, as if he were making "pictures rather than buildings." By designing "pictorially," or with a completed picture of structure and plan fixed in his mind, he could not satisfy his clients' changing needs. Looking back, Hudnut explained that by the mid-1920s, his church clients had begun to demand new types of spaces for educational and social functions that had no precedent in the traditional church. They sought modernizations for a simplified ritual and on a budget that "threw my composition completely out of balance."[74] Unable to achieve more than a tired Romanticism or to reconcile issues of form, function, economy, and structure in his architecture, Hudnut sought another way of reconciling them—as a teacher of architectural design and history. Teaching, he believed, would allow him the freedom to explore architectural ideas that his practice would not. "Clients tie us to our completed masterpieces and come to us for more of the same— but the teacher is not thus bound.[75]

Only on rare occasions did Hudnut's buildings surface after their publication in early 1920s. In 1945, a disgruntled critic of Hudnut's who had hoped to embarrass the outspoken Harvard dean suggested in a letter published in *Pencil Points* that the journal "devote a number of pages in the near future to a presentation of Mr. Hudnut's (1920s) architecture . . . in order to enlighten his fellow architects on modern

Joseph Hudnut, house on Burnley Avenue, Charlottesville, Virginia, 1924. (Photograph by the author, 1989)

Joseph Hudnut,
Sterling-Lewis
House, Charlottes-
ville, Virginia, 1923.
(Photograph by the
author, 1989)

architecture as he conceives it." The insinuation here was that if Hudnut did not currently practice, he should not preach. Lewis Mumford
had had this same charge leveled at him on many occasions, and other
nonpractitioner critics likely heard it as well.[76] William Wurster, then
dean at MIT, responded to Hudnut's critic in the same journal: "Those
of us who know Dean Hudnut well, and admire and respect his critical
judgment, know also his modesty when it comes to the few structures
he long ago designed. I am one, among the many, who feels no one has
done more to free the spirit of architecture from reactionary forces than
Dean Hudnut, by the nature of his critical writing and leadership in
education."[77]

Back to Teaching

Though he had not taught since his years in Alabama, Hudnut was appointed professor and director of art and architecture at the University
of Virginia's McIntire School of Fine Arts in 1923. The bureaucratic complexities of academic hiring did not yet exist in architectural schools,
and the offer came to Hudnut through his friend and predecessor in the
post, Fiske Kimball. Kimball, an architectural historian, also had close

ties to Hegemann, and he had come to know Hudnut through the German planner.[78]

As he moved away from his practice, Hudnut honed his administrative and teaching skills, and he came to regard himself as an educator "always eager for experiment."[79] He was one of two faculty members in Virginia's four-year program, which was modeled on the Beaux-Arts system and which Hudnut still viewed as "by far the best method for giving instruction in architectural design."[80] Hudnut took steps to bring the Virginia program up to date by adding design problems related to issues in contemporary practice and by revising the history offerings to include more recent architecture. He also tried to forge curricular links between the liberal arts and professional studies in order to encourage—here sounding like Gropius at the Bauhaus—"the co-ordinate development of mind and hand."[81]

Hudnut migrated north from Virginia in 1926 to the more prestigious Columbia, where he became professor of the history of architecture. Columbia offered many advantages over Virginia: first-rate equipment in an impressive space, a great architectural library, a far larger faculty and student body, and, of course, the architectural riches of New York. Furthermore, for Hudnut it held the possibility of an important promotion in the near future. The current dean, William Boring, intended to groom his former student to take over the top post after he retired.[82] The informality of both Hudnut's hiring as well as his anointment as head of the school still remained commonplace in architectural education. Hudnut took over as dean seven years later.

Before he did so, Hudnut reveled in his newfound freedom from practice. With his last architectural commission behind him, he began to consider seriously the limitations of contemporary Romantic architecture and of the Americanized Beaux-Arts educational system. He also recognized, during his first years back at Columbia, that in writing rather than in designing he could best express his ideas on architecture. His prose was far more eloquent, frank, and artful than his buildings ever were.

Somewhat surprisingly for a man who claimed that "my only important interest is architecture," Hudnut began his authorial career with a small book for a general audience entitled *Modern Sculpture* (1929). As was typical of Hudnut, he quickly made light of his own work—a brief survey of mostly European work from Rodin to Brancusi—claiming that the book "is now on sale at Liggett's Drug Store, rubber goods counter, at 29 cents."[83] Hudnut did make a few digressions into architecture in the book, merely hinting at the path his later critical writings would follow—as when he spoke of "humanizing" the "stark architecture of our new buildings" and of architecture revealing "a world made consonant with our most secret needs."[84] The People's Institute—the same progressive organization that had sponsored Hegemann's tour of American cities a decade earlier—sponsored the book, which grew out of a series of lectures Hudnut delivered on its behalf.

Hudnut also wrote a few architectural essays during his pre-dean years at Columbia in which he spoke of his dissatisfaction with the Romanticism of both the modern Gothic style and the classicism of his former hero, Charles McKim. The two architectures, Hudnut claimed, were symbols of "an opposed romance" that now offered merely a "sentimental attachment to form." Using the examples of McKim's Columbia library and Ralph Adams Cram's nearby Cathedral of St. John the Divine, Hudnut posited, in an appropriately Romantic tone, that

> each embodies in a manner more determinate than words, more provocative than thought, a creed in respect to the past. If one re-illumines the quiet light that shines around the brow of classical scholarship, the other wears, in a manner sure and assertive, the more authentic nimbus of St. Thomas Aquinas. The humanism that one celebrates—a humanism that ignores Darwin and the Revolution—is confronted by a mysticism that ignores the Reformation. Into one symbol a library is fitted; into the other, a church.[85]

Hudnut often used such "flowery and highbrow" prose when speaking out against the excesses of early-twentieth-century architecture. "I don't see what I can do about it," he once explained. "I am just *naturally* flowery and highbrow."[86] Instead of fitting our grand institutions into symbolic clothing, Hudnut challenged architects in 1930 to "belong to our own time" by allowing the "radiant spirit" emanating from "the city at our feet" to inform their work.[87]

Hudnut's "radiant spirit" bore no relation to Le Corbusier's, though he was already intrigued by the new architecture coming out of Europe. By the late 1920s, books and journals with modernist works from France, Germany, and Holland were finding their way into the libraries of those who cared to admit them. At Harvard, Henry-Russell Hitchcock recalled that he and other students had digested Le Corbusier's

Vers une architecture even before it appeared in the 1927 English translation.[88] By 1930, most American architecture students knew something of European modernism, though as one student noted, this knowledge derived "from what we read, not from what we were taught."[89] Students and interested others read articles on the Bauhaus and on individual architects and buildings, especially in the *Architectural Record,* though a few other architectural and cultural journals had occasional offerings.

Hudnut may well have been the first teacher in any American school of architecture to introduce students to Le Corbusier, Gropius, Mies van der Rohe, and other modern architects and to present their work in a positive light. He was surely ahead of others in allowing his Columbia students to experiment with the modernist aesthetic in the design studios. Hudnut came to be known as a "vigorous proponent of the International style" and appreciative students considered there to be "only one architectural school to attend: Columbia."[90]

Though it is not entirely clear how Hudnut first grew interested in the new modern architecture, he claimed that he was drawn to it in the late 1920s because it addressed important social issues and because he admired how it used new technologies to create a contemporary aesthetic.[91] He expressed concern, however, that the "doctrine of functionalism"—the idea that beauty simply happens if one builds logically— seemed to have "taken on an almost religious character" among young architects. Although the European modernists seemed to him—as they had to Hegemann—a bit too resolute, even strident in their "assertion of modernity," Hudnut did believe that their work offered a starting point "from which a new progress might be possible."[92]

It may seem unlikely that an educator with modernist leanings would hold an appointment as a professor of architectural history. It was especially unlikely in the late 1920s, when many accepted that being "modern" meant eschewing the harmful influence of historical buildings and plans. Hudnut never did subscribe to this view but always maintained great interest in the history of architecture and urban form. He claimed that studying this history afforded students an essential "experience of architecture." Through history, students learned to regard architecture and cities not as assemblages of individual elements but as a unified and inseparable whole. Seeing buildings or plans with their parts fused together allowed students to "feel" them with an "immediate" and "intuitive" sense and to experience what Hudnut called the "emotional content" of architecture.[93] Furthermore, he argued, students too often came to their studies "already engineers," with a far too developed "pragmatic habit of thought." For those who planned to be architects without having understood the significance of architecture, history would play a crucial role. It would "court them into aesthetic experiences, startle them into observation and new impressions, awaken them to the splendor of the art they have so fortuitously embraced."[94]

In his history courses, Hudnut taught students that cities and places are not "static things" but are rather "things in process," with a momentum generated by events that lie far back in time. Ideally, through studying history they would learn to think contextually and to make their own designs elements part of a larger, harmonious pattern.[95] Finally, because Hudnut viewed history as an endeavor that encouraged intuition, excellence, art, and a sense of continuity, he included modernist architects in his history courses, even in his years at Columbia, seeing them as part of the continuum of architectural history.

At the same time that European modern architecture found an audience in the United States, in the late 1920s, the Beaux-Arts system of education came under fire from educators, students, and practitioners who thought its methods archaic, its design projects useless, and the judgments of students' works unhelpful.[96] Critics charged that the system placed too much emphasis on elaborate rendering techniques and that its exotic programs were neither "human" nor "practical."[97] Even as late as 1934, a Columbia graduate described how, "on antiquarian boards we all wrestled with monumental schemes of a type never seen, or likely to be seen, on land or sea."[98] Many critics of the Beaux-Arts system objected to teaching design through competition, since it emphasized winning above learning. In too many cases, instructors would work out their students' *partis* for them, render large portions of their drawings, and even scheme to influence the juries judging the work.[99] Critics also accused the juries—often composed of visiting architects—of using inconsistent standards in their judgments and of making "superficial, hasty, and not well considered" choices that failed to measure the value of a student's performance.[100] These criticisms pertained not only to Columbia's School of Architecture but to the many other schools in the United States that relied on an Americanized Beaux-Arts system.

When the Depression hit, American architectural education was already in a state of confusion. As Henry-Russell Hitchcock noted in the

INVENTING AMERICAN MODERNISM

Architectural Record, if changes did not come, "we may expect to lose to Europe in this generation as many of our best students as we lost a generation ago."[101] The devastated American economy, the specter of unemployment facing those who had sought temporary refuge in schools of architecture, and the lure of steel, glass, and machine technology further opened the way for change and experimentation.

Hudnut launched the first attack against the French system with a decisive blow.[102] Almost immediately after he accepted the dean's position at Columbia in 1934, he renounced the educational and design principles that his patron had upheld during the fifteen years he had directed the program. With his characteristic diplomacy laced with irony, Hudnut declared in his first official report that "Dr. Boring maintained an ideal both in objective and methods, which we shall find hard indeed to maintain in years to come."[103] In place of Columbia's Americanized Beaux-Arts program, Hudnut introduced a new progressive agenda based, in large part, on the democratic educational principles of John Dewey.

There is no way of knowing if Hudnut had ever engaged in a serious study of Dewey's pedagogical philosophy or on what level he encountered the philosopher's educational ideas. It may well be that Hudnut became acquainted with some of Dewey's ideas when he was an architecture student at Columbia, given that Dewey was a highly visible figure on campus at that time. Education was an intensely discussed topic in many quarters during the first two decades of the twentieth century, and Hudnut's introduction to Dewey might have occurred outside the university.[104] He was definitely familiar with Dewey's progressive pedagogy by the time he returned to teach at Columbia. By 1926, several of Dewey's disciples had joined the Teacher's College faculty, making Columbia the national center for contemporary educational studies. Groups on campus often debated the new pedagogical methods while the *Columbia Spectator* highlighted speeches and studies coming out of Teacher's College. The idea of education as "both life and the preparation for life" and as "an organic creative process" circulated around the campus.[105] By 1929, Hudnut had undergone enough of a conversion to the progressive view that he argued before a national audience of architectural educators that "education is not instruction but experience."[106] The juxtaposition of two unrelated front-page articles in the *Columbia Spectator* underscores Hudnut's proximity to the pedagogical debates at

Columbia: while one headline declared, "Dewey Predicts New Education," the other announced Hudnut's appointment as the new dean of Columbia's School of Architecture.[107]

As Hudnut took the helm at Columbia, many aspects of Dewey's philosophy and activism appealed to him. Above all, Hudnut believed, as Dewey did, that education should play a key role in the formation of a democratic society, and he quickly made changes to shape Columbia's architecture program to accord with that view. Hudnut first abolished the Beaux-Arts design competitions. Rather than opposing one another for jury awards that advanced them in the school, students now worked on their designs openly and often collaboratively in the drafting room. Hudnut not only tried to foster a cooperative community of students in this way but also worked to encourage each individual's interests and talents. Much as Dewey had done in his Laboratory School, Hudnut tried to relate work in the architecture program to the life of the surrounding community. He replaced the typical Beaux-Arts design programs— grand tombs or Mayan temples—with more practical design problems that confronted the exigencies of modern life. No longer acceding to the idea of absolute truths, Columbia students would now learn from experience. They began designing housing for workers or low-income families while considering the demands of an actual site, economy, and function. The new design problems worked much like the "project method" that progressive educators championed at Teacher's College, hoping to rouse students' sense of moral obligation through projects emphasizing "purposeful activity."[108] Hudnut also eliminated the conventionalized drawings demanded of students in the French system and in their place required simple sketches, models, and working drawings.

Two principles gleaned from Dewey, and also from Werner Hegemann, lay at the heart of Hudnut's modern program at Columbia. To build in a meaningful way, Hudnut maintained, architects must have a wide understanding of the society in which they build, of its social, economic, technological, and intellectual currents, as well as its historical roots. Hudnut also set out to make his students into intelligent reformers—rather than mere embellishers—who used their art to reconstruct the human environment "for the better of the community as a whole."[109]

Hudnut found in Dewey a number of the same ideas that Hegemann had espoused. Indeed, the fact that Dewey reinforced for him many of Hegemann's principles may even have encouraged his interest in the philosopher. Hudnut's two mentors not only taught him to uphold the social aspect of design and interdisciplinary study, they both emphasized the importance of engaging a broad public in issues that affected their lives. Dewey, of course, was well known for having played a signal part in linking the academy to public life. In the end, Hegemann made his greatest impact not by designing but by bringing his planning expertise to the public realm: organizing, writing, and speaking out for his cause.[110] As dean at Columbia and at Harvard, Hudnut, too, considered it his duty to reach outside the academy in order to educate people and encourage them to participate in architectural and planning matters that affected their lives.

Hudnut identified not only with Dewey but with the "progressive" label. Disputed as that term may be among historians, for Hudnut it meant a concern for social reform, cooperative effort, experimentation, the conjoining of ideas and action, and participatory democracy. In the early 1930s, Hudnut liked to describe himself as a "*progressive* architect," in part because of the social aims he set out to achieve but also because of the design approach he favored. Progressives like himself, he maintained, tried to unify building construction and aesthetics and to avoid the formalism of the "conservatives" who viewed structure and aesthetic effects as "more or less unrelated."[111]

Hudnut regarded the new Town Planning Studio as his most important contribution to the progressive curriculum at Columbia. The new studio aimed at preparing architecture students for their part in the inevitable rebuilding of cities that would follow at the end of the Depression. To teach in the studio, Hudnut hired the regional planner and housing expert Henry Wright and his own mentor, Werner Hegemann. Hegemann had been in political exile in the United States for two years at this point and had been teaching city planning at the New School for Social Research. Since Columbia had no money to expand its faculty, Hudnut solicited the funds to pay Hegemann's salary himself.[112]

Wright and Hegemann engaged students in planning projects in neighborhoods near Columbia while encouraging them to regard the city as a composition of related buildings and spaces rather than as a landscape of frontages awaiting their constructions. They also encouraged students to see that through design they could help to improve the lives of individuals and communities. The two further acquainted students with a range of city planning techniques—site planning, housing development, and community organization—while demonstrating that planning and architecture are parts of a single design process, that is, civic design.[113] Hudnut had hoped to establish an "Institute of Urbanism" at Columbia, where researchers from a range of disciplines would explore the immediate problems of New York City, including those related to its administrative, political, social, economic, and physical contexts. This was the first time that Hudnut used the term "urbanism." While he might have used "civic design" instead, he cited the Institut d'Urbanisme in Paris as a model for what he had in mind, though he noted of the Paris model only that it served as a meeting ground for scholars and practitioners interested in a wide-ranging exploration of the city. His own plans for an institute never materialized for he did not stay long enough at Columbia to develop them.[114]

Creating a new kind of educational program at Columbia had meant bringing in new teachers. Along with Hegemann and Wright, Hudnut hired the housing reformer Carol Aronovici to teach seminars in housing and urbanism. To teach design, he also brought in a young modern architect from Sweden, Jan Ruhtenberg, who had apprenticed with Mies van der Rohe.[115] Ruhtenberg did not have the standing or talent of some other more famous European modernists, but because he offered a direct link to the modern movement, students found him an exciting addition to the school.[116]

Hudnut had probably met Ruhtenberg through Philip Johnson, then at the Museum of Modern Art, who had hired the young architect to help in designing his own residence. Johnson had approached Hudnut on an earlier occasion to suggest that he hire a modern architect for the Columbia program. Johnson had grand plans at that point, for he had proposed to Hudnut that he hire the Dutch modernist J. J. P. Oud. Hudnut never got the chance to consider the appointment seriously. When Johnson contacted Oud about such an appointment, the architect turned him down, citing poor health.[117] A year later, Hudnut had a second opportunity to hire a prominent European modern architect. In 1934, Lawrence Kocher, then editor of the *Architectural Record,* proposed to Hudnut that Walter Gropius come teach at Columbia. There was little work for Gropius in Berlin at this point, given the political climate there, and Gropius had expressed interest in such a position. If Hudnut even considered Kocher's proposition, he made no move to bring Gropius to New York.[118] He may have hesitated to do so for any number of reasons. The Columbia administration would likely have vetoed such a move either for economic reasons or because Gropius was too radical a choice.[119] Or perhaps Hudnut may have felt that his program there and his ideas for modern education were not yet ripe enough to include the formidable founder of the Bauhaus.

During his final years at Columbia, Hudnut established strong and lasting ties to the modern architecture community in New York and especially to the Museum of Modern Art, where he was much admired for having transformed "a Beaux-Arts Academy into a genuinely modern architectural training school."[120] Hudnut worked closely with the museum on its 1934 exhibition of "social architecture," impressing its director, Alfred Barr, enough that Barr put him on the committee overseeing the museum's architectural exhibitions. The committee also included H. R. Hitchcock, George Howe—who became a close friend of Hudnut—and the museum trustee and architect Philip Goodwin. Hudnut clearly made a good impression there as well since, in 1937, the Modern offered him a new salaried position as its president. Hudnut was at Harvard by then, with Gropius on his way, and he declined the offer.[121]

To Harvard

Hudnut accepted the deanship of Harvard's Faculty of Architecture at the end of a lengthy search process most unlike the informal one that had brought him to Columbia and Virginia. Harvard's new president, James B. Conant, who led the search, recognized that Hudnut's views on architectural education fit well with his own plans to usher in an era of modernization throughout the university. A chemist with no previous knowledge of the architectural field, Conant involved himself in the search for a dean (and all other tenured appointments at Harvard) to an unusual degree, ignoring the bureaucratic machinery that other university presidents relied on in the 1930s. He was determined to build up a distinguished faculty at Harvard for he believed that the university's ability to serve its true social function—guiding the intellectual growth of the whole country—depended on his finding the "exceptional man" in every field. To guarantee the quality of Harvard's faculty appointments, Conant personally headed every committee that named professors and deans to tenured positions in all departments of the university. Conant was also the first non-Brahmin president of Harvard (1933–52), hailing from Dorchester rather than Back Bay, and he was determined to transform it from a "fast-ossifying gentleman's club to a meritocratic, high-intensity" university.[122]

Conant's educational pronouncements and the actions he took at the helm of Harvard stemmed from his conviction that universities had the power to effect needed changes in American society and to set down a course for the future. He was heir to the tradition of liberal intellectuals who rejected excessive abstraction in the academic and professional fields and sought to bridge the gap between theory and the realities of social life. Dewey, of course, was prominent among these intellectuals, as were the "legal realists" who regarded the law as a tool of social policy and reform, and those historians who viewed history as a pragmatic instrument to be used in explaining the present and in controlling the future.[123] In his efforts to bring the university and the public together, Conant established the Nieman Fellowships, which allowed journalists a year of study at Harvard to enrich their work, and he created the Littauer School of Public Administration, which introduced midcareer public servants to new developments in their fields. Conant also established ties between Harvard and public broadcasting, and he launched a University Extension program that brought Harvard lecturers to locations throughout Boston.[124] He devoted his presidency to making a "modern" and "democratic" Harvard and to establishing "an educational basis for a unified coherent culture suited to a democratic country in a scientific age."[125] Conant's agenda fit well with the spirit of the New Deal, and many on campus regarded the sum of his efforts as a "New Deal" for Harvard (where, tellingly, voters chose Alf Landon over Roosevelt by a slim margin in 1936). Conant was independent-minded, "a progressive without being a radical or a freak," in a colleague's words, a registered Republican who voted four times for Roosevelt—which did not sit well with conservative alumni.[126]

Conant's first step in making Harvard a leading force for the intellectual growth of the whole country was to rebuild the faculty. As he sought a new head of the architecture school, he looked for guidance to the retiring dean, George Edgell, and to his own brother-in-law Harold Bush-Brown, who headed the architecture school at the Georgia Institute of Technology (and who, as a family member, was ineligible for the post). With their help, he made his way through the maze of architectural philosophies and began sorting out possible candidates for the deanship. Conant met with several architects and deans from across the country, learning about the issues facing the profession while

James Bryant Conant, Harvard president, in 1946. (Courtesy of the Harvard University Archives, call no. HUP Conant, James B. [17a]

also scouting out the best man for the Harvard post. Of the many architects he met, Conant had been most impressed with Hudnut. Hudnut seemed happily situated at Columbia, however, and Conant thought it unscrupulous to try to "steal" him away for Harvard.[127]

The Harvard deanship was a hotly sought after position among architectural educators who coveted the highly visible stage, ample resources, unrivaled physical plant, and first-rate student body that the post seemed to offer. Several serious candidates finally emerged including front-runner Ellis Lawrence, whose attempts to unite modern and traditional design at the University of Oregon had made him a contender for the deanship at Columbia in 1932. Conant also considered Roy Childs Jones from the University of Minnesota, who championed "functional, structural and social values" over the "highly artificial academic" methods of the Beaux-Arts. William Dinsmoor, a historian of classical architecture at Columbia, and Otto Teegan of the Harvard Visiting Committee, both great proponents of Beaux-Arts teaching methods, were the conservative choices if Harvard chose that direction. Nominations for a new dean, including several from self-promoters, and suggestions of strategies for Harvard's architectural future poured in from all sides of the divided professional community.[128]

Conant came to understand that the architectural field split into two camps. On the one side, he noted that the "archaeologists"—the name he gave to the Beaux-Arts contingent dominating Harvard and other elite schools—relied on past architectures as models for the future. On the other side, the "modernists" seemed to ally architecture with contemporary developments in engineering, economics, and politics. Given his own educational aims and scientific interests, Conant determined that Harvard must shift its program to the modernist side.[129]

Hudnut had not been looking to leave Columbia, but when President Conant finally approached him about a move to Harvard in 1935, he decided that he had "completed about as much damage as I could possibly do" at Columbia.[130] Harvard promised him more freedom and a wider field in which to create an educational program focused on modern architecture and modern civic design. At Harvard he believed he could establish a much-needed union among the appallingly disparate fields of architecture, landscape architecture, and city planning. As dean there, he would oversee the rebuilding of the three different schools that comprised the Faculty of Architecture: Architecture, Landscape Architecture, and City Planning. Each of the schools operated independently (as at other universities that offered all three in the 1930s), with its own pedagogy, teaching methods, and faculty, all of them specialized and disengaged from one another. Despite their autonomy, Hudnut regarded the three fields as "mutually dependent" and "a complement of the others." While "many factors" attracted Hudnut to Harvard, "none was so urgent," he claimed, as the opportunity "to forge into one strong school these three weak schools."[131] By working together, and *only* by working together, Hudnut believed that faculty and students might begin to tackle the ultimate design problem—the city.

The fact that President Conant shared Hudnut's progressive views and had come to favor modern architecture definitely influenced Hudnut's decision to leave Columbia for Harvard. Conant had the makings of an important ally, unlike Columbia's more conservative president, Nicholas Murray Butler, who cared little for new pedagogical methods and not at all about architecture.[132] As a scientist, Conant understood the power of cooperative research, and during his years at Harvard, he consistently encouraged connections between different departments of knowledge. It was Conant who loosened the bonds between departments by creating university professorships—appointments with roving commissions that allowed a handful of notable scholars freedom from departmental constraints—and who developed new interdepartmental programs.[133] In addition to his scientific background, Conant also had a deep interest in German culture and education, which further inclined him toward modern architecture and, ultimately, the Bauhaus.[134] As Hudnut anticipated, President Conant backed his efforts over the years, often against the opposing wishes of moneyed alumni, overseers, and resentful faculty.

2 MODERN MOVEMENTS IN THE IVY

In June 1935, Hudnut took over the Harvard deanship vacated by George Edgell, an art historian specializing in Sienese painting and the last of a particular breed of architecture deans there. Edgell had few ties, if any, with the architecture, landscape architecture, or city planning professions, and he offered no real direction in design or pedagogy to the Faculty of Architecture, preferring instead to act as a conciliator in administrative matters. Described as "a grand gentleman of the most polished, outgoing sort," he would apologize for his modest knowledge of recent developments in the field at the start of his epic History of Architecture course each semester.[1] Nonetheless, Edgell showed genuine sympathy for modern architecture when, in 1931, he supported a scheme for a radically modern addition to Robinson Hall, the McKim-designed Harvard architecture building. Two architecture students and a faculty member had publicized their sketch for a three-story brick addition set on pilotis with rows of horizontal strip windows that admitted abundant light into the different drafting rooms. Edgell defended the proposal in the *Architectural Record* against the criticism of Gothicist Ralph Adams Cram, who charged that this was "not architecture" but merely the joining of a "Queen Anne front and a Mary Ann back." Edgell politely differed and added that "as for Mary Ann—I visualize her as an honest little person, attractive even in a homely way, and primarily concerned in doing something useful."[2] Given this retort, it is not surprising that when it came to hiring his successor, Edgell urged President Conant to go in the modern direction and "get the best man in the country. That man is Hudnut."[3]

Edgell may not have led the Faculty of Architecture too far from the Beaux-Arts academic tradition during his thirteen years as dean, but with the exception of Hudnut at Columbia, neither had the deans of the

Proposal for addition to Harvard's Robinson Hall (1931). (Reprinted with permission from *Architectural Record* 70 [August 1931]: 126)

other architecture schools that had long been promoting Beaux-Arts methods. These universities—MIT, Penn, Cornell, California, and Princeton prominent among them—continued to offer Americanized Beaux-Arts programs in their schools despite criticism from both students and the more progressive practitioners interested in modern design. When the Depression hit and architects joined the ranks of the jobless, the academic system of teaching came under increasing fire. Teachers, students, and practitioners from all sides of the architectural spectrum joined forces to argue that the grand, anachronistic aspirations and theories of the French system had no place in a climate of mass unemployment, reduced wages, and widespread pessimism about the future.

As the Depression helped loosen the hold of the Beaux-Arts system in the schools, Harvard was among those adding a few courses that emphasized technical and economic aspects of building, including the Business Aspect of Architecture and Practical Requirements in the Planning of Buildings.[4] Also in the early 1930s, faculty began developing occasional projects that encouraged cooperation between students in architecture and landscape architecture—designing country residences, for example, or laying out educational buildings along the Charles River. In addition to these kinds of joint design problems, at least one design instructor, G. Holmes Perkins, who had just finished his own studies at Harvard, dared to experiment in his classes by substituting working drawings and research for the more elaborate *esquisse.* For all these efforts to surmount the shortcomings of the French system, before Hudnut arrived there was little difference between a Harvard architectural education and the traditional Beaux-Arts pedagogy. Even as late as 1933, the French government awarded Harvard a medal honoring its architecture school as the American school most accomplished in teaching along the lines of the École in Paris.[5]

An École des Beaux-Arts alumnus had, in fact, held the most prominent faculty post at Harvard (as at several other American schools) since 1911. Jean-Jacques Haffner, the 1919 Grand Prix winner, dominated architectural study at Harvard from 1921 until Hudnut arrived, setting the style and character much as the head design professor often did in architecture schools. Haffner's students thought him an excellent critic, though "a very stiff, very formal," and intimidating Frenchman, said to look something like Hindenburg. In the drafting room, he would visit the students' desks, sit at their stools, and mark up their designs with his pen. Holmes Perkins described that in his student days with Haffner, "the plan was *the* important thing. And out of that plan, everything else was to grow. In one sense, that's not very different from the modern. The difference was how you dressed the thing afterwards. Did you pick up some Gothic details or some Renaissance details? A new sort of clothes? In that sense, it was very eclectic. The designs were always deliberately chosen from some style or other."[6] Although Haffner generally upheld academic teaching methods at Harvard, he did so with a certain leniency after the Depression. He no longer required, for example, that his students do an *analytique,* the study of the Orders that traditionally introduced them to the elements and proportions of classical architecture. Perkins's own shift into modern design evolved as he and a few of his fellow students began to question this process of "dressing" and tried experimenting in a modern vein.

> Haffner would discuss a design with another student and you could hear what he was saying. He said to this fellow next-door, "ah, you should not do that modern!" I had been doing what I thought was the most modern thing and I said, "I overheard what you said." He said, "oh no no no no. That is all right for you. But he cannot do it." The only nice thing he ever said to me! In other words, the freedom to choose a historic style was absolutely contrary to the modern view where you were supposed to invent something using the latest techniques, reflecting the outlook of society.[7]

Haffner's measured interest in modern design spilled into his own work. As Melanie Simo has noted, Haffner's 1931 book, *Compositions de*

Jean-Jacques Haffner garden design. (Jean-Jacques Haffner, *Compositions de jardins* [Paris: Vincent, Fréal & Cie., 1931], 21)

jardins, addressed some aspects of modernism, such as the vast middle ground between "informal" and "informal" landscape design; a sense of continuity between house, garden, and the landscape beyond; and a frank recognition of the human presence in nature.[8] On curricular matters, Haffner supported the idea of integrating some courses in architecture with planning and landscape architecture courses, and he argued for stronger ties between the curriculum and the present circumstances of architectural practice. As for the buildings of the European modern movement—much on the minds of students in the early 1930s—Haffner and most other teachers in the Faculty of Architecture expressed no interest at all.[9]

Haffner had enthusiastically supported Hudnut's coming to Harvard, though not everyone involved approved. A few members of the Visiting Committee, the oversight group of alumni actively engaged with the policy and finances of the Faculty of Architecture, argued against the "reactionary" Hudnut, who championed "extreme modernistic architecture." Instead, they sought a more moderate candidate who sought "fresh creations evolved from a background of tradition."[10] The old-guard majority on the faculty also opposed Hudnut's coming to Harvard, including Henry Hubbard, longtime head of the School of City Planning, who had campaigned for the deanship for himself, and Bremer Pond, another longtime fixture at Harvard and chair of the School of Landscape Architecture. Both Hubbard and Pond represented the mainstream of their respective fields. The few younger, more progressive (and untenured) faculty members seemed "extraordinarily happy" about Hudnut's appointment, and students celebrated the news that Harvard had hired a dean with modernist leanings.[11] No middle ground seemed to exist in the polarized debate between traditionalists and modernists in 1935, even for those who may have sought it: one either belonged to the modernist camp, embracing technology and experimentation, or to the academic side, where tradition and precedent governed. All those who weighed in on Hudnut (even Hudnut himself) tagged him a modernist.

Deposing the Gods

Hudnut made his first act at Harvard a visible and symbolic one: he set out to redesign McKim's Robinson Hall into a space fit for educating *modern* architects and planners. As Hudnut described, "Harvard is filled

Robinson Hall, Harvard University, Hall of Casts, ca. 1925. (Courtesy of the Frances Loeb Library, Harvard Design School)

with cries of alarm and the noise of falling columns and arches, while I lead the attack against the Theseum and the temple of Nike Apteros, which have stood for generations in plaster form under our lofty ceiling."[12] Hudnut purged all vestiges of the academy from Robinson Hall, the conspicuous symbols and objects from the past adorning the great Hall of Casts: antique building fragments and sculpture that had filled the great two-story foyer since the building opened in 1904. After ripping Old Master copies, Beaux-Arts *envois,* and charts of the Orders off the many walls, he had the whole interior repainted a pristine modernist white. Where the Hall of Casts had stood in seeming perpetuity, Hudnut erected glass cases and spare white partitions for changing exhibitions of contemporary art.[13]

Hudnut not only gave Robinson Hall a new modern image, but he also redesigned its interior spaces in a way that expressed his commitment to a progressive, democratic form of education. He literally tore down the walls separating the architecture, planning, and landscape architecture schools and brought their classrooms and offices into proximity so as to promote cooperation among the fields. He removed all partitions in the drafting room, creating a large, open, common space where students in the three disciplines and at all levels of proficiency could collaborate on their work. To encourage individual growth, he designed a series of smaller spaces where a teacher could work closely with a small group or a single student.[14]

When Hudnut finished with Robinson Hall, he launched a similar attack on the adjacent Hunt Hall, the elegant old Fogg Museum building by Richard Morris Hunt that was used for the overflow of architecture, planning, and landscape classes and offices. Hudnut also purged these rooms and walls of the architectural past, joined spaces to foster cooperation, and even replaced the building's mullioned windows with large glass sheets of the latest manufacture, more pleasing to the modern sensibility.[15] By the time Hudnut finished his renovation, a Boston newspaper commented that, without "an overstuffed feature or a slanted roof in sight," visiting Harvard's architecture school was a "trip through the future, say fifty years hence.[16] Although Gropius was nowhere in sight of Harvard at the time of Hudnut's remodeling and the subject of hiring him had not yet been broached, historians have credited him and not Hudnut with remaking the buildings into modernist spaces.[17] Such has been the power of Gropius's reputation.

In his attack against academic "copyism," Hudnut went so far as to banish history books from Robinson Hall's library into storage elsewhere on campus—"deadwood" books he called them—thereby transforming "a reference library for the use of students in archaeology" into

Students copying drawings in the Robinson Hall library, Harvard University, ca. 1925. (Courtesy of the Frances Loeb Library, Harvard Design School)

a "working library accessory to the laboratories of design and construction."[18] The architect William Perry, an alumnus and devotee of Harvard (1905) and the École (1908), offered a detailed, personal account of the banishment. It begins with Perry, a protagonist in the story, receiving a phone call from the Robinson Hall librarian urging him to hurry over to the library.

> So I was there within fifteen minutes in a taxi. I came in, and there was a clean room; You have to go through the library to get back to the librarian's office. And as I walked through, everything was spic and span, and there wasn't a book to be seen, and I said, "Well you're really cleaning the library." She said despairingly, "Mr. Perry, it's being cleaned out!" And I said, "Well, please tell me!" She told me that every book on architecture published before the year 1936 had been removed from the library. . . . Shocked as I was by this method of negative approach to architecture, I asked Miss Cook if there were any books left. She said, "Yes, we have three volumes of first editions of Le Corbusier's *Oeuvre*."[19]

Some days later Hudnut and Perry happened to meet while at the Harvard Club for breakfast. According to Perry: "Hudnut looked up and saw me across the table and his eyes went down to his plate again. Architecture was so serious with him that I was not even an architect; I wasn't even an acquaintance." Perry then told the story of the library incident to those around him. When he finished, Hudnut stood up, slammed his fist down on the table, and disputed Perry's account as "absolutely false!" When Perry asked Hudnut for his side of the story, the dean explained: "This is a physical transfer of books. And I want it clearly understood that every book antedating 1932 has been taken out of that library."[20]

Although Perry most likely embellished the details of what he called "this very true story," Hudnut did replace the library's history books with blueprints of recent buildings, specifications, and manufacturer's catalogues.[21] This was a drastic measure and an almost inexplicable act, given Hudnut's serious interest in architectural history. The only explanation would seem to be that when he first arrived at Harvard, Hudnut was so intent on making rapid changes in the way students approached design, especially in preventing their copying from drawings of historical buildings, that he was willing to take radical measures. At the end of Hudnut's years at Harvard, the GSD librarian described that "the state of the Library during the ten years or so prior to the academic year

1953–54 was a sad one, and this after an enviable record of accomplishment since its beginning."[22]

Hudnut did not miss a detail in his efforts to modernize the Faculty of Architecture and its buildings. He even overhauled the *Official Register* of the architecture school, the catalogue that publicized a carefully constructed image of a decorous, high-cultured place. He streamlined the register's typeface, text and, remarkably, the frontispiece photograph of Robinson Hall's exterior, with its prominent bas-reliefs and plaques celebrating the Ancients. The new catalogue showed an old photograph, taken in 1906, before the details had been embedded in McKim's building. Though removing the ancient details from the building had proved too expensive, Hudnut modernized economically, with a mere sleight of hand.[23]

With changes in the spatial organization and detailing of Robinson and Hunt Halls underway, Hudnut began the radical administrative restructuring of the Faculty of Architecture. In February 1936, less than a year into his deanship, the university approved his proposal to dissolve the old Faculty and merge its three schools, Architecture, Landscape Architecture, and City Planning, into a single new school, the Graduate School of Design. Hudnut made "departments" of the three former "schools" at the new GSD, each with its own chair who would work collaboratively with the others under the leadership of a common dean. Hudnut had no choice to but to keep Hubbard as the head of City Planning and Pond in charge of Landscape Architecture, while for a short time, he himself chaired the Architecture Department.

Hudnut chose the name "Design" for the new School ("though I almost got thrown out on my ear for doing it") to emphasize the sense of unity he was trying to create among the three professions. As he explained it, "Design" described the fundamental and shared activity of architects, planners, and landscapers. Each of them arranged and interpreted ideas, both practical and aesthetic, into "visible patterns."[24] "I wanted to tell the people that we thought of city planning as design—and landscape and industrial design—and that all things which have to do with the creation of forms for civilized living, for the environment of man, are plastic design and are therefore basically one activity. To design a chair and to design a cathedral is the same process: the same evolution of form, the same evolution of technique."[25] Hudnut readily acknowledged that while the GSD's different departments shared important commonalities, each embraced "an area of human interest and

Above: Robinson Hall (ca. 1904) exterior, celebrating the ancients on the façade. (Courtesy of the Harvard University Archives, call no. HUV 52 [3–12].) *Below:* Robinson Hall exterior (ca. 1903), before the building was completed and details embedded in the façade. (Courtesy of Harvard University Archives, call no. HUV 52 [2–5])

a technique peculiar to itself and not included in the others." But because differences in the three fields had consistently raised barriers between them, Hudnut intended the GSD to stress their shared processes
and to emphasis the changed relationship among them. In the spirit
of collaboration, Hudnut even encouraged faculty members to regard
themselves as he now did, "as much a city planner and landscape architect" as an architect.[26]

The Old Guard

The old guard at the new GSD—Bremer Pond and especially Henry Hubbard—proved far less malleable than the bricks and mortar of Robinson
Hall. Hubbard remained Hudnut's most stubborn opponent at the GSD,
resisting all efforts to establish a cooperative design program and holding fast in his antagonism to modern architecture. He especially disliked
taking any orders from Hudnut related to the direction of city planning,
given Hudnut's limited experience in the field and Hubbard's lingering
resentment over the fact that Hudnut had won the deanship that he
himself coveted. As Hudnut told President Conant in 1938, Hubbard
"would if he could destroy my program for the School of Design."[27]

> Mr. Hubbard advocated a union of the three schools (architecture, land-
> scape architecture and regional planning) so long as he hoped to be dean
> of the reorganized faculty. It was after my appointment that he discovered
> the incompatibility of architecture and regional planning. His zeal for a
> separation of the two curricula grew as he approached the age when he
> might be retired as professor and chairman; while I waited as patiently as
> I could for that day to arrive.[28]

Hubbard had long been an important figure in the national planning establishment and at the forefront of planning education since its
beginnings in the United States. He had taught city planning at Harvard
from the time it was first offered within the School of Landscape Architecture in 1909, and he played an active part when Harvard made planning a field for graduate study in 1923. When the university opened the
nation's first school of city planning in 1929, Hubbard served as chairman.[29] Under Hubbard, Harvard took the lead ahead of other universities in educating planners: by the end of the thirties only three other
universities had planning schools or departments—MIT (1935), Cor-

nell (1935), and Columbia (1937)—though the field would grow rapidly, with fifteen new planning schools opening by 1950.[30]

Despite Harvard's early foray into planning education, the approach taken there had its critics, including Werner Hegemann and his partner, Elbert Peets, a 1915 Landscape Architecture alumnus. As Hegemann wrote from Germany in 1925: "In our common work, Peets and I revolted against the nameless reactionary attitude of the Harvard School of Landscape Architecture, out of which today the majority of American city planners are influenced. Out of this connection, you will understand how seldom I regret that I am placed living here."[31] Having worked with Hegemann and Peets only two years earlier, Hudnut likely knew how the two regarded the Harvard school. Whereas Hegemann treated city planning as an interdisciplinary endeavor rooted in the design fields, Harvard's faculty viewed planning instead as a highly specialized pragmatic discipline distinct from landscape architecture and architecture, and also distinct from the theoretical study of government, economics, and sociology.[32] This was the "reactionary" approach Hegemann referred to, and Hubbard had been instrumental in promoting it. The publications coming out of the Harvard City Planning Studies series give clues to the sort of planning promoted in the School, as do the kinds of positions that students took on after graduation. While the publications focused on airports, land values, traffic flow, transition zoning, and density studies, those who had studied planning at the Harvard went on to serve as administrators in the Federal Housing Administration, the Tennessee Valley Authority, and state or city planning commissions. Though they made decisions about the uses and appearance of the physical environment, they did so without much experience and with little training in design.[33]

Hubbard's writings and editorial work during his years at Harvard reflect a growing interest in dividing the fields of planning and design. Early in his career, Hubbard and Theodora Kimball, Harvard's landscape architecture librarian and Hubbard's future wife, coauthored *An Introduction to the Study of Landscape Design* (1917), which remained the classic student text for decades. The book considers landscape architecture as the fine art of subtly modifying the natural landscape, with the best designs revealing only slight evidence of human intervention. Its various chapters consider landscape styles, effects, composition techniques, and planting design, and it also includes a section on subdivisions and urban park planning. At the end of the book, Hubbard and Kimball proclaim that the "greatest opportunity for public service which is before the landscape architect of to-day is that he may bear his share in the complete organization of town and city and state and nation."[34] The book belongs squarely to the tradition of Frederick Law Olmsted, who conceived of landscape architecture and planning as a single field.

Olmsted's son, Frederick Jr., who taught landscape architecture at Harvard from 1900 to 1915, took the lead in moving the Harvard program away from his father's conception of the field. Unlike his father, who sought to humanize the commercial city and its workaday citizens through the design process, Olmsted Jr. looked to a new set of specialists, bureaucracy, and local government to plan and coordinate changes in the city.[35] Olmsted Jr.'s successors at Harvard, James Sturgis Pray and Hubbard, both members of the Olmsted Brothers firm, came to embrace a similar view of city planning. Hubbard made his change of heart apparent in his second book, also coauthored with his wife, *Our Cities To-day and To-morrow* (1929), which focuses on zoning, street systems, recreation needs, mass transit, and the legal and administrative means of planning. With city planning as his subject, Hubbard now had little to say about aesthetics or landscape design.[36] He similarly distinguished between design and city planning in the two journals he was editing, one aptly named *Landscape Architecture* and the other, fittingly enough, *City Planning*. Until *City Planning* began publication in 1925, articles on planning had always found a home in *Landscape Architecture*. After 1925, Hubbard placed all planning articles in the new journal, leaving *Landscape Architecture* narrowly focused on horticulture, parks, and gardens.[37] The Harvard curriculum followed the same pattern.

In 1929, Harvard won a grant from the Rockefeller Foundation to fund a new School of City Planning within the Faculty of Architecture.[38] (At several points, its name shifted back and forth between "City Planning" and "Regional Planning," although its educational mission remained much the same.) The grant also funded a new professorship, the Charles Dyer Norton Professor of Regional Planning, which went to Hubbard. City and regional planning now got official sanction as a discipline of its own at Harvard, much as Hubbard insisted it should, distinct from landscape architecture and also distinct from architecture. This was the situation as Hudnut found it when he arrived at Harvard. He was determined to change it.

With the backing of a like-minded committee of alumni, Hubbard fought hard to keep the GSD planning curriculum separate from architecture, against Hudnut's efforts to unite them. Hubbard had been instrumental in divorcing landscape architecture and city planning, and he had no intention now of allowing a marriage between planning and architecture. He considered architecture the "art of creating individual buildings." As such, it clearly differed from city planning, which he described as having a basis in "topography, economics, the law, the political machinery, and the predispositions and backgrounds of the people who are to be served."[39] For his part, Hudnut held fast to Hegemann's view that city planning was "the basis of architecture." Thus he would battle with Hubbard over the direction of city planning for the next six years.

Hudnut also had strong philosophical differences with Bremer Pond about the future of landscape architecture at Harvard, though he had a slightly less contentious relationship with Pond than with Hubbard. An alumnus of both the Harvard program and the Olmsted Brothers office, Pond had taught landscape architecture at Harvard since 1914, upholding its traditional offerings of art history, drawing, botany, and engineering. As Mary Daniels has written, Pond's education both at Harvard and in Brookline, along with extensive travel and his personal tastes, ensured his "fidelity to the value of traditional accomplishments in both design and its presentation."[40] A letter from Pond to a colleague in 1945—long after Gropius, Breuer, and others had made the modern idiom de rigueur at the GSD—sheds light on Pond's position as the world around him evolved in new directions.

> The Landscape Department is still trying to uphold the standards and type of instruction as we used to have it, with freehand and other things required; the architects look on us as old-fashioned. . . . I am quite willing to say that I am old-fashioned enough to believe most decidedly that design should be attractive to the eye as well as "functional" if it is to survive and not become merely a form of engineering.[41]

What were the standards that Pond fought to uphold? According to Hegemann's partner, Elbert Peets, who had penned a scathing commentary in 1927, those standards made Harvard "practically a branch of the Olmsted Office." Peets went so far as to blame the miserable state of landscape architecture practice in America on the Harvard program.

For fifty years Olmsted Sr. preached and practiced, and his faith has now spread to every corner of the country. His disciples have almost as tight control over American gardening as the Klan once had over Indiana politics. Large estates . . . are mainly in the landscape style. Every suburban lot breaks out in scalloped borders and specimen plants as naturally as a Plymouth Rock hen lays a brown egg. . . . Even when landscape architects do not get the job, the landscape idea usually does.[42]

Thanks to Pond and Hubbard—the "old Olmsted men," as Peets called them—landscape architecture at Harvard remained "separate and distinct from the contiguous arts." Furthermore, the "incredibly narrow taste" that Peets described—either "nature-imitative, informal, anti-geometric, opposed to the display of craftsmanship" or all "straightness, uniformity, economy, and equal balance"—ruled despotically at the Harvard landscape school when Hudnut arrived eight years later.[43]

A New Zeus

Although Hubbard and Pond did not budge either from their deeply rooted convictions or from their tenured positions at the GSD, Haffner submitted his resignation in 1936. He had always intended to return to France at some point, and though he got on well with Hudnut, he felt that the dean should be free to choose his own person to head the Architecture Department. Haffner returned to Paris to work as the architect of the Louvre at a convenient moment in his family life as well, for he did not want his daughters to come of marriage age in the United States.[44]

Hudnut immediately set to work on hiring a modern architect to fill Haffner's post. He was determined to bring a high-profile European modernist to the position, someone like Walter Gropius or Mies van der Rohe, both of whom he felt shared his views on architecture and education and whose presence would trumpet the GSD's commitment to modern design. Hudnut did not want a mere figurehead but a genuine collaborator to help him steer modern architecture and modern civic design in new directions. While he would oversee educational policy and administrative matters, Hudnut envisioned his new colleague bringing their common ideas into the design studios.[45]

President Conant fully supported the idea of bringing either Mies or Gropius to Harvard both because he sympathized with the new architecture and because he wanted the most distinguished leader in every field at Harvard. Conant no doubt found the prospect of bringing one of these two architects to Harvard intriguing, since they had each played an important part in German cultural developments during the Weimar years. Conant had developed a lifelong interest in Germany, especially in its educational and university systems, during a lengthy visit there in 1925. When he resigned the Harvard presidency in 1953, he did so to become the U.S. high commissioner to Germany.[46]

Hudnut carried on his search for a new design professor in secret, keeping only Conant and Alfred Barr at the Museum of Modern Art informed of the details. Hudnut told Barr of his plans because he knew that at the same time that he was looking for a modern architect for Harvard, Barr was trying to bring one of the modernists over from Europe to collaborate with Philip Goodwin, a museum trustee and architect, on a new building for the Modern. Barr left for Europe in mid-May to ask the architects J. J. P. Oud in Rotterdam and Mies van der Rohe in Berlin— and "failing these two," Walter Gropius, then living in London—if they would be interested in working on the museum building.[47]

Barr was already in London when Hudnut contacted him with the news that Harvard was looking to invite Mies or Gropius to fill Haffner's post. Hudnut asked Barr to discuss the possibility of a teaching post at Harvard with both of them, and if they expressed interest, he would follow up with a visit of his own. Barr suggested that Hudnut also consider Oud (whom Hudnut had supposed was still in poor health) as a possible candidate for the position. Hudnut cabled a message to Barr telling him to discuss the job with Oud because he believed Oud to be the "best of the three" and "the most likely to be successful in this country."[48]

Barr met with each of the architects at the end of June. Oud opted to stay at home in Holland, since after years of trying he was finally gaining recognition there. Mies expressed great interest in both the museum job and Harvard, and Gropius was also quite interested in the professorship at Harvard. Barr had barely mentioned the museum collaboration to Gropius, since Mies—whom Barr believed a far better designer—had already made clear that he was available.[49]

The day after he met with Gropius, Barr received news from the museum that the trustees refused to allow Goodwin to collaborate with a "foreign" architect on the building project. Barr quickly fired off a series of letters to New York saying that the museum was obliged, as the arbiter of the art and architecture of its time, to build the best modern structure it possibly could and that Mies was the right person for that task.[50] Barr also wrote to Goodwin asking why the trustees were "prejudiced against a foreign architect" when they "do not hesitate to buy English clothes or French hats (if not French pictures)—nor do they seriously object to the Museum's owning foreign paintings."[51] He hoped that news of Hudnut's interest in bringing Mies to Harvard might sway the minds of the xenophobic trustees in his favor, and he told them of Hudnut's plan in confidence. In the end, Barr's efforts to hire Mies were in vain. The museum instead hired Edward Durrell Stone to work with Goodwin. Stone was then a young architect with only a few buildings to his credit, but he had strong connections to a rather prominent trustee, Nelson Rockefeller.[52]

Toward the end of the summer, Hudnut went to Europe to follow the trail Barr had laid for him. He discussed the Harvard post with Mies in Berlin and with Gropius in London, where he had been living since he left Nazi Germany in 1934. Both badly wanted the chair at Harvard, especially since Hudnut also made clear his preference that they practice architecture at the same time that they taught. Hudnut returned to Cambridge clearly impressed with both architects. As he told Alfred Barr: "I have repeatedly weighed the qualities of each against those of the other, recognizing them as different in degree but much alike in quality. It is my present feeling that Mies would prove to be the more inspiring and perhaps more valuable man inside the School and that any work which he might do as an architect in this country would be superior in quality to the work which might be done by Gropius."[53] While this sounds like a ringing endorsement for a Mies appointment, Hudnut went on to sing the praises of Gropius, who "might have a greater influence upon the development of architectural education in this country as a whole and he would, I feel sure, be a stronger influence outside of our own classrooms."[54]

With their interviews over, the administrative process of hiring Mies or Gropius finally began. Hiring a famous modern architect for Harvard in 1936 was a bold move that required not only President Conant's consent and faculty approval but also an official vote by the university's governing boards. Conant counseled Hudnut to submit the names of two candidates to the boards on the theory that, if offered a choice of candidates, the chance for success was more likely. In response to Conant's suggestion, Hudnut prepared a lengthy memorandum introducing Mies and Gropius to the boards and discussing what each might contribute to the GSD. It is a remarkably evenhanded document and interesting enough to quote at some length, for it describes Hudnut's views on the two architects as well as the qualities he hoped to find in his future colleague:

> Mies is perhaps the most original architect among the modernists. He has arrived at his style by a long series of aesthetic experimentations rather than by a philosophical analysis. He is a sensitive artist with an extraordinary feeling for space and for the qualities of the planes which divide space. In his work he is somewhat extravagant, since he refuses to use any cheap materials. He despises ornament, believing that decorative qualities in work should be achieved by the richness of materials used, and he is especially famous for his successful use of glass.
>
> As a teacher Mies has contributed little to educational theory. His ideas may be said to be fundamentally those of his Bauhaus predecessor, Walter Gropius, but he has a peculiar quality of developing the latent powers of his students through their association with him and to win the devotion of those who work with him to a very extraordinary degree.
>
> I have had several long talks with Mies and I found him a person of vision, unusually informed in aesthetic matters, and with great distinction of manner. He impresses me as a vigorous and altogether honest person who seems to have every quality for leadership in the teaching of architecture. He is somewhat vain and I imagine that he might be more difficult to work with than Mr. Gropius.[55]

Hudnut predicted in the memo that Mies would be well received by "the more progressive element of the architectural profession in America," and that his coming to Harvard would pose a "distinct challenge to the conservative school . . . identified with the École des Beaux-Arts in Paris." But even this latter group, he suggested, would come to appreciate Mies's subtle technique and use of fine materials. Hudnut added that Mies was "an aristocrat who will not be appreciated by the mass of manufacturers" despite that they already imitate him.[56] On the subject of Gropius, Hudnut noted that his architecture is "less sensitive than that of Mies and in many ways lacks much of the latter's subtlety. He is less concerned with the fine use of materials and his detail is often times somewhat crude." Gropius's primary concern, he added, is with "the philosophy of architecture and the achievement of some integration between aesthetic expression and technique."

Gropius's achievements as an architect have been more significant than those of any other modern architect. As a teacher he has undoubtedly done more to advance the technique and theory of architectural education than any other man. He is a man of distinguished personality and of fine education, not only thoroughly informed in all of the arts, but also deeply interested in social, economic, and political movements. He writes in a convincing way, and has considerable command of the English and French languages as well as his own.[57]

Hudnut added that with his already wide reputation, Gropius would be well received in the United States: "He is favorably known to all the architects. Since his work is more reasonable than that of Herr Mies and since it has been more widely explained, Gropius is better understood." Hudnut also took pains to emphasize another trait he valued in a modernist colleague, that Gropius had already proved himself "an excellent propagandist."[58]

Hudnut tried to assuage any doubts the conservative Harvard boards might have had about Gropius's and Mies's political leanings. He acknowledged in the memorandum that the Bauhaus had been accused of "promoting Communist ideas," but he assured them that "neither Gropius nor Mies have any sympathy with Communism": "During Hannes Meyer's regime [at the Bauhaus] there was in fact some promulgation of Communist doctrines. And Mr. Gropius told me that he forced the resignation of Meyer immediately upon being told that the school was becoming a center of radical thought. Mies, who has never been suspected of such activities, is now a government architect."[59]

It is disconcerting to think that Mies's status as a government architect in Nazi Germany might have assuaged any skepticism the overseers had about Gropius's and Mies's political views. Hudnut also felt compelled to address concerns that Gropius might be Jewish. Although President Conant had discarded the quotas that his predecessor, Abbott Lowell, kept in place to restrict the number of Jews at Harvard, Hudnut knew that perception of a "Jewish problem" still lingered in some corners of the university:[60] "Another statement repeatedly made about Gropius is that he is himself a member of a Jewish family, or at any rate, has wide connections among Jewish people. I do not consider these charges to be of any importance, even if they are true; but as a matter of fact, they are not true. Gropius is a typical German of the scholarly university type."[61]

Hudnut kept up an active correspondence with Mies after their meeting in Berlin late in the summer of 1936, assuring the architect of his great wish to bring him to Harvard. While he did not quite promise Mies the appointment, Hudnut gave him every reason to feel optimistic. In September, for example, en route home after having visited Mies in Berlin, Hudnut wrote to him: "I should like, as soon as I reach Cambridge, to make a formal request to the President of the University in respect to the appointment of a Professor of Design. I hope that I may receive from you a letter telling me that you are able to consider favorably the acceptance of a chair should this be offered you by the President. . . . Some time may pass before you hear from the President."[62] For his part, Mies continued to assert his interest in coming to Harvard. Letters and assurances between Hudnut and Gropius were far less frequent.[63]

Why, then, wasn't Mies appointed to the professorship at Harvard? Ultimately, what Hudnut had referred to as Mies's vanity, his impatience with bureaucratic hiring procedures, and his dislike for Gropius cost him the job. Gropius's affability, in contrast, may also have helped move the decision in his favor. Hudnut had written to Mies that, at the president's request, he would be recommending two architects for the GSD position to the Harvard governing boards. Mies quickly sent Hudnut a note stipulating that if Harvard wanted him as a candidate for the post, no other person could be considered for it. Mies must have been stunned by the fact that Harvard was choosing between two architects for the professorship, for he seems to have been convinced that he would be offered the GSD post. Less than a week before he learned of the Harvard situation, Mies had turned down an opportunity for a professorship at the Armour Institute of Technology (now Illinois Institute of Technology) in Chicago. He had told Armour that he had "received an offer from another American university." Mies clearly believed himself a better architect than Gropius, and he believed that he would be a more suitable design professor. After discussing Mies's demand with Conant, Hudnut wrote to Mies that he had never intended to make it appear that he was technically a "candidate" for a position at Harvard. The tone of his letters to Mies subsequently cooled.[64]

Conant had as much say in the final hiring decision as Hudnut did. During a lengthy trip to England in the fall of 1936, Conant had a lunch meeting with Gropius in London, who seems to have won him over. Shortly after the president returned to campus, Hudnut sent Mies a letter that he would not be appointed to Harvard. At the same time, he wrote to Gropius offering him an "appointment for life" at the GSD and assuring him that he would be of "the greatest possible value" not only to Harvard but "to the cause of architecture in this country."[65]

After extending the offer to Gropius that December, Hudnut wrote to him and described the work that he intended the two of them to take on in the coming years. Hudnut's own grand but uncertain task, he wrote, is "that of devising a system of architectural education which will in some way be rationally related to the changing responsibilities of the architect in this country."[66] "I know quite well that no one can foresee definitely these responsibilities but I do know that the role of the architect in our civilization is undergoing a profound change and I feel deeply the necessity of attempting some general revision. I know of no one in the world who could be of greater help to me in this work than you."[67] Hudnut promised Gropius a group of fifteen or twenty of the country's best architecture students and the freedom to teach them as he saw fit so that "each year we may send out into the country a dozen or more young men who have come under your influence."[68] He further promised to help Gropius set up his architectural practice in Cambridge, and he reassured him that he would help him find opportunities to serve as an adviser or collaborator on important building projects. In effect, Hudnut, who was in a position to do so, guaranteed Gropius that he would be a significant player in creating a modern architectural landscape in America. Hudnut's final act of courtship was to send Holmes Perkins as emissary from the GSD to meet with Gropius in London to "clear up any doubts or misunderstandings that may be on his mind."[69]

Gropius eagerly accepted the GSD post for a number of reasons. In part, he wanted to leave London, despite the fact that he had developed strong ties there. He had grown particularly close to Jack Pritchard, owner of the modern furniture design firm Isokon, who, along with the author and critic P. Morton Shand, had arranged for his departure from Nazi Germany in 1934. Pritchard had provided Gropius and his wife, Ise, with a safe haven at the Lawn Road Flats, the ultramodern, white, ocean liner of a building that Pritchard had commissioned Wells Coates to design for a site in the middle of Victorian Hampstead. For a time, overlapping with the Gropiuses, Bauhauslers Marcel Breuer and László Moholy-Nagy also took up residence at the flats. The great white behemoth on Lawn Road not only housed the émigrés but also served as a central meeting point for the lively community of modern artists living in the neighborhood. Gropius befriended many people there, including the critic Herbert Read; artists Henry Moore, Ben Nicholson, Barbara Hepworth, and Naum Gabo; and the British architects affiliated with the Modern Architectural Research group, or MARS, who had banded together to promote the modernist cause. Pritchard not only housed Gropius, he helped him establish a partnership in London with Maxwell Fry, one of the MARS founders, and he tried to get them a number of different building commissions in Britain.[70] The arrangement between Pritchard and Gropius was not all one-sided: Gropius's affiliation with Isokon brought the firm a new level of international prestige, and the Gropiuses and Pritchards became lifelong friends.[71]

For all his friendships and contacts, the Britons did not appreciate Gropius's architecture enough to make life there either gratifying or economically viable. Gropius had expressed his dismay to Pritchard in 1935 that "after six months, I am not on my own legs," a situation that did not change during the next two years.[72] Although Gropius designed a few buildings in partnership with the young Fry, the larger commissions the two sought did not pan out. Much in line with the pattern that existed throughout Gropius's life, the famous founder of the Bauhaus had quickly overshadowed his partner, and he spent much time outside the office trying to develop contacts and clients of his own. Gropius's limited command of English did curb his well-known ability to promote himself in his new home. When he lectured, for example, he generally read a prepared paper, showed slides of his German works, and omitted the question-and-answer period at the end because of the

Lawn Road Flats, London. (Courtesy of the Pritchard Papers, University of East Anglia)

Walter Gropius with Maxwell Fry, "Unbuilt Project, Apartment Houses and Hotel, St. Leonard's Hill, Windsor, England," 1934–35. (Courtesy of the Busch-Reisinger Museum, Harvard University Art Museums, Gift of Walter Gropius, BRGA.78.2)

language barrier.[73] Gropius did not play the important role he hoped to in England in large part because the ground had not been prepared for what he had to offer. As Anthony Blunt confirmed in the *Spectator*, three months before Gropius left London for Harvard: "The Englishman in general dislikes functional architecture—the buildings of Le Corbusier, Gropius, Mendelsohn and the rest—because they are not *homey*. It is true that the Englishman is apt to make this accusation against all forms of foreign architecture—I doubt whether even the Italian villa or the smaller French château would pass muster as *homey*—but against functionalism the accusation is made with unusual venom."[74]

Though ready to move on from London because of his frustrating circumstances there, Gropius had not anticipated a departure anytime soon. In July 1936, he had entered into a permanent partnership with Maxwell Fry and had written to the under secretary of state in the Aliens Department asking permission for permanent residency in England.[75]

Even so, the idea that Lawrence Kocher had proposed to Gropius a few years earlier, that he find a teaching position in the United States and set up practice there, had always remained at the back of his mind. Gropius admired the "enthusiasm and eagerness of young Americans" along with their "optimistic and undaunted spirits," and he felt certain that his work would find a receptive audience in the United States.[76] Gropius had visited the United States in 1928 in the midst of its post-war prosperity, and he savored the freedom from constraints and openness to new ideas he saw in all areas, including the arts and politics. As he wrote to a friend in Berlin, "I have returned from America with precious gains, and I have truly come to love this country."[77] In Gropius's mind, America stood in stark contrast to England, where the "conservative attitude of the Englishman makes it difficult for him to recognize anything new."[78] Even his British friend Pritchard agreed: "I had indeed made a note that I would have a talk with you about America in view of my own feelings about developments there in comparison with here."[79]

In addition to the frustrations of refugee life and the limitations of his architectural practice in London, other compelling reasons drew Gropius to Harvard. It seemed clear to Gropius that the GSD under Hudnut shared the same basic principles of education and design that had governed the Bauhaus under his direction. He felt certain that he could accomplish at Harvard what he had been unable to in Weimar or Dessau—to create the world's premier school for modern architects. In Germany, the Bauhaus had been under constant attack, first by conservatives in Weimar, who drove the school out of that city in 1925, and then by the Nazis, who forced it out of Dessau in 1932 and caused its final dissolution in Berlin a year later.[80] Gropius had spent much of his time at the Bauhaus defending the school against government and public antipathy, and he did not achieve some important goals; notably, he managed to establish an architecture program there only after eight years had passed. The architecture program started in 1927, the year before Gropius resigned from the school.

Gropius knew that Harvard and America would allow him a freedom he had yet to experience, either in Germany or England, to pursue both his artistic principles and his social goals—essentially, to make good architecture accessible to all people.[81] The opportunity to hold an important post at prestigious Harvard was not lost on him: Harvard would offer him a highly visible stage from which to spread his ideas on modern architecture and urbanism. Gropius no doubt understood, too, that his offer from Harvard came at a most opportune time, when American architects were looking to fill the growing void created by the downfall of the Beaux-Arts educational system. And though Gropius voiced some doubts about universities as "healthy breeding grounds for architects," knowing that Hudnut had effectively purged his school of the academic system made him feel confident about "the practicability of my own ideas within the Harvard framework." In accepting the GSD post, Gropius told Hudnut, "I see clearly now that I shall not be isolated with my work at Harvard as we seem to go in the same direction."[82]

Gropius delayed his move to the United States for three months, until March 1937, leaving himself time to tie up his affairs in England. He and Ise said their good-byes at a dinner in London held in their honor and attended by an impressive number of guests. Of the more than seventy people who gathered to send off the Gropiuses, many came from the modern art and architectural communities, among them Patrick Abercrombie, Ove Arup, Serge Chermayeff, Wells Coates, Maxwell Fry, Sigfried Giedion, W. G. Holford, Julian Huxley, László Moholy-Nagy, Henry Moore, the Pritchards, Herbert Read, Morton Shand, and H. G. Wells.[83] Gropius made a farewell speech at the dinner in which he expressed his gratitude for the overwhelming tribute that the evening paid him and Ise and for the many friendships they had made in their two years in London. He also spoke of his disappointment at the state of architecture at that moment in England. While English architecture had expressed itself so perfectly in the past—"one need only think of Bath and the beautiful Georgian architecture"—in modern times this "pioneering and enterprising nation" seems unwilling to take "the same chance, to create a style in accordance with its social structure and twentieth-century way of living." Gropius told his guests that the future of English architecture lay in the hands of the MARS group (founded by his friends Coates, Fry, and Shand, all present at the dinner), who are working "to get rid of the imitation of old styles" and to confront "the problems of *our* day and *our* future." Finally, Gropius conveyed his excitement about "going to the States not as a stranger but as a collaborator and member of an institution of worldwide renown."[84]

While awaiting Gropius's arrival in the United States, Hudnut began seeking out architectural commissions for his new colleague. He thought it important that Gropius's hand be seen in the new buildings at Harvard, and he tried, though unsuccessfully, to persuade the administration to include Gropius in designing the new Littauer Center for Public Administration, to be built on a prominent site just beyond the gates of Harvard Yard. The building ultimately turned out as a stately, though mausoleumesque, neo-Bulfinch building by Shepley, Bulfinch, and Abbott. Hudnut also asked the well-connected Alfred Barr for help in finding projects for Gropius in New York, and Hudnut himself succeeded in interesting the various developers of an art center, a nursery school, and projects at Connecticut and Wheaton Colleges in the possibility of employing Gropius. In the end, only the nursery school project reached the negotiating stage, but Gropius's design for it was not accepted.[85]

Hudnut further laid the groundwork for Gropius's arrival in the United States by invoking his name wherever he could in the architectural press. In his capacity as a member of the Museum of Modern Art's Architecture Committee, Hudnut proposed the exhibition of Bauhaus work that ultimately took place there in grand fashion in 1938.[86] Hudnut also tried to make good on a promise to Gropius that he would help him "get big publicity" for his recent book, *The New Architecture and the Bauhaus.*[87] The book had been published in England in 1935, with an introduction by Frank Pick, a figure well known in London for having commissioned innovative modern graphic designs for the London Underground. Gropius had worked aggressively to find an American publisher, but even the Museum of Modern Art had rejected his book.[88] Gropius knew that a published volume would be a powerful tool for spreading his ideas in the United States, even more so than in England, where all the young modernists had read it and where it had put him on the lecture circuit.[89] Only days after Gropius accepted the GSD post, Hudnut wrote a preface for an American edition, and the Museum of Modern Art finally agreed to publish the book.[90] In his preface, Hudnut praised the Bauhaus for daring to create a new way of educating designers and architects for the modern mechanized world and for promoting a "mode of expression integral with our technical civilization."[91] Though he made no mention of any future for the Bauhaus educational system in the preface, that issue became the subject of heated debate from the moment word got out that Gropius was coming to Harvard.

A Harvard Bauhaus?

Partly that debate took place as the senior (mostly old-guard) faculty of the GSD considered Gropius's appointment as professor of architecture. Hudnut, Haffner, Hubbard, and Pond attended the meeting, as did three other longtime fixtures there: John Humphreys, who taught architectural design in a Beaux-Arts manner from 1911 until 1941; the construction teacher, Charles Killam; and Kenneth Conant, the GSD's historian, who specialized in medieval architecture.[92] All but Hubbard and Killam ultimately voted in favor of Gropius. As Hudnut confided to Holmes Perkins: "I have had a devil of a time getting the nomination of Gropius over, as you can imagine, but I think I am at last successful. I have used every possible device except murder and arson."[93] Hubbard expressed concern that Gropius would "establish a Bauhaus at Harvard" that would prove detrimental to city and regional planning. In Hubbard's view, Gropius's method of applying "logic" to modern materials and building methods in order to build effectively at the lowest cost "may have been successful at the Bauhaus, but it would require an enormous amount of adaptation to be valuable in regional planning." Gropius, Hubbard claimed, had no interest in the "illogical element" of architecture and planning, that is, in "matters of human customs, preferences, and matters of economic and legal habits of thought." Hubbard also doubted that Gropius would ever "master American conditions" enough to make any significant contribution to the planning field.[94]

Killam was far more adamant than Hubbard in opposing Gropius's appointment. A self-taught architectural engineer and a demanding construction teacher who ran his classes according to the systematized procedures of architectural offices, Killam absolutely rejected the idea of Gropius coming to teach and the prospect of a Bauhaus at the GSD. After twenty-nine years of teaching at Harvard, he resigned in protest against Gropius's appointment.[95] Killam explained his opposition to Gropius's appointment in a strongly worded essay, published in the journal *Pencil Points,* against modern education—by which he meant the Bauhaus, Gropius, and Hudnut—and against "extreme modern architecture." Pragmatic at heart and in mind, Killam argued that the purpose of architectural education was to prepare students to earn a living and to pass the exams that allowed them to practice. His essay articulated concerns that many in the architectural community shared, including the editors of *Pencil Points,* a journal that Hudnut considered "consistently unfair to modern architecture."[96]

Killam dismissed in his essay a fundamental principle of both Hudnut's and Gropius's pedagogical philosophies—that architectural education had a significant role to play in further developing the fields of architecture and civic design. Such advancements, he argued, could be made only by those with lengthy experience designing and constructing, while the schools could do no more than produce "competent" practitioners. Killam spoke out against the interdisciplinarity that Hudnut and Gropius favored, claiming that it distracted students from mastering basic architecture skills while forcing them to focus on useless skills from other fields. In a related vein, he ridiculed the "amateurish fumbling" that Bauhaus students had carried out in their experiments with hand tools on wood, paper, stone and other materials in the name of architectural education. Modern architectural education, Killam argued, did not even seem to focus on architecture—on designing well-planned, economical, and beautiful buildings—but on educating "young geniuses" who did it all, from planning buildings, cities, landscapes, to interior decorations and furnishings. Killam further derided the "extreme modernists who can give their clients bare boxes or glass hothouses," an "international style" that fits no one's needs or conditions. He even took a final and not-so-subtle jab at President Conant, Hudnut, and Gropius by deriding "the habit of some college presidents and professors who, unasked, advise the world on all controversial subjects."[97]

Killam's was a more elaborate commentary than most of the others who had spoken out against Gropius's coming to Harvard. More typical were reactions like that of Gilmore Clarke of the GSD's Visiting Committee, who expressed "shock" at the news of Gropius's professorship, which "may be good ballyhoo and might result in attracting students having a reactionary nature but not the type of men that Harvard has always stood for."[98]

At the other end of the spectrum, many architects celebrated the fact that the great German modernist was coming to Harvard. Hudnut received a huge stack of congratulatory letters from architects throughout the country to the effect that Gropius's appointment would result in "the most useful service that could be rendered to American architecture and to architectural education" or that "the influence of the Harvard architecture school will spread far beyond the limits of its drafting rooms." Harvard students rejoiced in the news that one of the famous pioneers of modern architecture would soon be among them. The *Harvard Crimson* anticipated that Gropius would "accelerate the motion of the School of Design toward the 'scientific' approach" by emphasizing "actual building problems, the nature of building materials, the place of modern industry in architecture and of the functions of building units within the community."[99] The *Crimson* also noted that Gropius "would like to teach courses here similar to those at the Bauhaus." After all, as Gropius told the reporter, the course of study he developed at the Bauhaus "enabled me to be asked to lecture here."[100]

However much Hudnut admired the Bauhaus educational program, he never considered it possible or desirable to rebuild it anew at Harvard. Both Hudnut and Gropius seemed to agree that the differences in time, place, and purpose, as well as the differing characters of the students and faculty at the two institutions, precluded the creation of another Bauhaus. Harvard and the Bauhaus shared little in common. As for students in the two institutions, those at the all-male GSD were a few years older than the young men and women at the Bauhaus; they had succeeded academically at the college level and brought an intellectual maturity to their studies that the Bauhaus students did not possess. As Gropius might have put it, the mental ability of the Harvard students far surpassed their manual ability. Thinking, reasoning, speaking, and writing had been the focus of their educations, while Bauhaus students excelled as artists, craftsmen, and designers. As for the faculty, the differences between the likes of Henry Hubbard and Bremer Pond at the GSD and Moholy-Nagy and Hannes Meyer at the Bauhaus could not be clearer. Hudnut always insisted that context, setting, and the people involved must be decisive factors in shaping an educational program. As he told Lawrence Kocher: "It is far from our idea to establish an imitation of the Bauhaus here. It is my feeling that any system of education has to be judged in reference to time, place, and circumstances and that philosophic abstractions in respect to it are decidedly dangerous unless clearly modified by a discussion of these realities. A system might be perfectly satisfactory at Paris in the time of Louis Napoleon which wouldn't function very successfully in Oklahoma under Roosevelt."[101] In hiring Gropius for Harvard—or Mies or Oud—Hudnut had intended to bring a modern architect to the GSD and not to import an educational blueprint.

Hudnut may have been zealous in his efforts to clear Robinson Hall of its Beaux-Arts past and to unify the three schools for the cause of civic design, but he was cautious in laying out a detailed agenda and curriculum for the new GSD. In part, he moved carefully because he understood the importance of diplomacy at Harvard, where offending the Visiting Committee and other conservative alumni might affect his school's budget. More important, Hudnut had determined to "proceed somewhat slowly" because he did not have—or want—an educational master plan for the GSD. Hudnut would never impose an ideal peda-gogical scheme on his school or apply a fixed approach that failed to consider "the particular circumstances which surround us." Under Hudnut, the GSD program would always be "in the making,"[102] con-tinually changing "as the conditions governing the professions and the architect's place in the world change. These factors have been changing so rapidly recently and the whole outlook is so uncertain that we, in the schools of architecture, might as well admit frankly that we do not really know the objectives of our teaching."[103] Hudnut not only admit-ted his uncertainty about the future of the architectural fields, but he made uncertainty a basic principle of his educational program, much in accord with John Dewey's pedagogical approach. "I am in a transitional period and I suppose I shall remain there for the rest of my life," he once told a colleague.[104]

Gropius seemed to agree with Hudnut's cautious, contextual ap-proach to education for, as he told Hudnut after he accepted the Harvard professorship, he intended to "keep reserved for some time after having started work, as I have to collect a thorough knowledge of the country first and its particular circumstances. . . . For the same reason, I dropped the idea of any present preparations of my own regarding teaching in the Graduate School, as mistakes can too easily occur by theoretical an-ticipations."[105] Holmes Perkins, who came to know Gropius very well, confirmed years later that "Gropius would never have said directly that he wanted to bring in something foreign and impose it. The one thing he insisted upon was that everything be democratic . . . and he tried also, in his very best way, to respect American traditions and culture." As Perkins described:

> Gropius went out of his way to do things which you could almost laugh at. The first thing he insisted upon was having a picnic with all his stu-dents. That had been unheard of before. Always the faculty was here and the students were there and never the twain shall meet. He was going to have a picnic, and once more, he insisted on playing baseball himself with the rest of us. And, he used to attend all of the town meetings in Lincoln. Every one. It wasn't just lip service. He believed in these things. Take a look at his own house in Lincoln. You will see that it is an attempt to relate to American colonial building. It is a white wood house.[106]

For all Gropius's sincerity, however, Perkins confirmed that "he really wanted to re-create the Bauhaus at Harvard."[107]

Gropius did not, of course, want to "re-create" the Bauhaus as it had been in Dessau when he was director—an applied arts school whose weavers, potters, metalsmiths, and designers in other media produced prototypes for mass production. He did, however, want to model the GSD curriculum after the Bauhaus's in a fundamental way, by establishing a first-year Basic Design preliminary course modeled closely on the famous *Vorkurs* that had served as the backbone of the German school. Required of all students for a six-month period before they pursued studies in their chosen field, that course had encouraged a thorough knowledge of and "feeling for" materials like wood, wool, glass, and stone as students experimented with them in a workshop setting. Basic Design had been intended to "liberate the student's creative power" and to introduce what the Bauhauslers believed were "basic principles which underlie all creative activity in the visual arts."[108]

At the same time that Gropius spoke of avoiding "theoretical anticipations" for the GSD curriculum, he held up the Bauhaus pedagogical scheme as a master plan with "universal validity." As he told numerous American audiences throughout his years at Harvard, "the Bauhaus education represents an objective method of approach appropriate for any country, any individual."[109] Gropius had wanted to initiate his preliminary course as soon as he arrived at Harvard, but he understood the need to be patient for a time. In his first years, there was much to be done to modernize the school and to combat the resistance of the old-guard teachers and alumni. From the moment he arrived at Harvard until he left fifteen years later, Gropius's conviction that the Bauhaus had offered the ideal program never wavered.

Before he had even left London to take up his Harvard post, Gropius began urging Hudnut to hire for the GSD one of the Bauhaus's "vital personalities," Josef Albers, who had been teaching at Black Mountain College in North Carolina since 1933. Gropius explained to Hudnut that Albers would offer GSD students a modern design education that no American instructor could match. Though he would never present it to Hudnut in that way, Gropius may well have seen Albers's coming to Harvard as the first step in transforming the GSD into an American Bauhaus.[110] In good faith, Hudnut brought Albers up to Cambridge for a series modern design lectures almost immediately. Hudnut wrote to Gropius that Albers had been a guest at his home, that he had "liked him immensely," and that he had learned a great deal from his talks. He explained to Gropius that getting Albers appointed to Harvard, since he

Josef Albers teaching at Black Mountain College, early 1940s. (Black Mountain College Research Collection and College Papers, N.75.10.269, courtesy of the North Carolina State Archives)

was a painter and graphic designer and not an architect, depended not on the GSD but on the Division of Fine Arts and that efforts to persuade that faculty to bring Albers would have to wait until Gropius had settled in Cambridge.[111] Hudnut seems not to have understood quite yet the role Gropius imagined Albers playing at Harvard, that of the master of a Bauhaus-like preliminary course at the center of the GSD curriculum.

Gropius's Arrival

The Gropiuses arrived in the United States in March 1937 and met with fanfare similar to what they had encountered on their departure from London. As Ise described, although "our farewell in London has made it very hard for the Americans to compete with, they are trying their best."[112] Their first weeks were filled with parties in both New York and Boston, where Gropius was introduced to the members of the progressive art and architecture as well as Harvard communities. The Gropiuses wrote to their friends in London of their new home, noting, along with the extraordinary number of parties, "the warm hospitality, blue skies, sun, the open landscape, and the white Colonial houses" with a "simplicity, functionality, and uniformity that are completely in our line." They added that "Dean Hudnut takes the greatest trouble to move every stone out of our way and we could not be better cared for as by him and his wife."[113]

Almost immediately after he took up his work at Harvard in April, Gropius proposed to Hudnut that, along with Albers, the GSD hire yet another of his Bauhaus colleagues for its faculty, Marcel Breuer. Breuer had not only studied and taught at the Bauhaus with Gropius, but in 1935 he had also emigrated to London, having been encouraged to do so by the Gropiuses. When Breuer had learned about Gropius's new position at Harvard, he had asked him to see if he could find work in the United States for him too, once he and Ise had settled into their new home.[114] In London, Breuer had formed a partnership with the young architect F. R. S. Yorke, another founding member of the MARS group, and he also designed furniture for Pritchard at Isokon. Although his work with Isokon took up much of his time, Breuer's practice with Yorke played a key part in his development as an architect. The two built several houses together, and they also designed a utopian model for a "Garden City of the Future." According to Isabelle Hyman, the Garden City project may have been "the most significant formalist invention of Breuer's career," granting him much fodder for future work and for his teaching at Harvard. The project allowed him to experiment at once with the structure and the nature of materials while also exploring issues of urban design.[115]

Gropius not only proposed that Breuer teach with him at Harvard, but he also wished to set up an architectural partnership together in Cambridge. The idea of a Gropius-Breuer partnership appealed enormously to Breuer and also to Hudnut, who was eager for his new colleague to open a practice. Hudnut knew that teaching would keep Gropius busy, but if Breuer would join him in practice, he imagined the two of them designing important modern buildings in their new country. Gropius had no trouble convincing Hudnut that Breuer would add greatly to the GSD architecture program, but the problem was money. Hudnut managed to solve that problem rather quickly; he secured a grant from the Carnegie Foundation to subsidize a two-year teaching position for Breuer.[116]

While still in London, Breuer had occasional doubts about moving to the United States, and he seems to have been unsure when he left England in the summer of 1937 that he would stay there. Within a month, however, he wrote to Yorke: "Before I left, everybody told me 'you will always stay in America.' I am afraid it will happen indeed. I regret it intensely that our collaboration which—as you know—has been very satisfactory for me always, would be cut short this way, but I trust that you will understand my feelings. The prospect to collaborate with my old friend Gropius is very tempting for me as you may imagine."[117] As for his thoughts on America, Breuer wrote of "the beautiful bathing

From left: Unidentified figure, Marcel Breuer, Ise Gropius, and Walter Gropius at the Lawn Road Flats, 1934. (Courtesy of the Pritchard Papers, University of East Anglia)

here, the Colonial style and the skyscrapers. . . . In New York I had one of the greatest impressions of my life."[118]

Just as he had helped Gropius with commissions and publicity when he first arrived at Harvard, Hudnut did the same for the Breuer, who was less renowned in the United States than his more senior colleague. Breuer's architecture was little known at the time he arrived in the United States, and in an effort to promote his buildings, rather than his better-known furniture and industrial design work, Hudnut arranged for an exhibition focused on the buildings in the pristine new galleries of Robinson Hall. Some ninety-eight Breuer items designed over the previous thirteen years filled the former Hall of Casts: architectural models, including the Garden City of the Future; photographs of buildings and models from England, Germany, and Switzerland; and some furniture pieces. To write the catalogue essay for the exhibition, which Hudnut scheduled to open at graduation (hoping for peak attendance) and run through the start of the 1938–39 school year, Hudnut commissioned the young historian and critic Henry-Russell Hitchcock, whom he knew admired Breuer's work.[119]

Hitchcock wrote in his essay that Breuer was "definitely not of the school of Gropius." Modern architecture, he explained, existed between two equally valued zones, one of "perfect adaptation" and the other of "outright creation." Gropius's work lay at the extreme of the former, since he approached the balance of function, structure, and design with "relentless intellectual analysis." Architecture at the opposite extreme depended on the qualities of "instinct, flair and imagination." Breuer's work fell squarely in the ideal place between the two zones for it combined an up-to-date technical approach with traditional materials and methods. Breuer exhibited in his work an "urbanity" rare in German modern architecture, free of "the raw edges, the abrupt transition," while offering the "color and vitality of traditional vernacular art."[120] Hitchcock anticipated that in his new home, with the different circumstances of American building and his respect for regional traditions, American construction methods, and modern technique, Breuer would provide much-needed leadership in the development of modern architecture. "He comes at a time," Hitchcock concluded in grand fashion, "when we need a leader and when he stands, we may firmly expect, at the opening of a productive and prolific career."[121]

The time was ripe, the stage set, leading members of the cast in place. By the time of the Breuer exhibition in 1938, Hudnut had laid the groundwork at the GSD for the opening of a new era in American architecture and urbanism.

3 MODERNISM TRIUMPHANT

Hudnut and Gropius worked extraordinarily well together during their first several years at the GSD, before their differences came to light in the early 1940s. As Gropius later described to President Conant: "The Dean had originally called me his 'keyman' for the whole School of Design. Before and partly during the war we collaborated very harmoniously and very efficiently."[1] Under Hudnut's and Gropius's direction in these honeymoon years, students and most faculty (with a few old-guard exceptions) easily accepted the idea, new to the Harvard School, that modern architects had a social responsibility to make good designs available to all people. They understood that modern clients had a new set of needs, both functional and spiritual, differing from those of any earlier era. Furthermore, the view was beginning to prevail at the GSD that in designing for the complex modern world, architects, planners, and landscape architects must work collectively, joining their expertise with that of colleagues from a variety of fields to seek the best solutions. Inside the GSD design studios, a modern aesthetic—flat roofs, ribbon windows, roof gardens, and open spaces—ruled unequivocally.

Hudnut and Gropius focused on two tasks in particular in their first years together at the GSD. Above all they set out to build a new faculty, to bring in a number of modern designers in all three of the School's fields who shared a progressive educational philosophy. They focused, too, on revamping the curriculum, devising new courses and eliminating outmoded ones so as to ally the GSD's three fields and to give them a modern bent. Almost until the postwar era, Hudnut and Gropius recognized only their shared beliefs and determination to make the GSD the world's leading school of modern design with superior programs in city planning, landscape architecture, and architecture.

City/Regional Planning

Henry Hubbard may have been one reason that Hudnut and Gropius so easily overlooked their philosophical differences in their first years at the GSD. Hudnut first did battle with Hubbard before Gropius arrived at Harvard, as Hubbard made clear that he would resist any changes that Hudnut might try to make in the Planning Department at the School. In response, Hudnut canceled all courses in Planning for the coming 1936–37 school year, refusing to renew any contracts for the untenured instructors, which left Hubbard as the lone faculty member, with the sole task of finishing research projects already in progress. Hudnut's move infuriated not only Hubbard and the few students enrolled in planning but also the alumni of the pre-GSD Planning School, who did not know of Hudnut's serious concern for the city and its future. They mistakenly feared Hudnut's action might mean an end to planning education at Harvard. Those supporting Hubbard's program waged a campaign in the national and planning presses, arguing that Harvard must "keep on planning," especially at this moment in time when "the American city leaves more to be desired than almost anything else in this country."[2]

Hudnut allowed the Department of Planning to offer courses once again the following school year, with three years' funding assured, two new visiting faculty members, and a focus now on physical planning. Still the problems persisted between Hudnut and Hubbard. When the latter refused to include "housing" as part of his departmental offerings, Hudnut managed once again to prevail, though this time using a different tactic.[3] Hudnut hired a particularly interesting new faculty member for the GSD, the German Socialist, modern planner, architect, and former *Stadtbaurat* of Berlin during the Weimar Republic, Martin Wagner. Even if Wagner's appointment did not push Hubbard into retiring as Hudnut hoped, it would surely bring a radically different concept of urban planning to the School.[4]

Gropius had been the one urging Hudnut to bring Wagner to Harvard. In 1933, the Nazi government had expelled Wagner from his position as *Stadtbaurat,* a wide-ranging post from which Wagner had directed Berlin's city planning and architecture department, choosing the architects for all municipal buildings, as well running all civil engineering, street design, construction, and landscape architecture projects.[5] Wagner subsequently left Germany for Turkey, where he served as Istanbul's counselor of city planning and professor of city planning at the Academy of Arts. From there Wagner wrote to Gropius in Cambridge asking for help obtaining a teaching position in the United States. Following the émigrés' unwritten code that once in America there were two things to do, "start a new life and rescue those we left behind," Gropius persuaded Hudnut to hire Wagner for Harvard. After getting President Conant to agree to an appointment for Wagner, Hudnut convinced the Rockefeller Committee on Displaced German Scholars to help fund his salary. Wagner came to the GSD as assistant professor of regional planning in 1938, and he stayed for the next twelve years.[6]

Wagner seemed a perfect addition to the GSD given his experience in Berlin integrating the many fields that helped shape the physical environment much as the GSD now aimed to do.[7] He was a perfect choice for teaching "housing" too, as he had a long-standing and deeply felt interest in designing low-cost housing by using standardization, rationalized building techniques, and prefabrication, and by trying to socialize the building industry. Students may have known some of Wagner's work already, particularly the well-published Britz Horseshoe Estate (built with Bruno Taut in 1925), a vast housing complex with 2,317 international-style units arranged in a semicircular pattern around a vast open space.[8]

Martin Wagner and Bruno Taut, "Housing, Berlin-Britz: Horseshoe Plan Surrounding Lake." (*Architecture* 60 [December 1929]: 337)

A committed and uncompromising Socialist, Wagner concerned himself more with the practical side of building construction than did most other radical architects, and he insisted that his buildings reflect their economic value in appearance. As an example of his planning work, Wagner had been the mastermind behind the famous 1929 competition to rebuild Berlin's Alexanderplatz as an "almost continually filled traffic sluice, the clearing point for a network of main traffic arteries" with "an uninterrupted flow of traffic."[9] He continued to view the car as a liberating force for all people, and he would give it pride of place while teaching in the GSD design studios. Wagner never compromised in his attitude toward the existing city, and he never minced words on the subject, even when he first arrived in the United States. In one of his earliest and typically undiplomatic lectures, Wagner railed against the "insoluble town-planning problem" of Manhattan, rejecting any schemes to renovate or maintain the city. "Hands off," he told the audience. "Let such cities perish, they suck the marrow out of our bones and money from our pockets." Rather than "pouring new wine into old bottles," he suggested mowing the city down and erecting a new one that suited "present and future needs."[10] This is precisely what Wagner did in a far-reaching design he made for Boston's center in the 1940s. Much like Gropius—though quite different from the stance that Hudnut would soon begin to take—Wagner championed "entirely new towns on virgin soil," functionally zoned and spacious, where "residence would be one of the highest fortunes of mankind."[11] Neither Wagner nor Gropius distinguished between the bombed-out cities of Europe and the decaying U.S. cities as they considered rebuilding. Cities in both places had fallen victim to modern capitalism and industrialization and would require the services of either a "great artist or planner"—or even a whole team of them—who understood future needs.[12]

One might have expected Wagner to have made a huge impact on students at the GSD for many of the same reasons that Gropius did. He was a somewhat exotic figure, coming from the front lines of Weimar's radical architecture culture to an eager student body. The fact that he cared passionately about social equality certainly appealed to the more idealistic Harvard students, who, urged on by both Wagner and Gropius, came to believe that they too would change the world through design. One former GSD student remembered Wagner as "very spirited, animated, and approachable. He encouraged the most radical political and design ideas."[13] But Wagner seems to have affected only a small number of students, perhaps because too many found him, as one student described, "totally out of place in the American scene and virtually incomprehensible to all but a handful of students, mostly, but not all, foreigners."[14] A dogmatic idealist by many accounts, Wagner's English never progressed very far, which occasionally made his relations with students difficult. Wagner worked well with Gropius, at least until 1940, when they had a falling out over Wagner's charge that Gropius had become too bourgeois, too fashionable in his work, and too much of a compromiser. Ultimately, as historian Jeffry Diefendorf has described, "a steely bitterness" developed between Wagner and Gropius, though they continued to collaborate on many student assignments and writing projects of their own. As they neared the end of their years together at the School, Gropius described Wagner as a "violent fellow, knowing front attacks only, without any subtle quality of tackling difficult problems with others. Wherever he has worked he has had violent clashes in practice. He is a research man and does very good work there but as soon as he steps into polemics, he hits people right in their center."[15]

Because Wagner could not work with most of the GSD faculty and had notoriously weak skills as an administrator, he never offered the counterbalance to Hubbard that Hudnut had hoped.[16] No matter what view one took of Wagner, however, no one doubted that he offered students a definite point of view and clear direction on translating his ideas on housing and urban planning into formal terms. He was devoted to teaching by all accounts, focusing almost exclusively on his students rather than practicing architecture or city planning. He even included students in his personal quest to solve the problem of mass-produced, low-cost housing. Holmes Perkins related that Wagner devoted himself "twenty-four hours a day to teaching. I never saw anybody so dedicated in my life. Not even Gropius."[17]

When he came to Harvard, Hudnut put Wagner under the auspices of the Architecture Department so as to keep him free of Hubbard's authority. Wagner taught the Housing course that Hubbard had refused to teach and also one titled Site and Shelter, the GSD's first course aimed at making architects and planners conversant with the problems of each other's field. Since Wagner believed wholeheartedly in the collaborative ideal, as Hudnut and Gropius did, he geared his courses to future "building masters" engaged in the "broader field of shaping and forming things."[18] In the Site and Shelter course, for example, his lectures advanced the notion that the best human shelters resulted when various building experts worked in concert. Each of his lectures focused on a particular area of expertise related to the shelter-making process and included such topics as: "Shelter from Bombs," "Smoke and Fire," "Noise," "Traffic," "Prefabrication," and "Organic Building." Because of his difficulty with English, Wagner typed out all of his lecture notes in a finished form and presented them in a way that inspired the students' alternative name for the course, "Sit and Swelter."[19]

Wagner's appointment to the GSD did not cause Hubbard to retire, though the battle between Hudnut and Hubbard finally came to a head during the 1940–41 school year. Citing budgetary reasons, Hudnut once again suspended courses in the Planning Department for the year. With a band of alumni and his department's oversight committee on board, Hubbard led a coup aimed at cutting all ties between the Department of City/Regional Planning and the GSD. If victorious, Hubbard planned to move the Planning Department either to the Engineering School, as at several midwestern land grant universities, or to the new School of Public Administration, akin to the program of the Institute of Planning, with its socioeconomic basis, that Rexford G. Tugwell would establish at the University of Chicago.[20] Hudnut, Gropius, and Wagner joined forces against Hubbard and his allies, though they recognized that losing the battle would not be catastrophic. As Hudnut told Wagner, "if the university authorities decide that city planning is unrelated to architecture, we can continue our instruction in this field as part of the work in architecture."[21]

Hudnut and Gropius together argued the case for uniting the fields of architecture and planning at the GSD. In an eloquent document written by Hudnut and addressed to President Conant, the *Minority Report of the Harvard Committee on Regional Planning,* they maintained that

> we conceive the regional planner as one associated in his struggle with men of other capacities and other backgrounds. . . . His part will include the effective use of the tools of planning—skill in the utilization of land, in the organization of transit facilities, in zoning, in statistics; but it must include also that power to reveal, through the command of form, the meanings which kindle the imagination and sustain the loyalties of men.[22]

While the *Minority Report* argued for a planning program emphasizing the "processes of thought and vision" related to planning, the majority on the committee—Hubbard and his cronies—wanted their program focused on the techniques and tools of planning. "The majority appear[s] to conceive design as a special technique and education as knowledge," Hudnut wrote. In contrast, the minority believes that "education is a discipline and growth."[23] With its appeal to progressive principles and interdisciplinarity, the *Minority Report* persuaded Conant. It also persuaded Lewis Mumford, who, despite his important position in the field of regional planning, would have little involvement with the GSD during Hudnut's and Gropius's time there. On this occasion, however, he received a copy of the report from Hudnut and declared it "nothing short of a little masterpiece . . . just what the intellectual and cultural groundwork of a School of Design should be."[24]

Hubbard's coup failed, and he finally left the GSD, retiring early though not quietly. The *Crimson* recorded the view from the old-guard side that in his effort to bring design back to city planning, Hudnut had effectively "ousted" Hubbard from the School. The paper quoted an angry alumnus who claimed that "Hubbard obviously cannot work under a man who is determined, as is Dean Hudnut, to wipe out both the School of Regional Planning and the School of Landscape Architecture." Calling the planning school a "tolerated poor relation in the house of modern architecture," the alumnus added that "there are also other ideas in the world, but Dean Hudnut wants to subordinate them to pure architecture."[25]

Given the impact that Hegemann's ideas had made on Hudnut and the strong personal relationship between him and his mentor, it is worth asking whether Hudnut might have brought Hegemann to the GSD to teach city planning, had Hegemann lived beyond 1936. I suspect that Hudnut would not have brought him there, despite his lifelong admiration for Hegemann's humanistic approach to planning, his intellect, and his ability to balance social, aesthetic, individual, and collective concerns. By 1936, Hudnut was "betting his life" on the new architecture, and Hegemann had always been skeptical of modern design.[26] Ultimately, Hudnut was looking to find a way for the Hegemannic tradition of civic design to coexist with modern architecture, to create cities and towns that expressed in contemporary materials and forms the essential qualities of the modern world—clarity, precision, objectivity, movement, and a sense of evolution and continuity.

Although Hudnut never directly addressed the question of bringing Hegemann to Harvard, comments he made at Columbia in 1937 about the teaching appointment of the British planner Raymond Unwin seem applicable to Hegemann as well. Unwin shared with Hegemann many planning concerns and principles, and their garden suburbs also had much in common. Hudnut did praise Unwin for having "demonstrated the necessity of a social basis for architecture," but he added that "recent progress has modified many of the principles upon which Sir Raymond's art is based. Mass production, machine technology, factory organization and distribution and the changed relations of state and individual have tended to outmode his architecture and his city plans."[27] In the same way that Unwin had not yet come to terms with such progress, neither had Hegemann. Had Hudnut brought him to Harvard, Hegemann would have made an awkward bedfellow for the likes of Gropius, Martin Wagner, Breuer, and the other modernists who would pass through the GSD.

Hubbard and his allies targeted Hudnut in his role as the chief administrator of the GSD, but Gropius came to the GSD with far more radical views of city planning. As he had made clear in *The New Architecture and the Bauhaus,* Gropius considered traditional forms of urbanism unsuitable for modern life, and against the "noxious anarchy" of existing cities, he championed functionally zoned cities with mass-produced, salutary high-rise housing set among broad open spaces, greenery, tranquility, and sunshine. Gropius's "City Verdant" was essentially that of the 1933 CIAM Athens Charter for a "functional city," with distinct residential, working, educational, and recreational districts set among alternating urban and rural zones.[28] His ideas for the modern city would develop during his years at the GSD, especially through his collaborations with Wagner.

Although Hudnut cared deeply about the city and its design, he made no significant changes in the GSD planning program during his first decade at Harvard, first because of Hubbard, and then because of the war, which interrupted new initiatives on campuses throughout the United States. Yet during wartime, Hudnut, Gropius, and the faculty who remained behind at the GSD began to wrestle with a new set of questions as they planned for the postwar world: How could cities be made to compete with newer and more open suburbs? What role should architects, planners, and landscapers play in the rebuilding effort? And, of course, the pedagogical question, How do we prepare students for the postwar reconstruction? As they began to address these questions, Hudnut's and Gropius's honeymoon years would come to an end.

Landscape Architecture

Early in 1938, the landscape architect Frederick Law Olmsted Jr., who remained deeply involved with oversight of the program at Harvard, complained to President Conant that under Hudnut's guidance, "the Department of Landscape Architecture at Harvard seems so little promising."[29] Olmsted Jr. and his supporters, including the department's chairman, Bremer Pond, persisted in advancing landscape architecture as a "distinctive" field, separate from the GSD's other two fields. Much like Hubbard, they rejected Hudnut's drive toward interdisciplinarity as well his embrace of modern design. Rumor had it in the late 1930s that Bremer Pond appended warning notes to his landscape design problems—any student attempting a "modernistic" solution would receive a failing grade.[30]

Despite the Olmsted group's efforts, by 1936 modernism was alive and well in the Landscape Architecture Department at the GSD, brought there by the now-famous trio of students—James Rose, Garrett Eckbo, and Dan Kiley—who worked surreptitiously on their modern designs in the basement of Robinson Hall. Eckbo, a Californian, had arrived at the GSD after studying landscape design at Berkeley, where Thomas Church, a GSD alumnus from the 1920s, had already begun to adopt a modernist vocabulary.[31] Rose had taken a few architecture classes at Cornell before coming to Harvard as a "Special Student" (since he was without even a high school degree), while Kiley had developed his design skills and horticultural experience working with Warren Manning. The three quickly became partners in rebellion against Harvard's landscape status quo, the Olmsted design legacy that they felt had been handed down as "routines for lesser minds" in previous years.[32] One might describe that legacy as favoring the informality of Humphrey Repton and Capability Brown on the one hand and the strict order of Le Nôtre on the other.

Eckbo related that when he arrived at Harvard, the landscape gospel held that "since trees were not made in factories," the profession need not concern itself with the issues of industrialization or modernization. The old "tried-and-true formal/informal system" of landscape design had worked for two centuries and would continue to suffice.[33] Hubbard and Kimball's *Introduction to the Study of Landscape Design* still served as the landscape "bible" at the School, and Eckbo recorded his frustrations with it in the margins of his copy of the book. In one section, he wrote: "Pictures, pictures, pictures. What about environment? How about three-dimensional space experience? Why must we be naturalistic *or* formal? What about all the gradations in between. . . . The fallacious nature vs. man concept. . . . Why is nature more perfect than man?"[34]

Writing under the pseudonym "Marc Snow" in his 1967 book *Modern American Gardens,* Rose colorfully described his impressions of the GSD from the perspective of a renegade modern landscape architecture student. Although "heads flew slowly by" with the "presence of Gropius and the clinically *un*detached administration of Joseph Hudnut," he wrote, the landscape faculty remained stuck in place.

> Apparently they had always thought that "modern" architecture was the result of whim plus glass-brick and chrome steel, rather than a changed way of looking at the objective world. "A tree is still a tree" was the defensive cry repeated so often that it became a kind of death-glub [*sic*] of the old school unwilling to recognize displacement. . . . Of course, the Harvard landscape school had never pretended to either seek or develop creative talent. Nor was it a mere trade school. Its continuing impact within the field of Landscape Architecture derives from the stable traditions inculcated in its practicing alumni. It was a professional school to train men who had already graduated from college to hold key positions in a gentleman's profession . . . and equip them to take their place in the hierarchy of landscape offices such as Olmsted Brothers. Talent was an obscure and unrecognized element, an unpredictable, slightly unsavory mutation which merely disturbed the well-organized routine.[35]

After Gropius arrived at the GSD, the students and faculty in Architecture housed upstairs in Robinson Hall eagerly debated the merits of the new European modern designs. Downstairs—though they claimed to have gotten no direct encouragement from Gropius above—Eckbo, Kiley, and Rose began to explore with great enthusiasm the new forms of space, modern technologies and materials, and the idea of the landscape as a changing environment where people hold the central place. As Eckbo remembered, "of the twenty students in landscape architecture—Dan Kiley, Jim Rose and I—were so turned on by the new ideas upstairs that on our own we began to explore new forms and arrangements which might reflect the new design ideas."[36] Inspiration for their modern landscapes came not only from upstairs but also from images of Christopher Tunnard's landscape designs in Britain, from his writings in the *Architectural Review,* and from reading Lewis Mumford. The three also thumbed through the latest architecture journals and books on modern art, admiring cubist paintings, constructivist sculpture, as well the pyramids, Stonehenge, and anonymous folk crafts.[37] As Dan Kiley recalled, thanks to Bremer Pond, the trio had little interest in history beyond these ancient and folk examples. Pond taught the history of landscape architecture course that Kiley noted was "so dull and so bad that we just hated anything to do with the past."[38]

Although Eckbo, Kiley, and Rose loved the now "charged, controversial and exciting" atmosphere of the GSD, they felt that Gropius had little interest in their field.[39] According to Eckbo, "Gropius seemed to think that some extension of architectural thinking about buildings, plus adequate horticultural activity would solve the landscape problem. He tolerated but did not encourage or seem to understand our efforts to develop concepts of positive landscape systems comparable to the Beaux-Arts in intensity though different in kind."[40] Gropius may not have been quite so indifferent to landscape architecture as Eckbo suggests. In a recent study of the 1938 Gropius House in Lincoln and its landscape, Eric Kramer showed that Gropius "undertook a deliberate integration of the house with the existing landscape through the intentional design of an intermediary space: the garden." Much like Kiley, Eckbo, and Rose, Kramer claims, Gropius believed in a "clear, logical, and distinctly modern philosophy about the landscape."[41] A number of the design problems that Gropius wrote at the GSD, often coauthored with Wagner, also point to a genuine interest in and sensitivity to the landscape and its design. In a typical example, Gropius with Wagner wrote of the New England region with its "special landscape character": "We may mention its scattered clumps of trees and patches of woods, and its sporadic ponds and lakes, so characteristic of all landscapes built on moraines. Such a landscape invites the artist planner to observe and preserve its variety of aspects."[42] Unlike his students, Christopher Tunnard seemed to think that Gropius had a deep interest in the landscape. Tunnard thought it significant that Gropius's architectural career began with a commission for cottages for agricultural workers. "Like Lord Shaftesbury," he wrote, Gropius's "roots were in the land. . . . He oscillated between a gas-lit apartment in Berlin and a close contact with his native soil." Gropius ultimately "saw in adaptations of nature at least a partial solution to some of our mechanized living conditions," according to Tunnard.[43] While Gropius may have *seemed* indifferent to landscape architecture to the students in the field, it may be the case that he *was* indifferent to the workings of the Department of Landscape Architecture at the GSD and to the workings of the mainstream profession.

Hudnut had a definite interest in landscape architecture, especially in integrating its domain with that of the architect, and he both lectured and published on this subject as early as 1938. A decade later, Hudnut would also write the introduction to the revised edition of Tunnard's famous modern treatise *Gardens in the Modern Landscape,* first published in England in 1938.[44] Like many others involved with the modern movement, Hudnut argued that the two realms, buildings and landscapes, formed parts of a single organism and that they should flow into and over each other. Hudnut did take issue with those in the modern camp who argued for only a minimum of landscape art in the modern garden. In the words of Henry-Russell Hitchcock, who subscribed to this view, the modern garden should preserve "all possible values previously in existence in the landscape setting with the addition of only the simplest and most practical provision for specific human needs."[45]

Hudnut argued against Hitchcock and others like-minded, claiming that a building on a site always altered the pattern of environment and erased the existence of any "natural" landscape setting. It was impossible to build on a site and, at the same time, leave it alone in its "natural" state. Therefore, Hudnut wrote, "I do not despair of gardens which are, I understand, bits of this earth which have been, like houses, designed." He insisted that the modern landscape architect must discipline the plants, contours, water, and necessary structure in order to integrate building and site. As architects and landscape designers worked in concert, Hudnut wanted more than a mere repetition of shared materials, scales, planes, and ornaments between house and garden. He argued for a meaningful expression that drew from the visible world but also from "the energies of the human spirit."[46]

Hudnut was not alone in promoting ideas of modern landscape architecture from within the GSD. While still enrolled at the School, Eckbo and Rose also began publishing both their ideas and designs, using a more polemical tone than Hudnut did. "This is the United States of America, 1937 A.D.," Eckbo announced in the first of their essays for *Pencil Points.* "Automobiles, airplanes, streamlined trains, mass production, the machine, new materials, new thoughts, new social concepts, a more abundant life." As an alternative to being "slaves to the ages," he offered his credo:

Plants are the important things in gardens. Every garden a stage, every occupant a player. . . . Gardens must be the homes of delight, of gaiety, of fantasy, of illusion, of imagination, of adventure, something more than an "outdoor living room." . . . Design shall be three-dimensional. People live in volumes, not planes. Things must be around us and over us, as well as under us. . . . Design shall be areal [*sic*], not axial. . . . Design shall be dynamic, not static. . . . Materials shall express their own inborn characteristics and possibilities.[47]

Eckbo illustrated his futuristic text with garden designs of his own that demonstrated abstraction from natural forms, simplicity, flexibility, three-dimensionality, and flowing (but still defined) space. These were among the first works of modern landscape architecture published in the United States.

The following year Rose similarly related landscape design and zeitgeist in another *Pencil Points* article, emphasizing the new possibilities of space derived from constructivist experiments. One could free landscape architecture from the strictures of the axial system, Rose posited, by translating into outdoor material the constructivist sense of transparency broken by a succession of planes.[48] Rose also addressed the qualities of landscape architecture that made it a unique art form, especially the fact that its materials live and grow and that the sky and surrounding environment determine its large scale.

Dan Kiley joined Eckbo and Rose in their journalistic efforts, coauthoring with them a series of articles in the *Architectural Record* in 1939 and 1940 that considered human needs in the urban, rural, and primeval environments. In their three articles, the students explored questions that landscape design in the modern world raised in their minds: "How can Man most constructively use his free time? What physical accommodations are essential to his recreation? Who will design them? And how?"[49] For answers, they looked to Lewis Mumford, Thoreau, and also to their own Christopher Tunnard, by then teaching in the Landscape Architecture Department at the GSD.

In 1939, Hudnut had appointed Christopher Tunnard, the British/Canadian landscape architect, to teach (untenured) at the GSD, assigning him first to the Planning Department and subsequently to Landscape Architecture. Hudnut had met the thirty-year-old Tunnard through Gropius, who, as Tunnard recalled many years later, "started me on my teaching career."[50] Tunnard and Gropius had come to know each

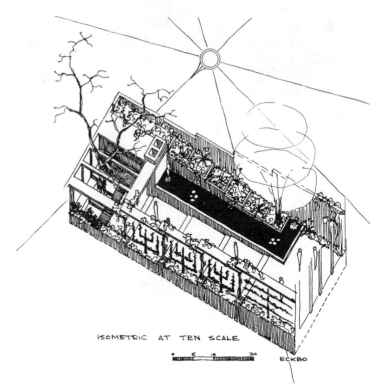

ISOMETRIC AT TEN SCALE

ECKBO

Garrett Eckbo, "Composition in Movement, ascending plant boxes versus descending ramps. Pool for length, statue for distinction, and espaliered fruits for wall pattern." (*Pencil Points* 18 [September 1937]: 578)

other in England, where Tunnard had worked with Gropius's British partner, Maxwell Fry, on a MARS plan for London. Tunnard had also designed gardens outside London with Gropius's friend Serge Chermayeff and had even proposed a scheme for the Lawn Road Flats.[51] Upon hiring Tunnard for Harvard, Hudnut called him "a great landscape architect" who represented a "point of view toward the modern movement in the arts which alone could bring the GSD departments into a spiritual harmony." Tunnard was also a "an excellent speaker and a man of personal charm," according to Hudnut, and therefore a figure well suited to help spread ideas of modern landscape design.[52]

Shortly before he arrived at Harvard, Tunnard had published *Gardens in the Modern Landscape,* in which he promoted ideas linking the modern garden to contemporary theories of art and architecture. From Le Corbusier and Adolf Loos, Tunnard had come to see "function" as the key factor in garden design: he argued that modern gardens must offer opportunities for rest, recreation, and convenience and must express the spirit of rationalism through an honest use of materials and simple, abstract design. Freed from formal conventions and from the drive to imitate nature, Tunnard experimented in his designs with the sculptural and tactile qualities of plants. Much like Hudnut (and Hegemann), Tunnard viewed the modern garden as part of the larger landscape, inseparable from housing and from urban and rural development. The ideas that Tunnard put forward in his book inspired many progressive practitioners and students, and it both scandalized and amused others with its polemical tone.

Like Hudnut (but unlike Gropius), Tunnard came to Harvard as "a modernist with a memory," in the words of a recent critic.[53] He not only advanced the cause of gardens for modern times—"the humanized landscape, the social conception of the countryside, and the garden of tomorrow"—but he expressed a genuine interest in the history of his field. Even *Gardens in the Modern Landscape* has a basis in history, perhaps a flawed or naive basis—"ludicrously cavalier" and "sloppy and useless," one critic has described it—but it does draw on history.[54] When

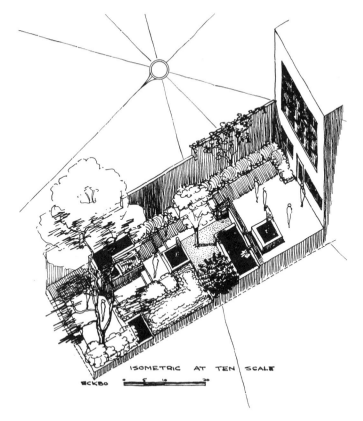

Garrett Eckbo, "Garden with abstract pattern of water, brick, and planting of various colors and textures." (*Pencil Points* 18 [September 1937]: 581)

Christopher Tunnard, ca. 1960. (Courtesy of Manuscripts and Archives, Yale University Library, Christopher Tunnard Papers 6082)

it was unpopular to do so in the modernist era, Tunnard treated modern landscape design as part of the historical tradition of landscape architecture. In their series of essays, Eckbo, Kiley, and Rose recognized Tunnard's debt to the past, and they quoted him as saying: "If, then, a new garden technique is to be evolved it need not necessarily reject the traditional elements of the garden plan. Rather, its aim must be to fuse them with new life."[55] Tunnard had found inspiration for his own designs particularly in works from the Edo period in Japan, the eighteenth-century Italian masters, and the French impressionists. He appreciated artistry and qualities of order and unity in gardens of all eras and believed that even historic landscapes could be preserved and, at the same time, intensely developed.[56]

Pond had never wanted Tunnard hired for the GSD, but Hudnut struck up a deal with him. If Hudnut brought Tunnard to Harvard, Pond could bring Norman Newton there, a Cornell alumnus from 1923 and a Rome Prize winner experienced in country house design and in the design of large-scale public projects. Interestingly, by the start of the war, Newton would come to embrace modern design and progressive education with a vengeance.[57]

As a teacher, Tunnard introduced his GSD students to landscape architecture as a field where issues of art, land, and community all came together, as his former student Lawrence Halprin has described. From Tunnard, who influenced him profoundly, Halprin has said that students learned "to design well and make an aesthetically and socially better environment for people to live in and thus in the broadest sense improve the modern world."[58] Tunnard's courses at the GSD included Site Planning, in which he covered a range of issues inspired by projects ranging from the Tennessee Valley Authority to residential densities, many of which had never been broached before in the Landscape Architecture Department.[59] Unlike the more typical small-scale landscape problems—such as Pond's assignments for courtyards, terraces,

Christopher Tunnard, "A Modern Dormitory Town for London." (Christopher Tunnard, *Gardens in the Modern Landscape* [London: Architectural Press, 1938], 151)

Christopher Tunnard, house with Tunnard-design garden near Halland, Sussex. (Christopher Tunnard, *Gardens in the Modern Landscape* [London: Architectural Press, 1938], 76)

or estate gardens—Tunnard introduced large-scale, complex problems to his students. In one example, his students planned a 1,200-family residential complex for a proposed industrial town in eastern Massachusetts. To do so, they carried out extensive research (much as they did for Gropius's and Wagner's design problems) on economic issues, land use, and manufacturing processes, learning the importance of collaborating with government officials, farmers, scientists, and others who might help them better understand the relationship between people and the land. Tunnard based his GSD design problems on a premise he would later come to reject: that because it is cheaper than rehabilitating existing cities, we should build new towns on undeveloped land.

Landscape historians generally discuss Tunnard's early design work in England, but he also demonstrated his ideas in a few gardens while teaching at the GSD, in Cambridge and nearby Lincoln. In the Koch House garden, for example, Tunnard showed his concern for three-dimensionality and spatial flow using screens, overhangs, and roof decks, along with an array of new materials, including glass, concrete paving stones, modern sculpture, and objets trouvés. Like his designs in England, this garden and his others in New England eschewed the traditional massing of plants for picturesque effect and instead used plants for their individual structural qualities. Tunnard also invited into his gardens views other than the traditional vast expanse of nature—allowing cities and ordinary buildings into sight. And instead of screening out the likes of garages or garbage cans, he embraced the Bauhaus principle of good design for all objects and structures.[60]

In 1943, the Royal Canadian Air Force drafted Tunnard into the war effort. When he returned injured from war that same year, Hudnut recommended him for a Harvard Wheelwright Fellowship to study city planning issues. With the fellowship in hand, Tunnard returned to the United States, but he then moved to Yale since Harvard had no open position in his field. With his departure, the GSD lost the world's leading theorist of modern landscape architecture. Indeed, Tunnard's theories as he had expounded them both in his 1938 book and in his GSD teachings remained the most thoughtful on the subject of landscape modernism for decades to come—with only Eckbo's writing close behind.[61]

Almost sixty years after he left Harvard, a Tunnard quotation from 1942 hung on a placard in the Landscape Architecture Centennial Exhibition at the GSD, effectively summarizing his teaching philosophy at Harvard:

Go out and study nature's living structures, the detail of a woodland scene, the balance held within a community of plants; there you will learn about materials. Study the larger works of man to gain a sense of scale; new forms of shelter, the gigantic sculptures of oil derricks, the simple pattern of a fish hatchery. Watch how water flows from a big dam; how steam shovels cut the mountainside in search of gravel for the roads. Books, studios, and dictated standards of beauty can never supplant the faculty of observation in design; this faculty can only feed on what is significant and real. And reality lies in the world between today and tomorrow, the realm of the modern movement in science and art.[62]

While at Yale in the years following World War II, Tunnard would grow disillusioned with the modern movement, despite having been its greatest proponent in landscape architecture. This too he shared with Hudnut, and it probably accounts for their lasting friendship and mutual professional support. While Hudnut continued to recommend Tunnard for prestigious posts, Tunnard occasionally invited Hudnut to Yale to address his students on civic design. By the time he died in 1979, Tunnard had moved so far from his earlier beliefs that he had become a major figure in historic preservation in New Haven and a member of the International Committee on Monuments and Sites.[63]

Hudnut was unhappy to lose Tunnard to Yale, though he would have delighted in Pond's leaving. That, unfortunately, did not occur until 1950. Melanie Simo has suggested that Pond may have survived the radical shift to modernism at the GSD because he had always viewed "space" and "spatial relations" as the traditional province of landscape architecture. With modern architects' new interest in space, students trained by Pond had something to offer in a collaborative situation. Holmes Perkins's description of Pond as a man "with no convictions at all" may also shed light on Pond's ability to survive at the GSD. By the time he left the School, he was assigning both collaborative design problems with the modernists and, at the same time, small-scale war memorials and courtyards "in the Chinese manner."[64]

The GSD Landscape Architecture Department would remain open during the war, with only a small number of students enrolled and hundreds of troops passing through to learn the art of camouflage and construction techniques.[65] The future of the department seemed uncertain then, as did the future of the profession. In 1940, Hudnut had warned landscape architects to move away from designing private estates to "public parks and recreational areas having as their central intention the communal health and happiness." To his own faculty, he advised that "some aspect of city or regional planning" be included in every advanced landscape architecture and architecture design problem.[66] Others in the architectural fields outside Harvard echoed similar sentiments, while practicing landscape architects voiced their fears that engineers had been adopting their ideas and the jobs they had traditionally held. The profession, and also the Department of Landscape Architecture at Harvard, needed to broaden the scope beyond horticulture to embrace a wider field. This was the primary task Hudnut set out for landscape architecture in the postwar era.

Architecture

Although Hudnut did not make the kinds of reforms he had hoped to in the Departments of Landscape Architecture and City/Regional Planning during his first decade at the GSD, the Department of Architecture was a different matter. Only three years into Hudnut's deanship, President Conant could rightfully boast that Harvard now had "the leading school of modern architecture on this continent and perhaps in the entire world."[67] Unlike in the Departments of Planning and Landscape Architecture, where Hubbard, Pond, and conservative alumni impeded change, almost no one interfered with Gropius and Hudnut as they worked to modernize the Harvard architecture program.

Soon after Gropius arrived at the GSD, Hudnut gave up his role as chairman of the Department of Architecture and appointed Gropius to the position. With Architecture in Gropius's hand, the dean now had an equal relationship to each of the three GSD departments, in keeping with the School's collaborative philosophy. Gropius and his larger-than-life personality quickly injected new excitement into the department. He encouraged students to develop their individual creativity and also their reformist impulses so that they designed for the benefit of all people. His students came to believe that they, too, now belonged to the architectural vanguard.[68] As Klaus Herdeg describes in his polemical book on the Bauhaus legacy at Harvard, Gropius demanded of his students "the role of true believer," that is, "believers in such things as progress through technology and 'returning to honesty of thought and feeling.'"[69] Summing up the view shared by many in the Master Class, one student confirmed that through Gropius "we went for a kind of apostolic succession—we felt that through him we could reach the roots of the modern movement."[70]

Students who had begun their architectural studies at the new GSD before Gropius arrived noted the enormous change that occurred at the School once the great "master" took up his post. Leonard Currie, who later taught architecture at Virginia Tech and the University of Illinois at Chicago, remembered:

> All that I was aware of in that winter of 1936–37 was that I was disappointed with the teaching at the GSD, which was caught up, like other U.S. architecture schools, in the moribund pedagogy of the Beaux-Arts system. As students we were asked to engage in endless copy-book projects, quite unrelated to the real world or to the needs of society. The arrival of Gropius promised an overturn of the entrenched traditional system and a new focus on creativity and the enhancement of the man-made environment for all of humankind. Much of that promise was subsequently realized.[71]

A number of Gropius students came to Harvard already impressed with the Bauhaus and interested in learning about architecture through its methodology. Others came knowing nothing of European modern architecture. Chip Harkness, who had "just stumbled in" with little knowledge of the current architectural scene, recalled being completely taken aback when, in a life drawing class, he noticed a fellow student's paper filled with cubes and triangles, the model translated into geometric shapes. Before long, he too came to appreciate abstract design and also to regard himself as an architectural "evangelist" who believed that architecture could "make a difference and change society, that it wasn't just a reflection of society." Unlike the advanced students who had studied earlier at Harvard or at other architecture schools, Harkness and those who began their studies at the GSD did not have to "unlearn" the Beaux-Arts ways of designing. From the start, they learned to design in terms of "societal needs, functional needs and building material." When these came together, "an aesthetic developed."[72]

Students frequently discussed the Bauhaus with Gropius and Breuer, and they came to know several former Bauhaus masters who passed through the GSD—Josef Albers, Herbert Bayer, and Xanti Schawinsky. On their own initiative, students read enormous amounts about the modern movement in Europe, familiarizing themselves with the MARS group and Tecton in England, the works of Aalto, Oud, Hans Poelzig, Hans Scharoun, among others on the continent. Frank Lloyd Wright seemed to them too mired in the Arts and Crafts and did not fit into their modern canon. As GSD alumnus Richard Stein related, "there was some familiarity with Wright's works, but not much veneration."[73]

Hudnut, Gropius, Breuer, and Wagner assured that design problems in the Architecture Department related to existing sites, that they were bounded by practical limits, and that they made research a significant part of the design sequence. As students carried out their problems—frequently houses, schools, apartments, or series of residential buildings in these early years—they often worked in groups and engaged with professionals from other disciplines: engineers, economists, real estate men, manufacturers, city planners, public administrators, and businessmen. Gropius invited participation from these fields so that his students could experience the broad range of concerns that affected architectural decision making.

In his own teaching, Gropius never offered his students any specific architectural solutions to their design problems, but he tried to make them think through the issues on their own. He never used his pencil to illustrate how students might improve their work but instead talked and asked questions that frequently led the students to abandon their earlier efforts and move in new directions.[74] As one former student explained, Gropius "taught me to look for form in the conditions of the problem—the program, the spaces needed, the material and structural possibilities for providing the space—and not in preconceived ideas."[75] His students understood that he "was not talking to us primarily about buildings as a new kind of style, but was attempting to interpret the vast changes of our age in terms of architecture and in terms of design as a process of doing." His strength, according to Paul Rudolph, lay in "his ability to analyze and make precisely clear the broad problems of our day."[76]

Gropius taught only some fifteen graduate students in a Master Class held in a small studio on Robinson Hall's second floor that accommodated just enough drawing boards for each member of the class. These students had all been trained in architecture already and came directly from their different schools in the United States or abroad, or from jobs in the field. Gropius and his select group of students shared an intense relationship, according to those both inside and outside of the group. He came to know his own students intimately, and many viewed his home in Lincoln as a second classroom.[77] With a few exceptions, Philip Johnson most notable among them, Gropius's students spoke of him with devout reverence: he was "the personification of a unified life";

"the spirit that made all things seem possible"; the man who "sees and understands relationships between things that escape most people."[78] To Johnson, a devotee of Mies rather than of his local master, Gropius was the "Warren G. Harding of architecture," an uninspired architect of "fine appearance and mediocre talents."[79] Despite his reverence for Mies, Johnson could not bring himself to move to Chicago and the Midwest, where Mies was teaching, over "mother Harvard."[80] That left him with Gropius.

As for the other approximately sixty architecture students working with other instructors in the large drafting room next door, they resented being shut off from the "purity of the Master class" and "envied and suspected" those inside.[81] As Henry N. Cobb has recalled, when he was a GSD student, "my colleagues and I resented the fact that Gropius just taught the Master Class. He never appeared at a review, he never participated in what was then the bachelor's degree program. And his class of fifteen students was an elite group. I wasn't so much offended by the fact that he didn't teach studio to the bachelor students, but I was very much offended that he didn't show up at reviews."[82] Though some students were offended by his seeming indifference toward them, others he did not teach directly felt the impact of Gropius at the GSD. As one student told Gropius years later, he had learned an enormous amount from him about building and design, "more by osmosis and example than any other way—for I admired you from afar and was never fortunate enough to be one of your students."[83]

Walter Gropius with students in Robinson Hall, March 1946. (Courtesy of the Harvard University Archives, call no. UAV 605.1.2, G422)

Gaining entry into Gropius's graduate student group was a simple process, especially in the first few years. Interested students with an architecture degree already in hand came to the first fall semester class, where Gropius assigned them a week-long sketch problem, each student's own house. On the basis of their designs, he selected fifteen from the thirty or so present, inviting the rest to take a preparatory year at the GSD and reapply.[84] Within a year or two, as the GSD's reputation grew and as President Conant pressed his case for admission to Harvard based on merit rather than familial ties, getting into Gropius's class and the GSD became extremely competitive.

Economic improvement and constant talk of an American building renewal boosted architecture enrollments across the country in the few years before Americans entered the war, especially at Harvard under Gropius. While enrollment in other architecture schools jumped 25 percent to pre-Depression numbers, the GSD's climbed as much as 40 percent in the fall of 1938, Gropius's first full academic year.[85] The lure of the Bauhaus master was great—especially as most other schools remained tied to the Beaux-Arts system until after the war. Gropius's GSD appointment—"a bomb placed in the foundations of academic training," in the words of his former student, the critic Bruno Zevi—ultimately triggered an important chain reaction: within a few years, Mies came to the Armour Institute in Chicago (1938), Aalto to MIT (1940), while Yale, Berkeley, and Oregon gradually reorganized their faculties after 1945. By the time Gropius had been teaching at Harvard for ten years, a modern pedagogical philosophy had supplanted the Beaux-Arts system in architecture schools throughout the United States; a similar pattern ultimately took hold in Europe.[86]

Those who made it into the Master Class took only one course, Gropius's, with Breuer as the assistant during the late 1930s, followed by Hugh Stubbins. Typically, Gropius and Breuer would explore a long-term design problem with their students, such as Gropius's house in Lincoln at the time it was in the planning stages, a school building, or an apartment house. At beginning of each of the four problems required to complete the master's degree, Gropius would talk in a philosophical way about the issues involved and offer a few of his "stock" lectures on wall openings or the nature of windows.[87] Offering a more cynical view on these lectures, Philip Johnson remembered that Gropius "went on and on about the value to the new architecture of his socialist philosophy in general, prefabrication and low-cost housing in particular—and teamwork."[88] When Gropius finished speaking, students would subsequently spend hours in the studio discussing stud construction, building orientation, building systems, the New England tradition, or sun control in the context of their designs. As work advanced, he would move from one student's desk to another, appearing faithfully two times each week at each desk, critiquing designs in a way that often led to general discussions about directions to explore. His comments usually attracted the surrounding students, who may well have benefited from them more than the nervous student whose work had raised the issues at hand. Gropius was said to be tireless as he moved around the drafting room, taking every problem and proposal apart. As the students finished each of their design problems, they presented their work to a jury of faculty and a large student audience, often intimidated as they did so, "stammering and stuttering . . . in awe of the great master, coming over from Europe to teach us the gospel."[89]

For all the many laudatory reminiscences of Gropius recorded by his GSD students, almost none of them spoke of Gropius as a great architect. Students often wrote of his extraordinary gifts as a teacher without even mentioning his buildings, though some did address Gropius's architectural work. As one student summed up, "it was generally agreed in the Master's group that he was a greater teacher than architect." Bill Lyman, a GSD alumnus who taught alongside Gropius, noted along the same lines that "for me the primary influence was in the area of character-building rather than design."[90] Garrett Eckbo also expressed the view shared by several others: "I have never thought of Walter Gropius as a great architectural designer . . . he was a great teacher and leader who had a faculty for looking at a student problem and commenting on it so constructively that all of the other students in the room always gathered around to listen."[91] Paul Rudolph more succinctly called his former teacher "a very powerful, but not a very good, architect." Rudolph related that Gropius "tried to reduce everything to a scientific basis, formulating charts about distances between buildings dependent only on the amount of sun and air that they needed, but the result was usually boring."[92]

Architectural critics outside the GSD seemed to agree that something other than Gropius's own architecture made him larger than life. In his obituary of Gropius, for example, Nikolaus Pevsner wrote of his "sterling human qualities," noting that "Gropius and Le Corbusier are the two greatest powers in architecture which the 20th century has so far produced—Le Corbusier as an artist-architect unfailingly brilliant to the very end, Gropius neither an artist nor brilliant, but unfailing as a moral force working towards aims which the century badly needed and still needs."[93] Ada Louise Huxtable went so far as to claim that, along with Le Corbusier and Wright, Gropius had "changed the world and we make no apology for that sweeping statement." And yet, she wrote, as a "great architect" Gropius does not share the stage with these other two or with Mies. Instead "the work of Walter Gropius was uneven, seemingly influenced in quality by the men with whom he collaborated." Huxtable concurred with his students that Gropius "did not produce buildings that shattered stylistic norms with the imprint of personal genius. Gropius's role in the front lines of modernism was something else again. That role was as a catalyst of ideas and practice during a period of radical change in a critically transformed world."[94]

While students looked to Gropius for his philosophical perspective, it was to Breuer they turned for inspiration and practical direction on building, planning, and the behavior of materials. Breuer served as the "artist" and "tastemaker" in the design studio, even the link between students and the revered grand master Le Corbusier, who never entered the GSD orbit in this high modernist era.[95] "We saw the International Style first hand through Breuer," according to Edward Larrabee Barnes. "He was young and talented and a great admirer of Corbu." Harry Seidler recounted that Breuer introduced him and his fellow students to "visual understatements that were at once lyrically romantic but also disarmingly simple solutions to planning and building." Even Philip Johnson admired Breuer's work. Gropius's house in Lincoln, Johnson felt, paled in comparison to the one Breuer designed across the street.[96] In recalling Breuer as a teacher, his former students invariably commented that his way of teaching resembled his way of designing—by instinct, seeming to follow no rules, and eager for inventiveness. In the drafting room, he was often heard encouraging his students with the phrase "why *not* to do it!"[97]

Breuer differed noticeably from Gropius in personality. If Gropius was the "Apollonian figure," Breuer was the "Bacchanalian . . . the one to revel with, the one to have a drink with."[98] He did not have Gropius's "severe integrity" or his organizational or systematic drive, and no one could imagine him promoting teamwork in practice or a methodical pedagogical scheme as Gropius did. Even Breuer's written design problems differed from Gropius's. While the latter tended to be long-winded and philosophical, Breuer would succinctly lay out the criteria students had to follow. As Breuer wandered through the drafting room to comment on student projects, he did so with a pencil in hand, though he did not draw over their work as some teachers did. He did not speak about the aesthetics of architecture, almost as if this were a taboo subject, but rather he ad-

Marcel Breuer with students Richard M. Stein and John Abbate. (*Architectural Design* 52 [July/August 1982]: 59)

dressed the layout of plans, whether or not something could be built, and how the individual elements might all work together.[99]

Breuer's sense of his own teaching accords with his students' memories of him in the studio. He tried there to prevent students from imitating his vernacular—"whether I achieved that or not is another question"—and to assure that they made their own decisions: "I very seldom drew on their drawings, adding my correction or showed them how to do it. I discussed principles of construction, solutions of function, what a window does, effects of daylight or sunlight, what is good or bad in a solution and so on. This was the criticism—not showing how a building should look. I wanted to encourage individual search and research by my teaching."[100] Barnes remember students holding Breuer's observations on design in the highest regard: "People were going to juries to hear him critique projects. Students from other classes would go to listen to him, even though he spoke only broken English and German. There was no question that he, as an instinctive designer, had the respect of the students."[101] It was unusual to find an intuitive, creative artist like Breuer in an architecture school, though he also thoroughly understood the details of construction, the nature of materials, and the possibilities of various joint systems.

Though they differed from each other in their teaching methods and styles, both Gropius and Breuer took pains to distinguish themselves as teachers from that other Bauhaus instructor then teaching in Chicago, Mies van der Rohe. Breuer contrasted his emphasis on getting students to "search and research" with Mies's preference for showing students "this is the corner solution, the brick solution, do it. With all respect for Mies—who knows very well what he does and wants, this approach is much too narrow." Gropius similarly described Mies as "too much the tyrant teacher who wants to impose himself instead of helping the student along with his, the student's, own framework."[102]

In their architectural office, Gropius and Breuer seemed to play similar roles to the ones they played at the GSD. For most of their four years in practice together, until the effects of the war began to be felt, the two kept up a vibrant practice designing a number of houses—most famously their own houses in Lincoln but also the nearby Chamberlain Cottage in Wayland; the Hagerty House in Cohasset, Massachusetts; the Frank House in Pittsburgh; and the Aluminum City housing group in New Kensington, Pennsylvania. They also worked on several unrealized college projects—at Black Mountain, William and Mary, and Wheaton—and they designed the interior of the Pennsylvania State Pavilion at the New York World's Fair.[103] In their architectural office, located for a short time in Hunt Hall and then on Massachusetts Avenue, Gropius and Breuer employed several GSD students as draftsmen, including Leonard Currie and William Landsberg. Both remember that Breuer acted as the primary designer in the small firm. According to Landsberg: "We saw very little of Gropius; It was all Breuer in the drafting room. Breuer was what in a bigger firm would be known as the Chief of Design. As far as the drafting room staff was concerned, Breuer was the person we dealt with."[104] Since Gropius did not like to draw, it is not surprising

Marcel Breuer and Walter Gropius, Hagerty House, 1938. (*Architectural Forum* 72 [April 1940]: 295–303)

Marcel Breuer and Walter Gropius, Chamberlain Cottage, Wayland, Massachusetts, 1940. (*Architectural Forum* 77 [November 1942]: 76)

that he did little of it in the office. As Isabelle Hyman has described, it was Breuer who drew many freehand architectural sketches and the assistants who did the finished drawings. This is not to say that Gropius had no input on the buildings designed during his partnership with Breuer, for he did.

The question of authorship during the Gropius/Breuer partnership is a complicated one, and several scholars have taken up the issue. Joachim Driller has written that the majority of the houses the two built in their firm were "principally or entirely the work of Breuer, for whom they represented the fulfillment of his long-standing wish to build." For Gropius, the houses were merely small scale "calling cards of his architectural ideas." Winfried Nerdinger also credits Breuer for much of the output of his practice with Gropius.[105] For the two architects themselves, the issue remained a sensitive one long after the demise of the firm in 1941. The acerbic architect Serge Chermayeff, a close friend of Breuer and a former friend of Gropius's, had likely heard from Breuer on this issue, for he asserted many years after the demise of the Gropius/Breuer practice that "Lajko Marcel Breuer did all the work that Gropius claimed. I didn't find this out until very much later. . . . He had left Gropius because Gropius claimed to be the author, the designer" of their projects together.[106]

It was likely Breuer's growing frustration that Gropius was getting undue credit for their firm's work that caused a major falling out over a seemingly trivial issue in 1941. Although Breuer had received tenure and his own students two years earlier, Gropius continued to invite

They lived like this . . .

They dreamed of this . . .

"... and this is what they got." Marcel Breuer and Walter Gropius, Aluminum City, New Kensington, Pennsylvania. (*Architectural Forum* 81 [July 1944]: 64)

him to participate in the advanced students' juries, which ultimately provided the setting for their dispute. When Gropius appeared fifteen minutes late to a jury in May, Breuer rebuked him on the spot and later that day wrote him an angry note: "During our jury meeting of today you handled the school business in a manner which I feel is below the level of the University and which I personally am not willing to accept. I strongly feel that you mis-used your authority and am deeply offended."[107] That same day Breuer sent Gropius a second "Dear Pius" letter:

I am now convinced that our partnership is objectively and personally possible no longer. As to the reasons, we each certainly have our own ideas, which I feel it would not help to analyze. I suggest that our office close with the first of August, when the New Kensington Housing job and the Abele [house] job will be completed. I also suggest that commissions we may receive before the closing of our common office be handled privately, according to which of us brought it in. This in effect would mean that our partnership ceases immediately, and that our collaboration is concerned only with the two jobs now in progress.[108]

The argument with Breuer took Gropius by surprise, and he accepted the dissolution of their partnership, adding in his response to Breuer, "nothing more can be said after your two amazing letters of May 23."[109] In recounting the dispute to Herbert Bayer, Gropius wrote: "What I feared for quite some time has now happened—a bust-up between Lajko and myself . . . the 'kleinmeister complex' against the former Bauhaus Director has brought him to commit betrayal towards me."[110]

Breuer and Gropius ultimately smoothed over their relations, though a certain resentment seemed to linger. For his part, Breuer assiduously avoided being cast under Gropius's shadow throughout the remainder of life, resisting any identification as a former "Gropius pupil."[111] Gropius seemed to hold a grudge against Breuer, at least in the short term: before Moholy-Nagy's death from cancer in 1946, Moholy recommended to the board of the Chicago Institute of Design that Breuer succeed him in his post as head of the design school, writing: "Although there has been a certain amount of friction between him and Gropius, I feel that he is one of the most brilliant architects of the generation after Gropius. . . . He has a great artistic sensibility which I am convinced is indispensable for the head of the Institute." Gropius, however, headed the institute's board, and he adamantly refused to allow any consideration of Breuer for the position. Gropius's stubbornness on the issue caused "a feeling of regret in most of us at the I.D. that Marcel Breuer should not be given a chance to decide for himself," according to Sibyl Moholy-Nagy.[112]

Although Breuer left Harvard for private practice in New York in 1946, GSD students continued to hold him in great esteem. Two years after he had left the School, a group of students "deeply concerned with the existing quality of work in the School" circulated a petition urging him to return to his teaching there. By the time it reached Breuer, ninety-five GSD students had signed it. Though he did not return to Harvard, the petition hung framed in Breuer's New York office for many years.[113]

Gropius, Breuer, and Wagner transformed the GSD Department of Architecture into a center of European modernism, but the department also included a number of other teachers who came with less exotic experience, among them two senior faculty members—Henry Frost and John Humphreys—the still untenured Holmes Perkins and Walter Bogner. An École alumnus, Humphreys was the sole old-guard figure left in Architecture, having practiced with Carrére and Hastings in New York and having taught at Harvard for nearly three decades before retiring in 1941.[114] If Humphreys objected to the department's new ways in his final years at the School, his voice was never heard since the balance had by then tipped in the modern direction. As for Henry Frost, Hudnut introduced him to Gropius as "the most sympathetic to modern architecture of all the GSD senior faculty."[115] Frost taught architectural design and construction at Harvard from 1905 until 1949, retiring only three years before Gropius departed. For many years, he shared a professional office in Cambridge with Eleanor Raymond, perhaps the most prominent woman practicing modern architecture in the interwar years. From 1916 on, Frost ran the Cambridge School of Domestic Architecture and Landscape Architecture for women, balancing it with his Harvard post. The Cambridge School had come into being after a Radcliffe graduate failed to gain admission to Harvard's all-male landscape architecture program. During the 1930s, Frost operated the school as a graduate division of Smith College, and it finally closed its doors when, desperate for students during the war, Harvard allowed women to enroll in the GSD. Frost's experience at the Cambridge School may have readied him for the changes he witnessed during his tenure at Harvard. At the Cambridge School, "we had no past, no older and wiser faculty members to advise us and dictate," so the spirit of experimentation prevailed.[116]

The two younger instructors, Perkins and Bogner, had both trained in the Beaux-Arts system—Perkins at Harvard, and Bogner at the Staatsgewerbeschule in Austria, followed by Harvard. Perkins had been one of a number of students taught by Haffner who moved away from the Beaux-Arts to modern in his designs and teaching methods. Along with his teaching, Perkins had his own architectural office, and he designed a number of modern houses in the Boston area. During his twenty years on the faculty, from 1930 to 1950, Perkins taught architectural design and occasional history courses, and in 1945, Hudnut appointed him chairman of the Planning Department. He would play a key role in helping implement design collaboration among the various fields. Perkins was widely respected by the students; even Philip Johnson held him in high regard. He remained a close friend and confidante to both Hudnut and Gropius, an unenviable position by the start of the postwar era.[117]

Bogner taught design and architectural practice at Harvard from 1927 until 1966, lasting well beyond the Hudnut/Gropius era. Described as a "nuts and bolts architect who knew how to build things," he appealed to students more interested in the technical rather than artistic aspects of architecture. Much to students' dismay, he had no compulsion about making abundant pencil marks—often accompanied by spilled cigarette ash—directly on students' work, even drawings they had worked on over long periods of time. Bogner came to embrace modern architecture enthusiastically and quickly after Gropius arrived, though as one student noted in 1940, Bogner had not quite "caught on to the true meaning of modern architecture."[118] A year earlier he had begun the design of his own modern house in Lincoln, which brought him other commissions for modern houses.

Of the others who taught in GSD's Architecture Department during the prewar years, Hugh Stubbins, one of Haffner's most accomplished students turned modern—"one of the coming men" in modern architecture, according to Hudnut—replaced Breuer in 1941 as Gropius's assistant. When he received tenure in 1946, he took on his own design classes. By the time he left Harvard in 1954, outlasting both Gropius and

G. Holmes Perkins, house in Brookline, 1939. (*Architectural Forum* 71 [July 1939]: 24)

Walter Bogner, Bogner's house in Lincoln, Massachusetts, 1939. (Photograph by the author, 2005)

Hudnut, he had served a brief term as both acting chair of the Architecture Department and acting dean of the GSD. He was one of few teachers at the GSD who would defend Hudnut's pedagogical ideas against Gropius's as their feuding began.[119] Stubbins, of course, went on to have a hugely successful practice that included such large-scale landmarks as the Berlin Kongresshalle (1957), Manhattan's Citicorp Building, and Boston's Federal Reserve Bank (both 1976), as well as several buildings on the Harvard campus.

History and the Liberal Arts

Shortly after Gropius's arrival in Cambridge, the Harvard administration decided to build on the excitement at the new GSD by bringing an architect as the next year's prestigious Charles Eliot Norton Professor of Poetry. At Gropius's suggestion, Hudnut recommended Sigfried Giedion, the Swiss architectural historian, for the year-long visiting lectureship that brought to Harvard for a series of six lectures "men of high distinction and preferably of international reputation."[120] If in 1938 Giedion did not quite yet fit that description, others who had held or who would later hold the prestigious post surely did, including Robert Frost, T. S. Eliot, Igor Stravinsky, and Leonard Bernstein.

Giedion, who had written his doctoral thesis with Heinrich Wölfflin on baroque and Romantic classicism, had by that time established himself as one of modern architecture's most active propagandists through his role in the CIAM, though he had not yet achieved acceptance in the academic world. Thus the prestigious Harvard post offered Giedion a helpful boost in this regard, and it also offered modern architecture and the new GSD a high level of publicity. Gropius had known Giedion since 1923, when he had paid a visit to the Bauhaus and, according to Gropius, "understood immediately." Their friendship developed through their work together in the CIAM, and Gropius came to appreciate his tireless support of the modern movement. In notifying Giedion of his election to the post, Gropius explained to him, "since by my coming and by the presence of Hudnut, the entire question of architecture has become topical here in all heads, I thought nobody could better enlarge the breach and give really fundamental explanations for our movement than you."[121]

To give Giedion an idea of the sort of scope he should aim for in his lectures and subsequent book, Gropius sent him a copy of Lewis Mumford's brand-new tome *The Culture of Cities,* along with a ringing endorsement of it. Giedion, too, admired the book but noted that he was "against condensing too much knowledge into one book."[122]

Not a laconic man, Giedion gave twelve, rather than six, lectures, and each ran beyond the allotted hour.[123] Because he was a great supporter and friend of Gropius's, nearly every GSD student attended the lectures, though most left them less than enthusiastic, "puzzled and bewildered," and even slightly amused by Giedion's grand and "unmistakably metaphysical air."[124] Giedion's lectures had combined both historiography and propaganda as he offered his view of why a new architecture was developing. Without much success, he tried to focus his argument around a single idea: "To show the tragic consequences of a

Sigfried Giedion with José Luis Sert, ca. 1953. (Courtesy of the Frances Loeb Library, Harvard Design School)

split-personality, of a split culture, to show the consequences of when thinking and feeling are moving on different levels."[125]

In 1941, three years after he delivered the lectures, Harvard University Press published a reworked version of Giedion's Norton Lectures as *Space, Time, and Architecture.* The time lag between the lectures and publication had occurred because Giedion's editor found his words as muddled as the students had. He insisted that Giedion rewrite the text in German and then had it translated back into English. The book became essential reading at the School and, moreover, for a huge international audience of architects, planners, art historians, clients of modern architecture, and students. Giedion's book also remains one of the best-selling books in the history of Harvard's press.[126]

After his year at Harvard, Giedion returned to Zurich, although throughout the war he traveled extensively, often passing through the GSD. It was not until after Gropius and Hudnut left Harvard that he returned for any length of time. From the mid-1950s to the early 1960s, the new dean, José Luis Sert, who knew him well from CIAM, brought Giedion to teach architectural history at the GSD.

The GSD's other historian, Kenneth Conant (no relation to the president), brought to the School an experience and a personality quite different from that of Giedion. A student of the medievalist art historian Arthur Kingsley Porter and a trained architect who practiced very little, he had spent much of his life at Harvard, where he became the first historian to achieve tenure at the School of Architecture, before the creation of the GSD. Conant specialized in medieval architecture, though he was well prepared to teach courses on all periods of European and American architecture, including modern. He was said to be an immensely knowledgeable and popular teacher with a teaching style that was "brisk and authoritative, gentlemanly, often good humored and notably unstuffy." In lecturing on Byzantine churches, for example, he might break into Byzantine chant himself, filling the halls of Robinson Hall with his "bass-baritone."[127] During the Hudnut/Gropius era, as the subject of history played a diminished part in the curriculum, Conant's status in the Architecture Department plunged. His classes, however, were still crowded with students from the Fine Arts Department.

The history of architecture would always play an important part in Hudnut's career, although when he first came to Harvard, he reduced the history course requirement—from four to three—even before Gropius joined the GSD faculty. He did so as a way of affirming the School's commitment to modern architecture, hoping to dissuade students from using only historical buildings as models for their own designs and to allow more time for other course work. In 1939, Hudnut reduced the requirement to a single course, and from 1946 until Hudnut and Gropius departed from the GSD, history became an elective field.[128] At least in the prewar years, Hudnut may have acceded to Gropius on the issue of history, for his Bauhaus colleague felt strongly that students beginning architectural studies should do so with an open mind, uncluttered by past architectures. By 1946, Hudnut had likely been pressured into making history courses optional rather than required, since by that time he had become known as an unabashed defender of the subject.

More in keeping with his humanistic nature than the reduction of history requirements might have indicated, Hudnut managed to admit design to the canon of the liberal arts for the first time in Harvard's history. In 1938, the GSD began its Architectural Sciences program, which allowed undergraduates to major in the "history and principles of design." In justifying the new program to the more skeptical members of the university administration, Hudnut set out the differences between design as a liberal and a professional pursuit. The undergraduate program, he explained, would provide an "intellectual discipline" rather than a professional training since it emphasized theory and history over practice. Whether or not one ultimately pursued architectural study after the program, Hudnut argued that because of its broad cultural perspective, architectural sciences would make a valuable course of study. Hudnut also defended the program by noting that it required students to take many traditional college courses: physics, geology, math, art history, and history, among others. Open only to a limited number of honors students, the major proved popular among students who saw it as the "only opportunity students had to express themselves" at the college level and the only program in which one learned to "understand the meaning of design."[129] One of the primary courses in the new major was modeled on Gropius's Basic Design at the Bauhaus. In a laboratory workshop, architectural science students developed a basis in design "through experience rather than precept" as in the famed preliminary course: they experimented with paper, pencil, scissors, clay, wire, and other materials, exploring the nature of materials and concepts of space and form. Along with this course, Hudnut himself taught the history of architecture in the new program, a clear indication that he remained tied to the subject. He lectured on buildings and cities from ancient times to the present in what students described as a "singularly unpedantic way."[130] For now, this juxtaposition of courses met with both Hudnut's and Gropius's approval, though it contained the seeds of their future troubles.

4 TRUMPET BLASTS

Amongst all architectural critics writing in America or for America,

Lewis Mumford and Sigfried Giedion are the most powerful. . . .

Their books, besides being works of scholarship, are trumpet-blasts.

—NIKOLAUS PEVSNER, 1949

Much like Giedion and Lewis Mumford, who straddled the fields of history and criticism rather than engaging in the practice of design, Hudnut made a great effort to bring his ideas of architecture and urbanism to a broad audience. Modeling himself as a public intellectual in the Deweyan vein, he promoted his case for modern architecture and civic design in a remarkable variety of outlets. Hegemann had likely set an example for Hudnut to follow in this regard, for he too had made his greatest impact not by designing but by bringing his expertise to the public realm: organizing, writing, and speaking out for the causes he believed in.[1] As his mentor had, Hudnut took part in numerous architecture and planning organizations, refereeing controversial competitions at the local and national levels, lecturing widely, and commenting frequently in the press on issues of design.

This chapter looks at some of the most significant of Hudnut's efforts to bring issues of modern architecture and urbanism beyond the confines of Harvard. In Washington, he led both the fight against the design of the Jefferson Memorial in 1937 and the controversial effort that followed to bring the first modern building to the Washington Mall. He also served as the leading force in bringing more than eighty modern architects and planners living across the United States into a new organization devoted to spreading modern practice—the American Society of Planners and Architects. Finally, Hudnut also brought ideas of modern architecture into the public sphere by publishing a great number of critical articles (roughly sixty during his years at Harvard) in a wide range of journals. Hudnut summed up his various activities—his writing, organizing, and debating—with the single word "propaganda," which he generously defined as a "process of enlightenment."[2] As a progressive educator, Hudnut felt it his duty to enlighten the public beyond the ivy walls. He devoted enormous effort to propagandizing on behalf of modern architecture and modern civic design, appearing on any stage that would have him.

The Love Nest Essays

By the mid-1930s, Hudnut had already established his modernist credentials through his educational work, but he was just then beginning to craft the first of his critical essays on modern architecture. It was his habit to spend mornings writing in the "Love Nest," his name for the isolated office at the top of Hunt Hall where he took refuge from daily GSD matters, and he rarely appeared in his administrative office in Robinson Hall before lunchtime. A narrow room about seven feet wide and sixty feet long, the Love Nest had earlier been the studio of Edward Forbes, longtime director of the Fogg Museum at Harvard (and Ralph Waldo Emerson's grandson) who had helped create the phenomenon of the university art museum in the United States. The Hunt Hall space offered Hudnut an ideal retreat, its walls tapestried with books, equipped with a bottle of sherry and glasses, books and lantern slides scattered on the tables, and velvet seats overlooking the rooftops of Harvard Yard.[3]

From the Love Nest, Hudnut wrote for professional and high-brow intellectual journals like many others in the academy, but he was likely among few Ivy League deans also writing for popular women's magazines. Hudnut styled his prose for a range of different audiences, always communicating rapidly with a journalistic bent and a penchant for generalized conclusions, not unlike Lewis Mumford.[4] In the *American Scholar* or the *Yale Review,* Hudnut would ruminate on the origins of modern architecture using Dewey as a touchstone, while in *House and Garden* or *Mademoiselle* he sympathized in flowery prose with the perplexed housewife and her hopeless quest to acquire good taste. No matter where he published, Hudnut aimed to share with his audiences what he described as "the philosophical or theoretical review of tendencies in architecture."[5]

Like Mumford and Giedion, Hudnut pitched his various writings to sound great trumpet blasts. Already widely published by the time Pevsner paid homage to these other two critics, Hudnut might well have placed Pevsner's tribute to them as an epigraph to his own critical writings, for he was the master of ironic self-deprecation. Though Pevsner did not mention Hudnut in his brief praise of Mumford and Giedion, others had kind words for the dean as critic. He was invariably noted as an "always quotable" commentator with "proved architectural wisdom," "dry insight into human nature," and an unparalleled ability to deliver the "elegant blast."[6] Another critic praised Hudnut's ability to balance propaganda and skepticism by describing him as "the most temperamental promoter of modern architecture in this country."[7] The *New Yorker* offered the following assessment: "Mr. Hudnut loves modern architecture well this side of idolatry and he writes of its problems with a catty aloofness charmingly disguised as sympathy. His demolitions are so bland that the reader hardly notices, till they are over, that they are also devastating. He has the skepticism and wit that are as disconcerting to a friend as to a foe."[8]

In his early Love Nest essays, those written before 1943, Hudnut admired the modern European architects—paying particular tribute to Gropius whenever possible—for their stand against mere formalism and against the idea that architecture is what comes about when one adds ornaments to buildings. Rather than applying art *to* building, Hudnut argued that the best modern architects were developing an "art *of* building" as they designed in the materials and forms of the evolving, technological world. By way of example, he held up Gropius's Bauhaus buildings for boldly displaying industrial materials and techniques in a vocabulary fit for the machine age, unlike the many recent buildings that masked their steel under neo-Gothic or Roman vaults.[9] Although Hudnut expressed admiration for Gropius, Le Corbusier, Oud, Mies, and others among the European architects for conveying the spirit of modernity in form, space, and technique, he tempered that praise by noting that their efforts were still too emphatic or "excessively heroic."[10] Despite his enthusiasm for the new modern architecture, even at the end of the 1930s he considered it at an early stage in the "process of formation." To achieve greatness, that is, to "command our hearts," Hudnut posited that modern architects must "develop, enrich, and amplify" what has so far only been "starkly given."[11]

Hudnut made two suggestions for moving past this early stage of modern design, the first clearly drawn from Hegemann. He advised that modern architects look beyond current technologies, methods, or rituals and conceive of architecture as an art that expresses in built form "the pattern of contemporary idea," that backdrop of general concepts that exists in every era.[12] In his 1938 essay "Architecture and the Modern Mind," which flaunted an image of the Bauhaus building on its first page, Hudnut posited that the new architecture must be shaped by "whatever vision we may form of the structure of the world, by whatever explanations of human experience we may accept, by whatever hope or despair is ours as we face the unknown and implications of that which is known."[13] No architect had yet fully interpreted in buildings or urban form the "clarity, precision, and devotion to objective truth," or that "sense of an evolving and continuing universe . . . the movement and tense energy" that are essential qualities of the contemporary world.[14] For this reason, Hudnut often spoke of modern architecture in the future tense, even as Gropius, Breuer, Wagner, and Tunnard taught in the studios of Robinson Hall.

Hudnut suggested that modern architects follow a second principle in order to bring their work beyond the initial, emphatic stage. Architects should emphasize the "architectural idea" as they design, by which Hudnut meant those qualities of expressiveness possible to buildings only. For all his effort at the GSD to unify the design professions, the notion that "architecture will yet be architecture"—distinct from all other art forms regardless of the many qualities they all shared—would remain central to Hudnut's concept of modernism.[15]

Hudnut identified three areas that architects should explore if they hoped to achieve a uniquely *modern* architectural expression: "space," freed by new technologies from the burdens of weight and mass; "human values"; and finally, "community." While space had always been a primary substance of architecture, in the modern age new technologies allowed architects to arrange and direct the flow of space in ways unimagined in earlier times, he explained. The new space was an actual physical material capable of being shaped, molded, or constructed—like a sculptor's mass—in almost limitless ways. It could allow buildings to reach out into cities or gardens, through courtyards, loggias, sheets of glass, and even over rooftops, dissolving the boundaries between buildings and environment. Although modern practitioners like Gropius, Mies, and Le Corbusier had begun to use the new space in these ways,

Hudnut did not think that even these architects had realized its full potential.[16]

No one had yet taken full advantage either of "human values" as a material of modern architecture. Hudnut explained that along with the "non-human" materials architects used in their work—stone, wood, or industrial goods—as builders of the "theaters of life," they must also design with the materials of "human affections and aptitudes." Even *modern* clients, he argued, those preferring a "collective industrialized" way of life and precisely mechanized homes, need expression in their environments. To achieve it, Hudnut challenged modern architects to "illuminate the material world with inward radiances," to create dwellings with "domestic happinesses," warehouses with "commercial enterprise," and universities with "a devotion to truth."[17]

Hudnut further maintained that modern architects had not yet given "community" the compelling role in their designs that it deserved. Architecture had always differed from other arts for the part it played in cities and regions, and yet the modernists had not played a large enough role in the war against "the mean, disordered, and inhuman shapes" of our contemporary cities. To do so, Hudnut urged them to "conceive their patterns of space and structure and life as integral parts of the larger patterns of cities: of cities which are not fortuitous complexes of streets and building sites but which are themselves evolving and unified works of design, conditioned upon science, directed towards human good."[18] Written in 1938, this passage was an early one in Hudnut's prodigious effort to champion a modernized form of civic design.

Though Hudnut would write an enormous amount about architecture and planning during his years at the GSD, he rarely suggested and never demonstrated any way to translate his ideas into buildings or modern plans. Because he never designed a single modern building or modern plan, the students claimed that Hudnut "never actually made his philosophy of art clear." In contrast, Gropius offered them a very "definite point of view."[19] The fact that Hudnut had given up practice years earlier and that he never taught any studios after his first semester at Harvard clearly limited Hudnut's impact on students at the GSD. Students were looking for absolute ideas and definite suggestions, and this gave Gropius a supreme advantage over Hudnut. Unlike Hudnut, Gropius believed, as many students seemed to, that a teacher must have "a clear ideological approach of his own [to be] able to give a student a definite conviction." And offering a definite conviction, Gropius insisted, "is the prime aim of a good architectural education."[20]

For his part, Hudnut believed that modern architecture could encompass a wide range of different forms, and thus he had no absolute principles to offer. As he told the social critic and journalist Frederick Lewis Allen in 1941:

> It is easier to say what the new architecture will not be, than what it will be. I think, for example, that techniques will play a much wider role in design than they have in the past and that people will be less concerned with formal or aesthetic values than they are at present. I think that the new architecture will recognize a changing and developing world so that people will be less impressed by permanence and unity and I feel that the important qualities to be looked for in architecture will be conditioned upon social and political relationships.[21]

Hudnut's writing and lecturing may not have inspired many followers among the students, but they did bring him celebrity in the architectural community, and they did lead to further opportunities to broadcast his views.

The Temple for Jefferson

Hudnut received the first of several national assignments in the spring of 1937 when a group of architects, artists, Democratic congressmen, and the editorial staff of the *New Republic,* all familiar with his talents for writing and advocacy, drafted him as the primary spokesman against the construction of the Jefferson Memorial that stands today in Washington. Safeguarding "our first great democrat," as Dewey called Jefferson, from deification in marble was a project well suited to Hudnut, given his own democratic ambitions in architecture and education. It allowed him to put to test the ideas he had been developing as wrote in his Love Nest. Hudnut also had a long-standing interest in Jefferson's architecture, dating from the time that he taught and practiced in Virginia.[22]

Surprisingly, the drawn-out, angry debate over the Jefferson Memorial would transcend architectural party lines: those against building a "pantheon" for Jefferson included a group of modernists led by William Lescaze, but also Elbert Peets, Hegemann's former partner, who had little sympathy for modern architecture; Olmsted Jr.; and the land-

John Russell Pope's Jefferson Memorial; Hudnut described the building as an "egg on a pantry shelf in the midst of a geometric Sahara." (Peter Aaron, Esto)

scape architect Gilmore Clarke, a vociferous opponent of Hudnut and Gropius on the GSD Visiting Committee. On the other side, Hudnut and Hegemann's old friend Fiske Kimball (who had appointed Hudnut to his University of Virginia post) led the fight for a classical memorial and for appointing the architect John Russell Pope to design it.[23] The case Hudnut put forward against the "temple" for Jefferson sheds light on his ideas of architecture in the late 1930s, while his role in the controversy points to his increasing prominence in pre–World War II architectural culture. Typical of Hudnut, he aimed his public relations campaign against the proposed memorial at a broad audience, avoiding any strong modernist rhetoric and using erudition and ridicule as his primary tools.

Hudnut articulated his case against the "egg on a pantry shelf in the midst of a geometric Sahara"[24]—his description of the proposed memorial—in every relevant public forum he could think of: newspapers, popular and professional journals, speeches in Washington, and comments presented to Congress during a hearing on the monument. Though he agreed with the monument's proponents that Jefferson might well have built a pantheon in own day, he argued that this meant only that Jefferson belonged to his own time. Even during his lifetime, Hudnut argued, Jefferson would never have offered the "impeccable classicism" of Pope's proposed monument but rather a more "naive" version like that of Jefferson's own architecture. Jefferson had tempered his classicism with the "Georgian rhythms, Georgian materials, Georgian scale, and Georgian taste" of his own era.[25] Hudnut argued that instead of the proposed imitation imperial temple, Jefferson's memorial should celebrate the lasting principles to which he had devoted himself: democracy, liberty, progress, truth, and simplicity. If Jefferson were living today, Hudnut posed, "is it not likely that he would yield himself to the currents of progressive thought of our day?" Since modern life is, above all things, about change and evolution, "it cannot possibly find aesthetic expression in a static or rigid architecture." Hudnut also relied on the Deweyan concept of organicism, which he would often return to in his architectural essays, as he argued against the proposed memorial.

> In a period when all of the world appears to us as an organic growth, when our mode of thinking is dominated by a conception of the organic in nature—of nature as an evolving, moving, growing and decaying order, in which human life is a necessary and essential element—we cannot possibly find in the static symbol, in formalized art of the classic period, any relation to our own needs or emotions . . . we can not conceivably find beauty in an architecture where all is complete, where all is fulfillment— an architecture which requires a permanent order.[26]

Along with condemning the static form of the monument, Hudnut also spoke out against the site chosen for it, a stretch of land frequented by visitors for its cherry trees and proximity to the Tidal Basin. The monument dedicated to the democratic Jefferson would destroy a "people's playground" if erected there. In addition, building on that site would also alter the character of the 1791 L'Enfant plan that Jefferson had favored for the capital city. L'Enfant, according to Hudnut, had created a "living organism," a city plan permitting growth and variation, rather than the fixed, perpetual classicism that the monument would impose.[27]

How to honor Jefferson then? Hudnut argued that his memorial must avoid all the indiscretions of Pope's proposed temple. To begin with, instead of simply handing the project to Pope, he advocated a democratic process for choosing the memorial's architect, a national competition that he believed would both result in a better design than the one proposed and incalculably aid "the cause of good architecture."[28] Furthermore, Hudnut argued—as he claimed Jefferson would have—for a serviceable memorial instead of an "archaeological monument," some kind of cultural center that would promote (in a phrase he often used) "the welfare and happiness of people." In its design, Hudnut insisted that the memorial must belong to the present time since "architecture extremely formalized in accordance with a past convention cannot conceivably attain an emotional significance."[29]

Hudnut knew that his side would lose the battle over Jefferson's memorial, particularly since the group had mobilized quite late in the building process. He was optimistic, however, that the huge public fight had brought on the "twilight of the Gods," that Jefferson's might well be the last ancient temple built in modern Washington. Even after John Russell Pope's grandiloquent National Gallery of Art opened its doors in 1941, not far from the Tidal Basin temple, Hudnut remained sanguine. As he noted in the review essay he wrote on that building, "yesterday when I passed the mighty steps of the National Gallery of Art, I thought that I could discern over its doorway the inscription, dim but growing distinct: *Ultimus Romanorum*."[30]

Smithsonian Gallery of Art

Hudnut's second national assignment gave him real reason for optimism that Washington had seen the "last of the Romans." His part in the Jefferson Memorial controversy brought Hudnut to the attention of Edward "Ned" Bruce, President Roosevelt's chief of the Treasury Department's Section of Fine Arts, who was leading the effort to build a museum of contemporary art on the Washington Mall.[31] At roughly the same time, Frederic Delano, who was also involved with the museum project, discovered Hudnut through an article the dean had published in the *American Scholar.* An influential figure in Washington—he was both President Roosevelt's uncle and head of the National Capital Park and Planning Commission—Delano forwarded Hudnut's article to the director of the Smithsonian, C. G. Abbot, advising him that as they proceeded in building the new museum, "we must listen to men like Mr. Hudnut."[32]

The Smithsonian Institution had already signed on to sponsor the museum for "living artists," and in 1938, Congress committed funds for an open design competition to choose the architect for a new building to house it. Even the idea of a competition caused controversy in Washington: no other federal building in that city had ever had its architects chosen by open competition. Money for the building would not come from Congress but would be raised from private sources after the jury selected a winner.[33] Though a few names were bandied about as possible donors, Ned Bruce was not entirely unserious when he asked Hudnut: "You don't know any nice friendly generous millionaire, do you, who wants to put up that Smithsonian building? I have been on a hunt for one for some time."[34] Nothing like the museum Bruce hoped to build existed in the United States, not even the Museum of Modern Art, which Bruce referred as "the little snob recently dedicated by the Rockefellers."[35] The new Smithsonian Gallery of Art—the name ultimately decided upon—would promote contemporary art through exhibitions, buying and selling recent artwork and reproductions, employing artists, publishing, and circulating art books in a great library. The Smithsonian Gallery would also act as a "feeder" to the National Gallery of Art, by handing on to it modern art no long considered contemporary but deemed to be of enduring quality. After a series of meetings and discussions with Hudnut, Bruce came to hold him in high esteem, and he believed, as he told both President and Eleanor Roosevelt, who followed the progress of the project, that Dean Hudnut is "blaz[ing] the trail which architecture is likely to follow in the future."[36]

Bruce assigned Hudnut the key role in the competition to choose an architect for the new building. Hudnut would decide the "thing to be done, the idea to be expressed" in the building, write the competition program, and handpick the members of the jury as well as direct the competition.[37] In these ways, Hudnut's ideas of architecture would finally affect the design of a modern building of national significance. His role in the project inspired the usual controversy surrounding the appointment of any modern architect to a significant position in the 1930s. His detractors accused him of being "intolerant of any architectural expression other than extreme modern and radical," and they worried that his prominent part in the competition would prevent conservative architects from even entering.[38] Ever the diplomat, Hudnut met personally with a few of his critics—those high-placed enough to impede his efforts, such as one C. L. Borie, a Philadelphia architect and member of the National Commission of Fine Arts—to assure them that he had "neither tail nor horns" and that the only thing "Red" about him was the "usual Harvard illumination."[39]

In the end, 408 architects from all types of practices—small-town, individual, large firms, varieties of traditional and modern—entered the competition to build the Smithsonian Gallery; the most well known of the entrants included Paul Cret, Ernest Flagg, Albert Kahn, Wallace K. Harrison, William van Alen, Clarence Stein, Philip Goodwin, William

Wurster, William Lescaze, Wallace Harrison, Eliel and Eero Saarinen, Edward Durrell Stone, Percival Goodman, and from the GSD, design professors Holmes Perkins and Hugh Stubbins and recent graduates Richard Stein, Leonard Currie, Robert W. Kennedy, and Eliot Noyes.[40] The competition attracted many architects with modernist leanings, partly because of Hudnut, but especially because of the jury he had assembled.

In keeping with a promise he made to Gropius when he hired him—that he would involve him where he could in important architectural events—Hudnut appointed Gropius to the jury. In addition, Hudnut made a juror of his friend, the architect George Howe, thinking he would be firmly on the modern side with Gropius, and he balanced the two against John Holabird and Henry Shepley, who he expected would take a more traditional stance. The final jury member, Frederic Delano, would fit somewhere between the two groups.[41] It was the first time, as Hudnut told Gropius, that "the modernists have had the slightest chance to build an important building in Washington. Your presence on the jury [will] give all the younger architects a tremendous incentive to do their best." Hudnut actually figured that the modernists had more than a slight chance, for as he confided to Gropius, "I'm sure you can persuade Delano."[42]

Hudnut's program for the building competition encouraged a modernist sensibility by emphasizing the museum's "dynamic rather than static" quality, calling for galleries laid out "not as a series of permanent or monumental rooms" but as great open spaces with temporary partitions appropriate for changing exhibitions, and with the building as a whole flexibly planned for future growth.[43] Hudnut emphasized the terms "movement," "maximum flexibility," and "freedom of extension" throughout the whole competition program. Though it may have seemed contradictory to the modern spirit of the program, Hudnut also insisted that materials associated with permanence and grandeur—marble, limestone, or granite—be used for all of the Smithsonian Gallery's exterior surfaces, much as in the existing traditional-style Mall buildings.[44]

By demanding a sense of permanence and grandeur for the building, Hudnut anticipated the debate over monumentality that would break open among modern architects in the mid-1940s and continue throughout the decade. Lewis Mumford sparked that debate with his 1938 observation in *The Culture of Cities* that "if it is a monument, it can't be modern," meaning that modern buildings, by definition, precluded such features as symmetry in design, hierarchy in massing, overtly symbolic content, and decorative elements.[45] In 1943, Sigfried Giedion brought the issue to the fore by insisting that modern architects, who had been focusing on the immediate need for housing, must begin to build monuments, symbols, or "human landmarks" that served to express society's "highest cultural needs."[46] This is exactly what Hudnut had intended for the Smithsonian Gallery on the Washington Mall.

Though he wanted the new building to fit well into the larger landscape of the Mall, Hudnut did not want it to seem part of a fixed master plan, and he added a phrase to the design program stating that "nothing in this program is to be interpreted as requiring a formal or balanced relationship to other buildings."[47] Finally, Hudnut made clear to the architects entering the competition that no museum building could be built without the final approval of the Commission of Fine Arts, which advised Congress and the president on all matters pertaining to architecture in the District of Columbia.[48]

In many ways, the Smithsonian Gallery project resembled the efforts Hudnut was undertaking at the GSD. Hudnut imagined the gallery as an "active influencing agency" that both encouraged the creation of new works of contemporary art of distinction as well as the appreciation of them. He also wanted the museum to be "educational in the broadest sense," to reach out to other large institutions but also to those in small communities by using both popular and scholarly formats. Ultimately, much as he intended for the GSD, the new Smithsonian Gallery would "restore to American art a healthy relationship to the life of the community."[49]

In the summer of 1939, the jury for the Smithsonian Gallery competition unanimously awarded the grand prize to Saarinen, Swanson, and Saarinen—with Eliel Saarinen in charge—praising the firm for having designed a masterfully sited building, clear in its composition in mass, dignified in expression, with a fine use of materials, and an interesting and imaginative exterior.[50] In advance of the criticism that he knew would come from the nonmodern camp, Hudnut publicly praised the building for, of all things, its classicism, declaring that "nothing more is needed in Washington than a recovery of the classic spirit."

For fifty years architects have tried to make Washington classical by hanging colonnades and porticoes on the sides of buildings but they have only succeeded in making these buildings complicated, false, and restless. Mr. Saarinen has put aside the futile grasping at the externals of the antique architectures in order to recapture, not Hellenic form, but the Hellenic way of working. For the purpose to which it is addressed his building is as perfect as the Parthenon, being animated by the same faith, the same passion for truth, and the same clarity of expression.[51]

Hudnut's commentary on the winning Saarinen project helps clarify for us the qualities that he sought in modern architecture, or at least in modern public buildings. In addition to the project's classicism, he praised the architects for having designed the building from the inside first, working outward only after satisfying its occupants' needs and the "demonstrable laws of structure and use." When they moved to the outside of the building, the architects then reworked their design to relate to the broader pattern of the Mall and to the plan of Washington.[52] Many others in the competition did not take this second step.

As for the issue of monumentality in relation to the winning building, Hudnut recognized that many of the people who opposed the Saarinen design did so because it lacked the obvious heaviness that one associates with majesty and endurance. He conceded that a modern building with light, thin walls hung on metallic frames such as theirs could not emit the same kind of authoritative air of one with massive stone walls or heavy columns: "I am inclined to think," he wrote, "that a genuine monumentality is definitely prohibited by our contemporary technique of construction and also by contemporary use." Rather than seeking refuge in *"fake* monumentality"—hanging classical elements on a concealed scaffolding, for example—Hudnut urged architects to follow the path of the Saarinen project, which offered a "compensatory quality" in its shaping and arranging of enclosed space.[53]

As expected, the Saarinen design raised a storm of protest among what Ned Bruce described as "almost the entire architectural profession, more particularly by the older entrenched architects."[54] Gilmore Clarke, a sparring partner of Hudnut's in this battle too, was among those accusing the Saarinens of having won the competition by "'playing up' to the jurors." He claimed that the Saarinens understood the biases of the various jurors and designed the building to conform to them. The building in Clarke's view—and his view mattered since he sat on the Commission of Fine Arts—was "totally unsuited for the Mall," where all other buildings have, "or appear to have," structural bearing walls. A

Publicity photo for the Smithsonian Art Gallery, February 1940. *Left to right:* Robert J. Swanson, Eero Saarinen, Eliel Saarinen, Walter Gropius, Jean Labatut, Joseph Hudnut, and Antonin Raymond. (Copyright Cranbrook Archives, no. 5476–24, Richard G. Askew, photographer)

Model of the Smithsonian Art Gallery, February 1940. (Copyright Cranbrook Archives, no. 5476–20, Richard G. Askew, photographer)

number of other critics opposed the design for its "factory-like" appearance and construction, and for the obviousness of its steel frame with a thin stone and glass veneer.[55]

The Smithsonian Gallery of Art did not get built and for a number of different reasons. To begin with, the Commission of Fine Arts rejected the design, and no one ever solicited any of the funds needed to build the museum. If the untimely death in 1940 of Ned Bruce, the greatest champion of the project, did not mean the end for the Saarinen building, the war in Europe certainly did. Beyond the politics of architecture, the prospect of American involvement in the war loomed large early in 1941, when the Smithsonian project got banished to the archives.[56]

Before the project was cast aside, however, Hudnut, Bruce, the jurors, the Saarinens, and others who championed the building managed to get enormous national publicity for the winning design. The national press covered the competition thoroughly, and a large-scale model of the Saarinen project, along with the ten finalists' drawings, toured museums and architecture schools throughout the country, including the Harvard GSD. Though it was never built, the Saarinen project at least brought the concept of a contemporary national museum housed in a distinguished modern building on the traditional Mall into the realm of possibility in the public mind. In her catalogue essay for the Museum of Modern Art's 1944 exhibition, *Built in the USA, 1932–1944,* Elizabeth Mock pointed to the Saarinen's Smithsonian Gallery design as one of the occasional buildings that are needed to "raise the every-day casualness of living to a higher and more ceremonial plane, buildings which give dignified and coherent form to that interdependence of the individual and the social group which is of the very nature of our democracy."[57] Hudnut would later pose the question in the title of an essay he published years later, "Can Modern Architecture Build a Symbol?"[58] In the case of the Saarinen Smithsonian Gallery, he seemed to think it did so.

Though a decade too late to save the Saarinen project, Hudnut ironically would himself be appointed to the Commission of Fine Arts in 1950 to fill the seat vacated by Gilmore Clarke. The august body of commissioners had not changed much in the intervening years so that Hudnut's appointment, and that of the modern architect Pietro Belluschi at the same time, would finally "hearten those who have been hoping that the monopoly of a small conservative clique of column architects on the commission could be broken."[59] President Truman would appoint Hudnut and Belluschi after purging the committee of several of its members, including Clarke, who had opposed Truman's wish to add a balcony to the White House.[60]

The ties between Hudnut and the Saarinens (Eliel particularly) extended beyond the Smithsonian Gallery episode. More than any other architects, the Saarinens' work of the 1930s and early 1940s seemed to express in built form many of Hudnut's ideas of architecture. Also, at Cranbrook, where Eliel Saarinen taught for many years, the architect seemed to be advocating ideas of design that accorded well with Hudnut's. Historian David De Long has described, in a passage equally suited to Hudnut, that at Cranbrook, Saarinen "encouraged diverse expressions linked not by appearance or even clearly specified principles of design, but rather by a consistent attitude toward place and materials. It was a philosophy that safeguarded both values of personal expression and public good."[61]

Both Saarinen and Hudnut rejected the Romanticism of their own architectural educations, but they also refused to embrace, as Saarinen's biographer, Albert Christ-Janer, has written, "pure rationalism when the move was toward the coldly rational."[62] A few contemporary critics noticed the connection between the Saarinens and Hudnut. A 1947 *Architectural Record* article on the Saarinens' new buildings at Drake University included a bold-printed caption noting that the buildings "present the thinking of one man of proved architectural wisdom and academic experience—Dean Hudnut of the Harvard Graduate School of Design." The author had connected Hudnut to the Drake buildings since he was well known for encouraging projects like the Saarinens' that anticipated further growth and recognized the evolving nature of the larger fabric.[63] Christ-Janer also mentioned Hudnut in his discussion of the Saarinens' work on the Cranbrook campus. The Saarinens' campus designs, he wrote, are an excellent illustration of Dean Hudnut's principle that "you need not build in a similar style to attain unity. A good design in proper scale will bring the harmony you desire."[64]

In 1941, Hudnut reviewed two new Saarinen buildings for *Architectural Forum*—the most progressive of the architecture journals—in which he wrote of his admiration for "the great and just renown of Eliel Saarinen."[65] Hudnut first of all celebrated the usefulness of the Saarinens' Kleinhans Music Hall in Buffalo. Delighted that on the brink of war the Saarinens could engage the city's interest in music and in making a living memorial rather than defense housing, aerial torpedoes,

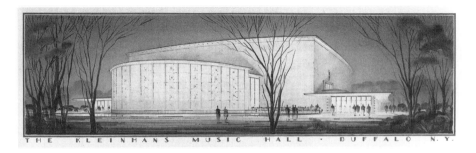

Eliel and Eero Saarinen, Kleinhans Music Hall, 1938. (Copyright Cranbrook Archives, no. 4778, Richard G. Askew, photographer)

or merely decorative memorials, he praised the building as a symbol of "civilized living." Hudnut had a particular interest in music (perhaps encouraged by his wife's accomplishments as a pianist), and he likened this building to a Steinway for its organic nature. As in that perfect instrument, Hudnut described that the Saarinens shaped space and fabric in an eloquent way, as if they were parts of a single organism. "This is the thrilling fact about modern architecture and it is the one fact which distinguishes modern architecture from all those which have preceded it since the Gothic era," Hudnut wrote in praise of the Kleinhans.[66]

Hudnut identified even more with the Saarinens' Crow Island School, a progressive school building located in the suburbs of Chicago's North Shore that, according to Hudnut, encouraged both social usefulness in its constructed form and "making and doing and expressing in ceaseless variety." The Saarinens had designed a series of hospitable spaces, according to Hudnut, an assembly room that "gathers the children into its arms" and classrooms that communicate both an understanding of youth and of the teacher's way of working. Once again he praised the Saarinens for shaping the building's individual elements first and then submitting them to a larger "organic" order.[67] For all his critical writing and lecturing about architecture, Hudnut rarely addressed specific buildings, the Saarinen projects being an exception to his usual fare of larger subjects: housing, city planning, and modern architecture writ large. Occasionally he narrowed his field to consider building types; churches, schools, and university campuses always interested him greatly.

Hard as it is to gauge his persuasive powers as he sought to mold public opinion, on one occasion in 1945 Hudnut delivered a lecture in downtown Chicago that made a direct impact. He referred to the University of Chicago at one brief moment in a wide-ranging lecture as "that horror out on the Midway." A university trustee in the audience stayed after the lecture to ask Hudnut for clarification. Hudnut explained that while a Gothic cathedral like Chartres recorded the changes in ideas and temper over the centuries of its building, the "static" Gothic of the University of Chicago captured neither the spirit of Gothic architecture nor of a modern university. Buildings housing contemporary ideas and people, he continued, must reflect contemporary thought and life. The trustee brought Hudnut's argument before the board at its next meeting, and as a result, the prepared blueprints for a new Gothic administration building were scrapped. Letters of protest from indignant alumni poured in, but as the trustee later wrote, "the way was opened to future commissions to the great: [Eero] Saarinen, Mies van der Rohe, etc."[68]

Hudnut had specifically recommended these two architects—and only these two (Eliel had by then given up practice)—to the president of the University of Chicago. While Hudnut spoke to President Colwell of

Eliel and Eero Saarinen, interior of classroom at Crow Island School, 1941. (Copyright Cranbrook Archives, no. 5657–3, Richard G. Askew, photographer)

his "lively admiration" for Eero Saarinen's "vigorous style and fine understanding of group composition," he saved his greater praise for Mies van der Rohe, "probably the ablest of modern architects now practicing; he has a vigorous and original mind and . . . is capable of great elegance in his work and his feeling for form-space is quite sensitive."[69] By 1948, when Hudnut offered his advice to Colwell, he had long since finished his propagandizing on behalf of Gropius.

Apart from his writing and lecturing, Hudnut's propagandistic activities included the oversight or jurying of other design competitions both small and large—a municipal airport building in Fitchburg, Massachusetts; a civic design scheme for Boston;, the Hidden Talent Competition, which offered its winner publicity rather than a commission; and finally, the Franklin D. Roosevelt Memorial Competition in 1960, none of these nearly so significant to Hudnut or all-consuming as the Smithsonian Gallery. Hudnut took part in all these events because he believed in the idea of open competitions, persuaded that they drew the best designers in the profession and perhaps even led to the discovery of new talent, all the while stirring up public interest in architecture.[70] In addition to these activities, Hudnut served on numerous national and local commissions related to architecture and planning, for he hoped that in this way too he could disseminate his ideas of modern design while also encouraging citizen interest and participation. Along with the National Fine Arts Commission in Washington, Hudnut headed the Metropolitan Housing Association in Boston and sat on a committee investigating correctional and mental health buildings and on the commission overseeing urban renewal in Baltimore. He also remained actively involved with the architecture department of the Museum of Modern Art.[71]

It was by *not* belonging to the American Institute of Architects (AIA) that Hudnut tried to affect the direction of that organization, and the architectural profession in general. Unhappy with the AIA for a number years, Hudnut resigned from the institute in 1945, convinced that it had become merely a trade organization of architects who cared about their work only insofar as it offered a means of livelihood. As for the AIA's journal, Hudnut disliked its editorial policy of putting forward many divergent opinions, which he believed resulted in a journal offering no opinion whatsoever. In complaining of the journal to the AIA president, Hudnut told him, "It happens that I *do* have an opinion and I might go so far as to say that I am chiefly interested in opinion."[72] The resignation of the Harvard dean caused quite a stir at the AIA, for the organization feared his departure might influence GSD students to avoid membership when they became practicing architects. The AIA sent several different emissaries to Harvard to dissuade Hudnut from leaving the organization but to no avail.[73]

Hudnut's relationship to the AIA did not end with his resignation in 1945. He rejoined the organization in 1951, only to resign again in 1953, this time because he was retiring from the deanship at Harvard. The AIA discussed granting him emeritus status, but those inside the organization with longer memories opposed such a move. As the head of the AIA Boston chapter, Harold Willis reminded his colleagues that, back when Hudnut first resigned in 1945,

> we heard quite a spate of words from his famous large vocabulary. We were told that the AIA was no more than an organization of old traditional architects and that he had no further interest in it. . . . His poor opinion of the AIA was by no means kept to himself, but broadcast throughout the School of Design to faculty and students. I obtained the impression that he was largely responsible for the antagonistic and sneering attitude toward the AIA which the students and some of the faculty at the Harvard School of Design had at that time. [The AIA president] entirely agrees with me. At all times he found Mr. Hudnut most uncooperative when asked to write articles or do anything else for the AIA. To make him a member emeritus would establish a most undesirable precedent.[74]

Though Gropius may also have had philosophical differences with the AIA, his relationship to the organization was far less rocky than Hudnut's. He never considered resigning since his doing so would have been viewed as anti-American, especially by those already skeptical of him. Staying in the AIA, of course, benefited him in the long run, for without doing so, he would not have won the AIA Gold Medal in 1950.[75]

Gropius as Propagandist

During Gropius's first year at Harvard, Hudnut had loudly trumpeted the accomplishments of his new colleague to American audiences. For his efforts on Gropius's behalf in seeking commissions and jury positions for him and in arranging exhibitions and celebratory gatherings, Gropius reported to his friends in London that Hudnut was "a brilliant impresario."[76] After having been in the United States for just over a year, however, the tables had turned. Gropius grew concerned that Hudnut himself was "too much in the shade," and he set out to draw public attention to the dean and his achievements. He turned to Walter Saunders of the *Architectural Forum* for assistance, telling Saunders that he had "no doubt [Hudnut] is the first man who has found a practicable way of bridging the old and the new in architecture, following this course very decidedly and with greatest care." But Hudnut was too modest, he said, "and people generally do not know of his rare qualities and strength." Gropius suggested that the time had come for the *Forum* to publish a "good, elaborate article about his work, his intentions, and his achievements."[77] Saunders replied that the *Forum* editor found the idea of a full-blown article on Hudnut "questionable" and suggested instead a larger article on the state of architectural education in the United States.[78] This may be one of the few times that Gropius's propagandistic efforts did not succeed.

Gropius had long understood the power of propaganda, and he was, by all accounts, a celebrated master of the trade. This aspect of Gropius appealed enormously to Hudnut, who had, during the process of hiring a modernist for Harvard, related to President Conant that Gropius had already "proved himself an excellent propagandist."[79] Since then, historians who have written about Gropius seem to agree that his talent for public relations was "nothing short of fantastic." At the start of the Bauhaus, for example, Gropius set out to create "an idea that we shall promulgate with every means of publicity at our disposal . . . we shall draw grand designs and also propagate them."[80] He surely succeeded in doing so, and his efforts to spread his ideas while at Harvard were equally grand.

Once he settled in the United States, Gropius became an indefatigable lecturer, symposium participant, and writer, with at least 150 public lectures and articles to his credit during his fifteen years at Harvard and others to follow in subsequent years. Like Hudnut, Gropius worked hard to air his ideas, though he preferred to address a narrower range of audiences than the dean did: architects, planners, industrial designers, and educators in the design fields. Much of Gropius's writing and lecturing focused on what he called educating architects for "creative design." An interesting fact of his enormous output on this subject was that since Gropius regarded his educational ideas as "universally valid," he delivered nearly identical lectures and wrote many similar articles from the start of his career at Harvard through to the end.

Gropius essentially argued in these essays and lectures that architectural education had become too timid, too scholarly, and too rooted in the past. American architecture schools needed a new way of educating their students, one aimed at releasing and increasing the creative powers of each individual. Architectural education should model itself on the Bauhaus system and begin with all first-year students taking a common preliminary course modeled after the Bauhaus's. Gropius described the course for his many audiences, noting that students who took the course would develop the all-important habit of integrating issues of form, construction, and economy as they considered any design problem. They would learn to invent "independently, true, genuine forms out of the technical, economical and social conditions they find themselves in."[81] After completing the six-month preliminary course, students would be ready to begin their studies in one of the narrower fields of concentration—architecture, planning, or landscape architecture. Gropius not only argued for Basic Design in his various lectures and essays, using language similar to that used by John Dewey and American progressive educators, he also described to his audiences the importance of "learning by doing" and "experience" in architectural education. Hands-on experience, he claimed in one of his stock formulations, "would help to bridge that fatal separation between craftsmanship and academic learning which weakened the art of design during the development of the machine age."[82] Gropius always spoke with great self-assurance, with a British-like rectitude, and he was sometimes prone to underestimating his audiences. After one lecture in which he had described the tenets of progressive education to a rather well-informed Museum of Modern Art audience as if he were their inventor, Alfred Barr took him to task: "We should be most unhappy if you should find yourself handicapped through your misunderstanding or underestimation of American culture. For example, in your lecture to our members you took great pains to explain to our members the elements of 'progressive' education—methods which have been employed in America for a quarter of a century."[83]

Although both Hudnut and Gropius spread their ideas through publishing and lecturing, Gropius did not share Hudnut's interest in effecting architectural change by participating in the kinds of local and national institutions that Hudnut did. Gropius did, however, play a role in several organizations allied directly with the cause of modern architecture and the Bauhaus legacy, and, for a while, he encouraged Hudnut to join him. Gropius took a great interest in the Institute of Design (ID) in Chicago—briefly called the "New Bauhaus"—where his friend and former colleague from the Bauhaus, László Moholy-Nagy developed a design school and curriculum closely modeled on the German Bauhaus.[84] At the time of the school's founding in 1937, the Association of Arts and Industries in Chicago had in fact approached Gropius to serve as the school's first director. Gropius had just arrived at Harvard and was not interested, but he recommended Moholy, "my nearest collaborator in the Bauhaus."[85] Under Moholy, the Institute of Design trained students in a variety of fields, not just architecture but also metalwork, glass, textiles, and stage display. The ID required its students to begin their studies with the Foundation Course, a basic design course very much like the one Moholy had taught at the Bauhaus and very much like the one Gropius was determined to start at Harvard.

Gropius acted as the official "consultant" of the ID, and in this capacity he invited Hudnut to participate as one of the institute's trustees, or "sponsors," as they were called. Gropius helped assemble a group of distinguished sponsors: John Dewey, Julian Huxley (the English zoologist who knew both Moholy and Gropius in London), Alfred Barr, and the publisher W. W. Norton. Although the sponsors apparently never held a meeting nor offered financial aid to the School, Moholy still considered Hudnut an important advocate of the ID. He told Hudnut that "one day I wrote Gropius that I envied him that he has you on his side. I said this merely because of your reputation. Now I am even more conscious about it. It makes one feel so optimistic to see how generous, human, and wise you are."[86] Though Hudnut had little to do with the ID after Moholy's death in 1946, Gropius continued to play an active part in the often-stormy affairs of the school.[87]

Gropius also continued his affiliation with the CIAM during his years at Harvard, and he tried to help those members who were dislocated because of the war find jobs in American architecture and planning schools.[88] The CIAM never had a strong organizational presence in the United States, with its center of activity in prewar and postwar Europe. During the war years, as Sigfried Giedion described in 1943: "CIAM has been silenced and dispersed by the course of inexorable events. Today it lives only in individuals whose spirits were disciplined by a decade of close collaboration."[89] On several occasions, a number of CIAM members and friends did meet in the United States, the first time in 1939 at Oskar Stonorov's farm near Phoenixville, Pennsylvania. Hudnut was one of the few Americans attending, along with Edward Durrell Stone and Wallace K. Harrison. Others present included Gropius, Giedion, Breuer, Madame de Mandrot, Richard Neutra, Alvar Aalto, and Knut Lonberg-Holm.[90] There is no record of Hudnut commenting on the organization at this point, either in his published writing or in any remaining archival materials. Since he was always eager to find ways to advance the new architecture in the United States, he was likely exploring the possibility of the CIAM's help in doing so.

Hudnut made an important contribution to the CIAM in 1942. He lent the group a public relations hand by writing the foreword to José Luis Sert's *Can Our Cities Survive?* (1942), the book that introduced the CIAM's urbanistic program to English-speaking audiences. Hudnut's foreword was his first of many essays on modern urbanism, and though he expressed optimism about the CIAM's program for urban improvement, he kept it general in tone and did not consider any particular aspects of their program. As in many of his other essays, Hudnut's foreword called for "spiritual forces" to shape our evolving cities and not the dictates of logic or formalist aesthetics.[91] Hudnut also used his connections to facilitate an agreement with Harvard University Press to publish Sert's book. Acting "in the name of CIAM," Hudnut signed the contract with the press and announced that the book would become a GSD textbook.[92] Hudnut had likely signed on to help with the project as a favor to Gropius without having seriously considered the implications of the CIAM planning proposals, for within a few years, he would openly oppose many of the ideas advanced in *Can Our Cities Survive?* Sert did present the CIAM's theories and remedies for urban ills in a rather vague fashion in the book, which may have eased the way for Hudnut to pitch the project. It is likely, too, that the book's devastating and highly effective visual analysis of existing cities grabbed Hudnut's interest. Though Hudnut helped Sert and the CIAM publicize the book, the group's planning agenda made little impact on the GSD Planning Department—that is, in the prewar years.

Interestingly, Sert had first asked Lewis Mumford to write the introduction to *Can Our Cities Survive?* but Mumford declined the offer. Though Mumford told Sert it was "a very able piece of work," he also found the book seriously flawed. He did not like the fact that Sert had identified in it only four functions of the city—dwelling, work, recreation, and transportation—and that he completely neglected the political, educational, and cultural aspects of urban life. "The organs of political and cultural association are, from my standpoint, the distinguishing marks of the city," Mumford explained. "I regard their omission as the chief defect of routine city planning; and their absence from the program of the CIAM I find almost inexplicable."[93]

Hudnut also attended some CIAM meetings in New York, and in 1943, the *New York Times* reported he had been named an "incorporator" and "director" when the CIAM formed the New York CIAM Chapter for Relief and Postwar Planning.[94] The significance of Hudnut's role in the CIAM, which may suggest something about the importance of the New York chapter more generally, is noted in a letter Hudnut wrote to the architect George Keck one year after the chapter had formed. "I was just a little surprised to learn that the CIAM had organized a chapter in this country," Hudnut told Keck. Moreover, "I was quite surprised to find myself elected a director of the CIAM chapter."[95]

The *New York Times* article also named William Wurster, Moholy-Nagy, Wallace Harrison, Oscar Stonorov, and Serge Chermayeff as officials in the New York chapter. Though some of the members continued to meet on occasion, Gropius, for one, questioned whether they should bother keeping an American branch of the CIAM at all. As he explained, a new group with a growing membership had come into existence in 1944, the American Society of Planners and Architects (ASPA).[96] Within a short time of the ASPA's founding, the New York chapter members all joined the new organization, while their own group remained only loosely intact.

American Society of Planners and Architects

Hudnut was a central force in the ASPA, serving as its premier organizer, first president, and the author of its constitution. With a starting membership of about seventy and no clear set of goals, Hudnut claimed that "the thing that I care most about in this whole business of the ASAP [*sic*] is this idea of organizing the liberal wing of our profession. . . . The mere fact that we stand together in a society is in my opinion an aim which will justify our existence."[97] Other groups of modern architects and planners in the United States had begun forming a few years earlier, most notably "Telesis" in the Bay Area, which aimed to promote environmental design and regional planning as well as to increase concern for architecture's relation to society. Another group in Cambridge, mostly GSD and MIT students and teachers, put out the magazine *Task,* which offered a "social and cooperative" agenda.[98] Though the liberal wing Hudnut referred to might also have organized under the CIAM umbrella, a number of architects, Hudnut among them, felt the need for a clearly American organization. As he wrote: "I think it would be greatly to the advantage of our cause if our organization could have from the beginning an American flavor and look less like something imported. In my judgment, the word 'international style' has done infinite damage to the cause of modern architecture, and the sooner the word 'international' is forgotten, the better."[99]

Hudnut's comments did not represent any change of heart; he was indeed more responsible than anyone for the presence of foreign architects and planners in the United States during the 1930s and 1940s. In fact, when Philip Goodwin expressed his concern that the ASPA might have "an un-American flavor," Hudnut shot back: "No one seems to have noticed that the Beaux-Arts Institute was un-American, although in my opinion it was intensely so. The young men who organized *our* Society were all Americans and we are not conscious of imitating any foreign organization."[100] Hudnut understood that in the wartime climate, when American patriotism ran high, the spread of modern architecture in the United States depended on its breaking out of the circles of international radicalism.

The ASPA ultimately steered clear of direct connections to political organizations for precisely this reason. When the group had held its first meetings in 1944 at the Museum of Modern Art and Harvard, a few representatives attended from FAECT, the left-wing Federation of Architects, Engineers, Chemists, and Technicians. FAECT, said to be the most powerful labor union backing architectural workers with its roughly 6,500 members, led the fight against low wages and high-handed decision making in the professions it represented. Continuing to affiliate itself with connections to organizations like FAECT, some ASPA members worried, would only hurt their efforts to advance the case for modern architecture in the United States.[101]

The ASPA subsequently tried to distance itself from obvious left-wing, international affiliations while still offering a clear alternative to the staid AIA. As Hudnut noted, those of the modern persuasion "are not represented in the Institute of Architects and never will be."[102] When Hudnut resigned from the AIA, he had told its president that he had transferred his loyalties to the ASPA and would render whatever services he could to the architectural profession through the new organization.

Joseph Hudnut (*left*) and George Howe (*right*) at the 1945 ASPA Meeting in New York. (*Architectural Forum* 82 [March 1945]: 7)

With characteristic diplomacy, he added, "I do not like to make this reason public because I do not wish to emphasize in any way whatever differences may obtain between these two professional groups."[103]

Membership in the ASPA was an "invitation only" affair at first, with invites extended to those who had "taken a stand on behalf of modern architecture and have given some proof of accomplishment in this field," either in built form or in writing.[104] Before long, so that the ASPA might become a national organization with active chapters in different cities across the country, membership became less restrictive, and the number of members peaked roughly at eighty. To advertise the ASPA, the Executive Committee urged its members to use the ASPA acronym when signing their names, on their letterheads, in publications, and in the signing of all works, just as AIA members often did.[105]

Educators and soon-to-be-educators from the Harvard, Yale, and Penn architecture and planning programs took the leadership roles in the new organization: Hudnut, Louis Kahn (who followed Hudnut as president), George Howe, Hugh Stubbins, and Holmes Perkins. Other early members of the ASPA included several émigré architects, many American-born practitioners, a handful of critics, and a few staff members from the Museum of Modern Art: Alfred Barr, Elizabeth Mock, Catherine Bauer, William Wurster, Eero Saarinen, Paul Rudolph, Marcel Breuer, Serge Chermayeff, J. L. Sert, Sigfried Giedion, George Howe, Philip Johnson, Lawrence Kocher, Pietro Belluschi, Richard Neutra, Christopher Tunnard, and Gropius had all joined the group. Interestingly, Lewis Mumford was not a member, for he did not quite fit in with

MEMBERSHIP

American Society of Planners And Architects
As of January 4, 1947

Charles Abrams	Robert Allan Jacobs
Lawrence B. Anderson	John M. Johansen
Edmund Bacon	Philip Johnson
Mary Cook Barnes	Louis I. Kahn
Alfred H. Barr, Jr.	Edgar Kaufmann, Jr.
Herbert Bayer	George Fred Keck
Pietro Belluschi	Robert W. Kennedy
Richard M. Bennett	Morris Ketchum, Jr.
Hans Blumenfeld	Frederick J. Kiesler
Simon Breines	Carl Koch, Jr.
Marcel Breuer	A. Lawrence Kocher
Gordon Bunshaft	Jules Korchien
Charles H. Burchard	Robert A. Little
Serge Chermayeff	Bernard E. Loghbough
Alfred Clauss	William W. Lyman, Jr.
John P. Coolidge	Robert B. Mitchell
Jacob Crane	Elizabeth B. Mock
Leonard J. Currie	Rudolph Mock
Frederick L. Day, Jr.	Dorothy Schoell Montgomery
Kenneth Day	George Nelson
Vernon DeMars	Eliot F. Noyes
Merrill Denison	Janet H. O'Connell
John W. Edelman	Stamo Papadaki
Hermann Field	Ieoh Ming Pei
Jean Bodmann Fletcher	G. Holmes Perkins
Norman Fletcher	Eero Saarinen
Clark Foreman	Xanti Schawinsky
Mary Goldwater	Jose Luis Sert
Walter Gropius	G. E. Kidder Smith
Frederick A. Gutheim	Oscar Stonorov
William Hanby	Hugh A. Stubbins, Jr.
John C. Harkness	Christopher Tunnard
Harwell H. Harris	Konrad Wachsmann
Douglas Haskell	Martin Wagner
Alice Carson Hiscock	Roland A. Wank
Henry-Russel Hitchcock	Paul L. Wiener
K. L. Holm	Elizabeth Wood
George Howe	Henry Wright
Joseph Hudnut	Catherine Bauer Wurster
Huson T. Jackson	William W. Wurster

the modernist circle.[106] Gropius played a remarkably small part in the ASPA, surprising for someone who rarely played a small role in anything. He may have decided to curb his involvement since Hudnut was so deeply engrossed with the society and relations between them had already begun to sour. Furthermore, the ideas that the ASPA was putting forth were exactly those Hudnut was trying to advance at the GSD, and they stood in contrast to those that Gropius sought to put forward.

Because Hudnut often acted as scribe for the ASPA, even the language the organization spoke in was his. Essentially, just as Hudnut was trying to unite the three disciplines of planning, architecture, and landscape architecture in the School of Design at Harvard, so was the ASPA trying to deepen the connection between planners and architects through a common professional organization. (The fact that the ASPA completely brushed aside the field of landscape architecture does bring to mind the complaint made by GSD landscapers that the School ignored their field during the Hudnut/Gropius era.) To explain the nature of that connection, the ASPA used the following paragraph in an official document, issued after its first annual meeting. It is the exact same paragraph—minus the word "landscape architecture"—that Hudnut wrote five years earlier for President Conant when he described the close ties between the disciplines represented at the GSD. The substance of the paragraph also appeared in a number of Hudnut's articles, especially those published after 1944, when the bulk of his writing began to focus on civic design and on the relationships between the fields of architecture and city planning.[107]

> Architecture and city planning are social arts. Each is inseparable, except in rare instances, from the collective life, the smallest unit of which is the family, the largest the population of a city or region. The materials of each art, if not the same, are at least alike in character since they comprise, first, those aspects of human existence which invite structural adaptations, and second, space and the material substances capable of such adaptations. They are alike also in that each is integral with both the physical and social sciences and attain their vitality and usefulness from that integration. Identical in origin and tradition, similar in their basic processes, architecture and city planning attained their individualities as the consequence of a growing diversification of social activities; and yet they have in fundamental intention and technique an unequivocal—and, until recently, acknowledged unity.[108]

In its official documents, just as in many of Hudnut's essays, the ASPA also advanced the idea that architects must regard the city, rather than the individual building, as the basic unit of design in architecture, just as Hegemann had taught Hudnut.[109]

The ASPA tried to advance its twin causes of spreading modern architecture and unifying the fields of planning and architecture with the usual fare of conferences, speeches, and publications. And as the *Architectural Forum* reported, the group was also "dedicated to action and opposed to fruitless verbiage."[110] Indeed, the society set out to demonstrate its objectives by undertaking actual building and planning projects; it quickly adopted as its cause célèbre, the building of the United Nations headquarters. The ASPA and the New York CIAM chapter shared double billing in heading a public debate over the selection of the site for the UN and the design of its building.

The two groups submitted a position paper outlining their views on the project to the UN secretary general, and since Hudnut authored that document, he had a good deal of power to shape the debate. Not surprisingly, the ASPA and CIAM rejected the overblown monumentality and anachronistic styles used in buildings akin to the UN, like the League of Nations Building in Geneva and the International Court at the Hague. They further opposed the creation of a fixed formal master plan for the UN complex. Hudnut's hand in the project clearly showed in the ASPA/CIAM brief, as it urged planners and architects involved in the project to employ "whatever advanced theories of planning and design may develop during the progress of the work," rather than adhering to a set approach, including the set functional planning approach of the CIAM.[111] It was also like Hudnut to insist that "considerations of economy should not weigh too heavily" in the design of the buildings and plan. By the time of the UN project, Hudnut had begun to argue that modern architects focused too much on economizing in their designs, at the expense of greater issues of meaning. Finally, the ASPA and CIAM urged the UN to select an architect for its project through a "democratic" international competition.[112] The two groups laid out a set of guidelines for the competition that, based on the Smithsonian Gallery model, would select architects and planners for the project rather than the design of a building and site. Unfortunately, the ASPA and CIAM contributions to the debate on building the UN complex abruptly came to naught after the UN General Assembly accepted John D. Rockefeller's gift of a six-block site along the East River in Manhattan.[113]

The ASPA took on no other projects as grand as the UN, nor did it actually complete those it set out to work on, including Louis Kahn's suggestion for an ASPA-designed urban community.[114] Kahn, who took over the presidency of the society in 1947, had always been an active member, and it was on the basis of their collaboration in the ASPA that Hudnut offered Kahn a position teaching design at Harvard in 1946. One can only speculate on how different the GSD's fate might have been if Kahn had accepted Hudnut's offer. Kahn turned him down because he wanted to remain near his native Philadelphia and because he did not want to take time away quite yet from his own practice.[115]

By 1948, the ASPA effectively ceased to exist, though it never officially dissolved. Hudnut's opponents at the AIA gloated that "Dean Hudnut and his colleagues were not successful in establishing a progressive association of contemporary architects."[116] Holmes Perkins's comment that "we succeeded so well that we didn't need it any more" may have been more accurate.[117] By the time the ASPA folded, many of its members—including Gropius, Breuer, Stubbins, and even a number of their students—were all running thriving modern practices. Perhaps the demise of the ASPA also points to Hudnut's failure to interest modern architects in that which mattered most to him—the union of the architecture and planning fields and modern civic design.[118]

Overall, Hudnut and Gropius succeeded in their many efforts to advance both modern architecture and the interdisciplinary GSD. By the time of the last ASPA meeting, modern architecture had become the new orthodoxy while the GSD ranked as the dominant force in American architectural education. Hudnut's and Gropius's numerous publications and public lectures helped advance both causes, as did their parts in the national debates over the Jefferson Memorial, the Smithsonian museum, and the UN building. These activities, as well as their successful attempts to organize the "liberal wing" of architects practicing in the United States, also brought them attention they would rather have avoided—from the Federal Bureau of Investigation.

The FBI had first targeted Gropius as a subject of investigation because he was a German citizen residing in the United States during wartime, but his active public life further piqued their interest and caused the size of his FBI file to thicken. Hudnut's propagandizing activities—especially his part in organizing an exhibition of American architecture in the Soviet Union—as well as his fraternizing with possible enemies, also earned him an FBI file with his name on it.[119] One entry in Gropius's file explained the nature of the FBI's interest in him and Hudnut: (the strikeout here corresponding to blacked-out text on the official papers):

> Investigate suspected Nazis, Walter Gropius, ——— and ——— Harvard University. The Dean of this school, Joseph Hudnut is in perfect sympathy with these men and possibly is in active co-operation. He has fought hard to get these Germans established here during the last few

years. Gropius poses as a "refugee"; one of his first activities upon receiving his present appointment was to try to place as many other Germans as possible in similar positions all over the country. . . . Do not be misled by any American sponsors these men might have.[120]

A final amusing entry in Gropius's file does show that the FBI had an interest in—and, alas, ignorance of—Gropius's architecture. The entry expresses concern that while Gropius had published plans of his 1938 house in the book *The Modern House in America* (1940), he had neglected to include the plans of his basement. That basement, the center of Gropius's, and perhaps also Hudnut's, subversive activities—did not, of course, exist.[121]

5 CONFLICTING VIEWS
OF HOUSE AND TOWN

In her obituary marking Gropius's death in 1969, Ada Louise Huxtable wrote that although other modern architects held similar convictions, Gropius was "the man in whom philosophy coincided with history." He assumed his professorship at Harvard at the right moment with the right ideas, and this "prophet whose time had come," as Huxtable called him, had immediate influence and eminence on the American scene.[1] Huxtable's remark surely pertains to Gropius's teaching of housing and town design in his years at Harvard. Gropius instructed his receptive young students in these fields in ways that fit perfectly into the course of history and of American building.

Hudnut had no such luck with timing, and the views of housing and urbanism that he held ultimately conflicted with those advanced by Gropius. Tensions between the two mounted by 1943 as Hudnut began frankly criticizing in the press and in lectures the approach to housing design he saw inside the GSD studios. Hudnut objected to what he viewed as Gropius's overemphasis on economy, flexibility, utility, and, oddly enough, formalism in housing at the expense of any substantive meaning or emotional content. By the end of the war, Hudnut also began speaking out against the anticity attitude that Gropius was promoting. In contrast to his colleague, Hudnut campaigned in favor of traditional urban elements—lively streets, mixed-use neighborhoods, and "skyscrapers, theaters, gardens, . . . and shops innumerable, crowded together" and forming the framework of a lively community life.[2] Though it was never Hudnut's practice to name a specific target in his criticism, his barbs landed squarely on Gropius.

Housing and the New Deal

Gropius arrived at Harvard at the right moment in the history of American housing to advance the building of both low-income high-rise housing and the single-family decentralized modern house. In the years prior to his coming, the Depression had wreaked havoc on American housing conditions and the housing industry. At its lowest point, housing construction fell 95 percent while at least ten million families lived in substandard dwellings and conditions.[3] A vast Dickensian literature described the astounding conditions in which the lower economic classes lived, which resulted in soaring crime rates, infant mortality, and deaths from tuberculosis and pneumonia. As never before, Americans were willing to consider new, and even "foreign" ideas to solve the housing problem.

One idea gaining currency—that government should provide subsidies to help wage earners buy or build homes—had met with great hostility before the Depression. Most Americans then rejected the "un-American" notion of government intervention and believed that buying a home should remain one's private concern. Many even agreed with the conservative housing reformer Lawrence Veiller, who argued that while cities must clear their slums "because the public interest indicates that their demolition is required," the government must not rehouse those displaced, for that would be "foreign" to American practice and principles.[4] Finally, in 1937, the Roosevelt administration declared that neither private enterprise nor local governments had yet managed to provide decent homes for low-income citizens.

In order to help the many Americans living in conditions "injurious to health and morals, conducive to delinquency and destructive of family life," Roosevelt advocated government-supported, long-term, low-interest loans to individual home builders and building societies.[5] That year Congress enacted the U.S. Housing Act, marking the first time in which the federal government took on the responsibility for constructing sound, low-cost housing. The act established the United States Housing Authority and empowered it to fund local housing agencies that would, in turn, would provide "decent, safe, sanitary, dwellings for families of low-income." As houser Catherine Bauer noted, passage of the Housing Act of 1937 "found democracy functioning rather better than usual in America." The *New York Times* editorialized that America had finally taken a "real start toward wiping out its city slums."[6]

By the start of the 1930s, a growing number of American housing reformers had begun holding up European housing practices as the model for the United States to emulate, Bauer foremost among them. She pointed out that while Americans had enjoyed great prosperity during the 1920s and Europeans lived in political and economic chaos, the Europeans had nonetheless managed to build some six million units of "modern housing." These included many high-standard, low-rent, modern dwellings in pleasant neighborhoods. What did America have to show? "Congested tenements, wooden three- and four-deckers, and jerry-built, jostling bungalows; foreclosures, evictions, worthless mortgages . . . vacant lots and expensive rotting utilities."[7] Bauer herself became a strong proponent of clearing slums and rehousing people in new, planned suburban communities with the help of government funds. Dr. Edith Elmer Wood also claimed that the high quality of new state-funded working-class projects going up in Europe showed that government monies could help solve the colossal housing problem in the United States.[8] By the mid-1930s, a growing number of architects, planners, laborers, mayors, bankers, clergy, and social workers were joining Bauer, Wood, and other liberal-minded housing reformers to form a genuine national housing movement. For this group, Gropius's arrival in the United States offered a boon to the cause.

Gropius's coming to Harvard also coincided with a series of other U.S. government housing initiatives. Among them, the towns designed as part of the Greenbelt Town Program—brainchild of economist Rexford Tugwell, who headed Roosevelt's Resettlement Administration—resembled in a number of ways the "townlets and towns" that Gropius and Wagner would create with their students at the GSD. Undoubtedly, as Tugwell laid out his towns, the low-cost housing communities in suburban settings that Wagner and others in Germany had built provided a source of inspiration.[9] Tugwell favored buying cheap land at the edge of population centers, constructing self-sufficient model communities with modern houses, surrounding them with a greenbelt to prevent encroachment from the grim outside world, and luring in residents from slums and blighted areas. Once people moved into the new towns, he planned to "go back into the cities and tear down whole slums and make parks of them."[10] The idealistic Tugwell considered the Greenbelt towns to be utopian schemes with their residential areas, surrounding green space, and pleasant town centers. Critics considered the towns unnecessary at best, while at the other extreme, they accused them of imposing "foreign, socialist, or communist, ways of life on the American people." A few newspaper headlines fanned the flames with headlines such as, "First Communist Town in U.S. Nears Completion" and "Tugwell Abolishes Private Property."[11]

Construction of the towns began in 1936 in Maryland, Wisconsin, and Ohio, but the Greenbelt Town Program ended after only two years because of exorbitant building costs. The towns had not turned out exactly as planned either: residents came from the middle rather than the lower classes, and the promised industries or businesses necessary to achieve their independence did not materialize.[12] As commuter towns, then, the Greenbelt towns failed to offer the model for future metropolitan development that the Roosevelt administration had anticipated. They did serve an important purpose, however, even beyond that of housing some thirty thousand Americans. With their attractive garden paths, green spaces, superblocks, and modernistic architecture, they sparked a widespread interest in the planned residential community and inspired many Americans to demand good, and suburbanlike, planning in their own towns and cities.[13]

New Deal policies also allowed many middle-class Americans to purchase their own first single-family home, which they almost always did outside the city. The federal government subsidized the single-family suburban house through mortgage insurance and tax laws but also through the building of the same highways and infrastructure that made suburban living possible.[14] Not just policies but also New Deal rhetoric encouraged the move to suburbia. For example, one key government report described the American city as a center of congestion, crime, and "material decay and human corrosion," and it argued for building housing outside it, somewhere between dense concentration and "wholesale decentralization."[15] Although the history of American settlement had always been that of a people trying to spread itself out, New Deal programs and official discourse helped pave the pathways that led the middle class to abandon the inner city in droves. Many of the people who were unable to follow those pathways before World War II would get their chance to do so after the peace, when—thanks to the programs put in place during the thirties—suburbia would boom at the expense of the city.

Hudnut versus Gropius on Housing

Hudnut had identified "scientific instruction in Housing" as the most pressing need at the time he established the Graduate School of Design in 1936. With the addition of Gropius and Wagner to the faculty, housing quickly become a central concern throughout the School.[16] Harvard had lagged far behind Columbia in the housing field, where, during Hudnut's brief deanship, Henry Wright, Werner Hegemann, and sociologist Carol Aronovici had all made housing for the masses of Americans the primary focus of seminars and studios. These three had brought their experience from the trenches of the American housing movement to the Columbia classrooms. In contrast, Harvard had no faculty and no courses dedicated to housing when Hudnut arrived there. Hudnut recognized Gropius's coming to teach as an important step toward filling this huge void at the GSD. As he assured President Conant during their search for a modern architect, Gropius is "deeply interested in housing problems and has contributed many of the fundamental ideas now universally accepted for the design of workmen's houses."[17]

The *Architectural Forum* made a similar point in its article announcing Gropius's arrival at Harvard in 1937. Gropius's "life-long rebellion against eclecticism" and his "deep interest in the social and philosophic aspects of housing" put him "at the very spearhead of the Modern movement," the *Forum* noted. To introduce Gropius to its audience, the journal compared him to "that other distinguished European architect now lecturing at an American university" and engaged in housing issues, Raymond Unwin at Columbia. The article described that while Sir Raymond's pioneering work in English garden cities had recently won him the highest honor of the status quo, the Gold Medal of the Royal Institute of British Architects, no such accolade would go to the unorthodox Gropius. Noting housing as a central preoccupation of both architects, the *Forum* clarified the difference in their two approaches: while the venerable Unwin "is an ardent believer in the spread-out, row cottage type of development," instead "Gropius, with Le

Harvard's modern Gropius. (*Architectural Forum* 66 [March 1937]: 14)

Columbia's not-quite-so-modern Unwin. (*Architectural Forum* 66 [March 1937]: 14)

Corbusier, is among the foremost exponents of the skyscraper type of city planning."[18] The article even included photographs of both architects, Unwin, older, bespectacled, with a worn floppy stovepipe and out-of-date suit, while a youthful Gropius stood in front of his Chicago Tribune skyscraper project, looking severe, exacting, and modern like the building itself. The not-so-subtle subtext: out with the old, in with the new. After all, the *Forum* noted, "the civilized sons of Harvard" had just appointed the fifty-three-year-old Gropius to a tenured professorship.[19]

Gropius had first introduced his views on housing to an American audience during the celebrated 1934 Museum of Modern Art Housing Exhibition. Aimed at arousing public interest in housing for lower-income workers, that exhibition portrayed photographs of the dismal conditions in which millions of Americans lived, while offering up contrasting images of successful new housing being built in Europe. Gropius's 1930 Siemensstadt project got pride of place on the cover of the exhibition's catalogue, which also contained an essay he wrote on housing alongside essays by the Columbia trio—Aronovici, Henry Wright, and Hegemann—as well as others by Catherine Bauer, the exhibition's primary organizer, and Lewis Mumford.[20]

Gropius's essay, "Minimum Dwellings and Tall Buildings," clarified his "universally accepted ideas" for urban housing that Hudnut had spoken of to President Conant. Whether in a house or an apartment building, Gropius argued, all dwellings must meet two basic requirements: a private room for every person (no matter how small that room) and enough window space to allow ample light, sun, air, and views to greenery below.[21] Gropius also weighed the question of the ideal type of dwelling in his essay and concluded that, while the single-family house offered both serenity and privacy, in heavily populated cities that house-type made little sense. For urban settings with high land costs and limited space, Gropius argued in favor of ten- to twelve-story apartment buildings set widely apart on landscaped plots, ideally with each dwelling unit occupying a single floor. Finally, Gropius also argued in his catalogue essay for a broad activism in housing on the part of all city residents. Nature can only penetrate our cities and homes, he insisted, if citizens demand new zoning laws regulating population density, the cubic content of a building in relation to its plot, as well the amount of sun exposure for each residential unit. With an activist citizenry, he promised that the apartment house of the future would bear no resemblance to our "squalid, cramped tenement house of the past."[22]

In Germany, Gropius had worked in a similar vein for the cause of working-class housing, both as propagandist and designer. To the architects and planners gathered at the 1930 CIAM meeting in Brussels, for example, he delivered the keynote speech, "Low, Mid- or High-Rise Building?" in which he first argued that single-family houses on the outskirts of cities worked well for higher-income families, while high-rise units better suited the finances and needs of the working class. Only the high-rise, he claimed, would allow the latter group "the biologically important advantages of more sun and light, larger distances between neighboring buildings, and the possibility of providing extensive connected parks and play areas between the blocks." Since the mid-rise allowed neither adequate sunlight inside nor green space outside and cost too much to build, "its disappearance can only be called progress."[23] Gropius lobbied for high-rise housing in newspapers, on radio, and in a number of different lecture halls. Ever the master propagandist, in housing exhibitions in Paris and Berlin Gropius displayed large diagrams he had made to "prove" that the high-rise offered more open space, sun, light, and air and greater opportunity for informal social contact than any other form of housing. Lest the illustrations failed to persuade, he embellished them with compelling slogans: "Apartment high-rises in green spaces—an urban form of living for the future!" and "Living in a high-rise—urban dwellers: own up to the big city!"[24] Gropius also hammered home the same theme in articles with titles like "Cry Stop to Havoc, or: Preservation by Concentrated Development."[25]

Gropius not only spoke out for high-rise living, he also designed (though never built) several high-rise projects, including a twelve-story building for the 1929 Siedlung Haselhorst competition in Berlin, later reduced to ten stories in several detailed drawings.[26] Though at the forefront of housing debates in Europe, Gropius was not, of course, alone in championing high-rise urban housing during the interwar years. Among others, Le Corbusier had exhibited his Ville Contemporaine in 1922, Richard Neutra his "Rush City Reformed" in 1926, and in 1927,

Walter Gropius, high-rise steel-frame apartment, 1929–30, perspective.
(Courtesy of the Busch-Reisinger Museum, Harvard University Art Museums, Gift of
Walter Gropius, BRGA.44.27)

Ludwig Hilberseimer had laid out his residential city of *Zeilenbauen* (straight rows). Marcel Breuer had also proposed three different high-rise housing projects by 1928.[27]

It is interesting to note, given the important role Martin Wagner would play in teaching housing at Harvard, that Wagner openly opposed Gropius's arguments for high-rise residential blocks. In his capacity as Berlin's *Stadtbaurat* in the 1920s, Wagner charged that Gropius had failed to consider practical issues like heating, water pressure, safety, and, more important, the psychological aspects of high-rise living. He argued that "no ten-story apartment machine will provide the elbow room which the urban resident desires."[28] Despite their fundamental difference of opinion on this issue, Gropius had still urged Hudnut to hire Wagner for the GSD precisely because of his expertise in the housing field.

Throughout his career at Harvard and after he left in 1952, Gropius continued to advance the cause of high-rise, widely spaced, residential urban buildings for the working class. Once he settled in the United States, however, Gropius also developed a great interest in designing decentralized single-family housing.[29] Perhaps Wagner's opinions made some impact on his thinking as the two worked closely together at the

GSD. More likely, Gropius was responding to American enthusiasm for suburban life, the abundant land available for such houses in his new country of residence, and especially the type of private patronage he found in the United States in contrast to Socialist Germany. Gropius never even got the chance to build any high-rise apartment blocks until the post–World War II era, when he received commissions to build several in Berlin. His most visible high-rise project in that city came five years after he left Harvard, at the invitation of his old ally, former Harvard president James B. Conant. In 1957, in his new capacity as U.S. high commissioner to Germany, Conant invited Gropius and his firm, The Architects Collaborative (TAC), to prepare guidelines for laying out the vast housing scheme ultimately known as Gropiusstadt. After doing so, TAC also designed several buildings within the large complex.[30] Criticized soon after its completion as a jungle of faceless thirty-story towers, the name of the project did not quite confer on Gropius the honor intended.

Despite the small number of them he actually built, Gropius ranked as one of the world's great proponents of modern, low-income, high-rise apartment blocks. As Richard Plunz has written in his history of housing, "The combined sentiments of Gropius and Le Corbusier produced a formidable polemic, both social and aesthetic, visual and verbal, which conformed perfectly to the economic realities confronting housing design in Europe and America."[31] If Gropius did not assure his own place in the history of high-rise housing projects, critics and historians—Plunz being one of many—have done so for him.

The growing controversy between Hudnut and Gropius might even have first started over the issue of high-rise public housing for it was on this subject that their differences first surfaced. In 1943, Hudnut attacked the modern housing project in a remarkably prescient article, "Housing and the Democratic Process," that set him apart from Gropius, from a number of other modern architects, and even from many liberal housing reformers.[32] Hudnut's trenchant commentary on the high-rise projects and on the direction in which public housing was moving in the United States anticipates by nearly two decades the criticism Jane Jacobs offers of these "hostile islands" in her *Death and Life of Great American Cities* (1961). Hudnut railed against the inhuman, sterile, institutional way of life imposed on the occupants of the tediously uniform high-rise projects set on islands sequestered from the heart of the city. Though he believed in publicly funded housing and the use of public funds to raze urban slums, and though he declared himself on the side of housing reformers, Hudnut condemned the way in which the idea of public housing was being translated into practice. "No one in the lower income-group could, I think, have invented the housing project," he wrote. "They are, rather, products of theory—things contrived by men who, however anxious for social reform or for the relief of suffering, yet stand a little aside from the forces engendered by social conflict. [The lower income-group] as I remember it, was first even a little resentful of our efforts—or at least our attitude—and had to be teased into our shining new paradise with the promise of mechanical refrigerators."[33] Hudnut argued that public housing projects emanated from the crisis of unemployment rather than from the crisis of housing conditions. "They are a means of creating economic activity" and have clearly been shaped by intentions that too often relate only incidentally to social objectives. This explains the character of the housing project, he continued, "its machine-like processes, its tedious uniformity, [and also] the lavish expenditures for labor and the strict economies in the purchase of brains." The creators of the high-rise projects wanted little more than "a standardized industrial product capable of being turned out rapidly in the largest possible units and with the maximum utilization of labor."[34]

Hudnut further described the housing project as "an act of segregation," with people from certain social and economic categories pulled away from the excitement of urban life and reestablished on new sites cleared precisely for that purpose. These new sites stood out conspicuously from the rest of the city with their uniform architecture and landscape and by the arrangement of these things. Inside the projects, he deplored how "a new habit of life is invited: not invited merely, but demanded and—by methods which have at least the color of science."[35]

Hudnut offered an alternative to the high-rise housing project and isolated superblock idea that was prophetic of Jane Jacobs and others decades hence. His suggestions distanced him not only from Gropius but also from other housing reformers who rejected the high-rise, low-income project, including Lewis Mumford and Catherine Bauer. Unlike these two decentralist housers who favored low-rise dwellings outside the city for those displaced by slum clearance, Hudnut suggested returning public housing to the city's institutions and especially to its streets. "You can have good housing without eliminating the street: the street, which is integral with the tradition of cities, the most active channel of human intercourse, the oldest theater of democracy," he argued. "The more I think of the average housing project, the better I like the dynamite idea. A good explosion would not only open a space at the center but would, at the same time, scatter the low income dwellings out into the wider complex of the city and open channels for an admixture of other dwellings. Some housers, I suppose, would consider the method drastic; and yet I wonder whether, in the long run, it would prove more disruptive than their own."[36] While Gropius may have had a great sense of timing, Hudnut clearly did not. Scattered, mixed-income, subsidized housing for an admixture of peoples in the heart of the city was an idea whose time would not come for several decades.

At the time Hudnut spoke out against the projects, very few had actually been built in the United States. The "tower in the park" idea would begin to flourish only after World War II in cities across the country. While many later critics would attack the monoliths and their superblocks, especially from the 1960s on, Hudnut was challenging them in 1943 for what they were *about* to do.

Teaching Housing at the GSD

The design and social issues of housing loomed large in Gropius's courses and in those taught by a number of different faculty in the GSD's three departments. A few courses even focused entirely on the subject of housing, the first of them taught by Walter Bogner, who had no particular expertise in the field. When Martin Wagner arrived in 1938, he took over and developed a course that stressed the design of low-cost housing and the possibilities that prefabrication techniques might offer. His students in Housing I explored current housing practices and theories, governmental efforts in the field, and the relation of residential areas to city plans; they also designed both private houses and multiple dwelling units, always with an underlying effort to understand what humans require in their home and surrounding environment.[37] Although the GSD would shift its focus in design to the larger rebuilding of cities and towns in the postwar era, housing continued to have an important part in the curriculum. Catherine Bauer Wurster taught a housing seminar at the School from 1946 to 1949 with a social scientific approach rather than architectural. Her course examined housing policy and administration, housing's role in the national economy, and the production and consumption of housing for all income groups, as well as issues of land ownership and control. After Wurster left Harvard for Berkeley, William Wheaton, a city planner and former FHA official, took her place in the course.[38]

Apart from these offerings in housing and Gropius's emphasis on the subject, Breuer, Perkins, Stubbins, Frost, and other faculty in the three departments of the School all had their students designing a range of residential building types—large apartments, urban housing groups, small prefabricated shelters, and most often, single-family houses for suburban or country settings. Students certainly designed other types of buildings in their courses—schools, community and recreation centers, town halls and small offices, most commonly—but for faculty and students alike, designing housing for all economic classes was definitely a primary subject of interest.

The GSD housing problems, now found in the Harvard archives, offer a rich source for exploring the ideas and the approach to housing taught at the School in the Hudnut/Gropius era. It is clear after looking through them that the two leading the charge in housing, Gropius and Wagner, confronted quite different concerns from those Hudnut expressed. Their design problems deal overwhelmingly with issues of economy, flexibility, utility, and new building technologies. Although many of Gropius's and Wagner's problems include lengthy preambles that clarify their philosophies of housing, none of these preambles addressed what Hudnut called "the art in housing" or "the *idea* which is the essential substance of a house."[39] Instead, a typical Gropius or Wagner housing problem might state that "the main objective of this housing problem is to show by plans, and to prove by figures, how to achieve real low-cost housing." Or, as another problem advised, students must "above all . . . deal with the economic problem," and still another, that "great emphasis should be laid upon low building costs." Gropius frequently told his students that "the economic factor should be the leading one" in planning the design of dwellings, instructing them in one problem to design "shelter for less money in shorter time."[40]

Clearly related to economy, the idea of "flexibility" in the modern home also got great play in Gropius's and Wagner's teaching. The two encouraged their students to design flexible homes that could grow or shrink according to client need and without any costly rebuilding. Ideally, clients could "demount" their homes and move them from one location to another, not just accommodating a transient lifestyle but assuring steady site values. Over and over Gropius's and Wagner's design problems insisted that the modern home must "fit the family in any state of its size, its age-composition, its income," and its other varying demands. To meet client needs in the modern era—an "unstable period of shifting social standards," as the problems described it—a home had to offer "the *utmost flexibility*."[41] How to achieve both flexibility and affordable cost? By turning to prefabrication and standardization, both subjects of enormous interest to Gropius and to Wagner.

After his partnership had ended with Breuer, Gropius had shifted his attention in his practice to prefabrication. With the German architect Konrad Wachsmann, Gropius worked on the design of a flexible "packaged house," a dwelling with interchangeable walls, floors, ceilings and even roof.[42] Wachsmann took the helm of operation and together with Gropius devised a demountable system of interlocking panels with a standardized joint detail and wedge connector. A group of entrepreneurs formed the General Panel Corporation to market it, though the venture never flourished.[43] Wagner also had his own prefabricated housing projects underway at the same time.

Not surprisingly, then, prefabrication played an important part in the housing design problems that Gropius and Wagner assigned students. However, Gropius did not want students developing or even working with actual systems of prefabrication as they carried out their projects, for he believed that doing so would prove too difficult a task for inexperienced architects. Instead, he encouraged students to conceive their projects "from the point of view" of prefabrication—to simplify building methods, to use some modules or standardized parts, and to

Dahong Wang, GSD student project for a flexible house made from prefabricated units, 1943. (*New Pencil Points* 24 [December 1943]: 77, 81)

I. M. Pei, GSD student project for a flexible house made from prefabricated units. (*New Pencil Points* 24 [December 1943]: 77, 81)

strive for the economy and flexibility in their buildings that prefabrication allowed.[44]

Of greatest importance and fitting with Hudnut's critique, Gropius's housing design problems especially asked students to confront the aesthetic issues raised by prefabrication or partial prefabrication. Gropius noted frequently in design problems and in his lectures and essays that prefabricated building posed a particular aesthetic dilemma: "The more standardization and prefabrication is used—and for good social and economic reasons—the more will be needed the vision of the designer to secure individual variety."[45] In other words, as Gropius also put it, the modern architect "who refuses to live by repeating the forms and ornaments of our ancestors" must learn to "enliven the regimentating [*sic*] starkness of machine-made repetition."[46]

One way to enliven this starkness, Gropius suggested, was by contrasting "industrial processes of surface treatment" with different materials and different textures, including "ribbed, corrugated, punched, spotted or mottled," or to alternate surface finishes, such as mat and polished, dark and light, rough and smooth.[47] At the same time that he looked to industrial processes, Gropius also argued for "another healthy way in which to overcome our bastard civilization of borrowed ornaments" and enliven modern buildings—by fusing architecture and vegetation. Gropius proposed that the textures and materials of walls, combined with "the shadows of trees, shrubs, and flowers, in sunlight or in artificial light," furnished the client with "a beautiful screen of patterns which impregnates our imagination with ever-changing vivid impressions."[48] Not just Gropius but also others on the GSD faculty tried

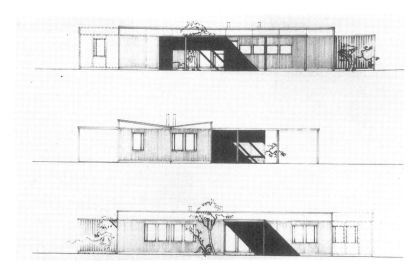

E. Chin-Park, dwelling type, GSD student project, 1946. (Courtesy of the Frances Loeb Library, Harvard Design School)

K. H. Cheang, two-story row house, GSD student project, 1943, uses a mixture of surfaces and textures to provide "visual variety." (*Architectural Forum* 79 [December 1943]: 76)

H. Mck. Jones, one-story row house, GSD student project, uses vegetation to provide "visual variety." (*Architectural Forum* 79 [December 1943]: 77)

to bring visual variety to their sterile buildings. In one example, Walter Bogner told students outright to make designs that "catch the eye" and "consist of something new and startling in character." A number of landscape problems also stressed the importance of "pictorial effects" and designs with "more interest."[49]

Just as the GSD students explored surface decoration in their individual house designs to achieve visual variety when designing groups of houses, their design problems instructed them to experiment with plan and elevation for much the same purpose. Year after year, Gropius required students to design "the post-war shelter for the average family," a house-type for repeated use in the same neighborhood. After students completed designing a single postwar house, the problem then suggested ways to vary the appearance of that house "without abandoning the economic advantages of its repetition":

a. Use alternately the plan as well as its mirror.
b. Place the house at different angles to the sun.
c. Alternate the materials, their textures and colors and alternate the bright and dark effect.
d. Confine the adjacent outdoor living space around the house by varying combinations of pergolas, trellis [sic], screens, hedges, fences, shrubs, and groups of trees.
e. Place the garage or car port at different angles to the house.
f. Add a screen porch to the house in different positions and angles.[50]

According to the problem text, this exercise aimed to develop an attractive neighborhood of similar but varied buildings. It is important to point out that the suggestions above did not ask students to think about how buildings work together to form a neighborhood, or even how they work with the natural setting. Instead, each of the six suggestions relates to the single house without larger context. The goal of the exercise was simply visual variety.

In his critique of Gropius's teaching method developed in *The Decorated Diagram,* Klaus Herdeg uses a 1950 GSD design problem, "Site Development for Family Residences," which offers students the same six suggestions for varying the appearance of their houses.[51] Herdeg's conclusion that "a preoccupation with pattern and texture seems to govern all scales from the site plan to the wood grain of a trellis" seems right on target, even when it came to buildings larger than houses. Herdeg also points out that the design problem offers students no motive to "go

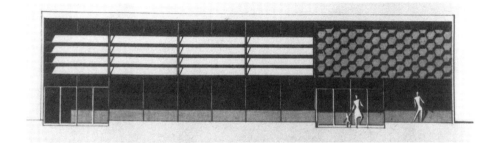

Charles Forberg, exhibition building, GSD student project, 1946, showing a pre-occupation with pattern and texture typical of work in the GSD design studios. (Courtesy of the Frances Loeb Library, Harvard Design School)

beyond achieving a nice arrangement of objects and surface elements in the service of 'visual variety.'" Thus he claims, much as Hudnut did forty years earlier, that "what was meant as an exercise in 'reconciling the economic advantages of mass production of standardized building parts with man's desire for individuality'—a rather good objective, then and now—turned out to be a prescription for almost meaningless production of visual variety."[52]

Gropius went even further than Herdeg knew in the postwar shelter version of this problem. He also suggested to students six ways in which they could "counteract a rigid effect of regimentation" in the neighborhood of the postwar house. To make the neighborhood itself visually interesting, he advised students to consider:

a. Street systems; optimum lengths of streets; the effect of bent or curved streets.
b. Interruption of streets by squares.
c. Optimum lengths of rows of houses or house blocks. Staggering.
d. The use of natural contours.
e. The use of natural views.
f. The use of groups of plants and trees.[53]

The idea of a residential neighborhood played no part in Gropius's conception here. He considered streets only for the "effect" they might offer, and he regarded squares as "interruptions" that might visually enliven monotonous streets. At the heart of these suggestions, Gropius wanted a variegated neighborhood to make dull houses in a dull setting seem interesting.

Victor Lundy, nursery school, GSD student project, 1947. (Courtesy of the Frances Loeb Library, Harvard Design School)

As Gropius and his students sought aesthetic effects to mask the monotony of the money-saving machine, Hudnut argued against such formalism. "Variations made to avoid monotony," he insisted, "only make the monotony more evident."[54] Instead of looking for "sight-relief" to decorate monotony, a phrase that appeared in one problem, Hudnut proposed an architectural solution to neighborhood design: focus less on "surface effects and more on 'arrangements': that is to say, on the shapes, proportions and relationships of buildings, and on the shapes, proportions and relationships of the spaces between and around buildings."[55] Instead of the "postwar house," Hudnut proposed the "post-*modern* house." In his 1945 essay of that name, Hudnut distanced himself from the brand of modernism represented by Gropius's "engineered" shelter. Hudnut's "post-modern house" would rely on modern structural techniques to express "the idea of *home*"; it would exploit the new freedom to model space and direct its flow, and it would embrace new qualities of light, new relationships to site and nature, and the diversified palette of new materials. But the post-modern house would not merely display the wonder or drama of these modern inventions as the postwar house did, in a way "detached from the idea to be expressed."

Hudnut's house would use them for "the purposes of a language," to convey the "*idea* which is the essential substance of a house."[56]

Hudnut further explained that his house would belong to "a post-modern owner," a person not so different from the "modern owner," with visions, tastes, and habits of thought "most serviceable to a collective-industrial scheme of life." The world might even appear to the post-modern owner, too, "as a system of casual sequences transformed each day by the cumulative miracles of science."[57] But the "post-modern" owner would differ from the modern owner insofar as he would claim for himself, "some inner experiences, free from outward control, unprofaned by the collective conscience." Even when all the world is "socialized, mechanized, and standardized," Hudnut wrote, those experiences "will yet be discoverable in the home." Hudnut ended his essay with the simple declaration (and he never minded sounding corny) that in the post-modern world, "houses will still be built out of human hearts."[58]

Hudnut's 1945 "post-modern house" essay has recently brought new fame to the man who hired Gropius for Harvard. In recent years, the essay has been anthologized, included on course syllabi, and mentioned in various treatises on postmodernism.[59] Despite his 1945 coinage of that now pervasive word, Hudnut did not try in this essay, or ever, to advance a "post-modern" movement. With his appeal for symbolic richness, the expression of inner experiences, and beauty "unexplained by economic necessity or technical virtuosity," and his call in other essays for history and communication, it is tempting to put him forward as a precursor to the "right" kind of modernism or even postmodernism. Clearly, Hudnut's criticisms of Gropius's modern architecture and urbanism did anticipate in a number of ways the postmodernist critique that came several decades later.

Hudnut was not alone at the GSD in criticizing Gropius's turn toward formalism. As early as 1940, Martin Wagner had also argued that Gropius's concern for economy and technology had turned into a mere quest to avoid the tedium of standardization. But whereas Hudnut objected to Gropius's preoccupation with the economic and technical aspects of architecture, Wagner took Gropius to task for neglecting these same considerations. He did not want Gropius to teach students how to decorate prefabricated buildings but rather to teach them the practical aspects and methods of prefabrication that they could apply to solving the "real problems of our time."[60] As one who believed that "ideals in this world cannot be realized without staking one's whole personality," he expressed to Gropius his deep disappointment in the direction his colleague was moving.[61] In an angry letter to Gropius, Wagner asserted that "Bauhaus Gropius" had not hesitated to introduce students to the practical field of prefabrication, despite "the danger of making mistakes. . . . All progress has to pass through the stage of experiments and mistakes." The "Harvard Gropius," however, believes "he can or should stop students making mistakes in pioneering new building fields."

> Here, I am afraid, errs my beloved Goethe-Gropius of Weimar. I never have seen students—and teachers too—making more mistakes in imitating Corbu and Gropius than in our school and I have never seen more students and teachers coming to wrong inferences than in Robinson Hall. What is the difference between the ossification of the shapes as are to be seen in the École des Beaux-Arts and [the] drawings we can observe in our School? The shapes, indeed, have changed, but the principles of shaping and forming are damned alike, at least in imitating the teachers and what they like.[62]

Wagner challenged Gropius on one other point: has the "old Weimar-and-Dessau fighter Walter Gropius lost his fighting power of 1924 or is he going to be satisfied with what he has reached up to today?" Wagner was clearly not satisfied with the state of architecture in 1940. As he told Gropius, "You might think—I do not know—we have reached a final shape of architecture, while I think that we are still far away from the holy of Holies in shape and form and that we are still living in a transition time that will last far beyond our own life time."[63]

In "The Post-Modern House," Hudnut made a point similar to Wagner's last charge against Gropius. In what was surely a dig in 1945, Hudnut praised the "architects of the 1920's," naming Gropius among them, for certain achievements they had made in their work of that decade. But what these architects had accomplished then, Hudnut said, was "never meant to be definitive—or international," implying that they had not advanced terribly far in the last twenty years. What they had created two decades earlier was a strong "base from which a new progress might be possible." Hudnut added—and here differed from Wagner—that modern architects should develop this base with a "peculiar countenance in every nation and in every clime."[64]

Hudnut never entered the debate over regionalism in modern architecture—over the Bay Region style or the New Empiricism—in any explicit way, but the statement above indicates where he stood on the issue of a regional expression. Hudnut had always believed in adopting a sense of the region in buildings and in civic design. This had even been an important part of his architecture in the early 1920s, and certainly of his work with Hegemann, and he had not wavered on the issue. Hudnut's close friend and confidante William Wurster, who had spent the 1943 school year at Harvard before moving down the road the following year to the deanship at MIT, was at the center of the regionalist storm. Lewis Mumford had unleashed that storm in a 1947 *New Yorker* "Skyline" column in which he argued that Wurster's houses in California, and those of a few others, exhibited a "free yet unobtrusive expression of the terrain, the climate, and the way of life on the Coast" that was far superior to the sterility and abstraction of so many other modern examples—namely those of "international style." Mumford described these West Coast buildings as belonging to the "Bay Region" style.[65]

Mumford's column offended many architects, and to debate its merits, the Museum of Modern Art invited a group of them to take part in a formal symposium early in 1948 entitled "What Is Happening to Modern Architecture?" Gropius, Breuer, Hitchcock, Mumford, Tunnard, Philip Johnson, and Barr were among the dozen or so speaking at the conference. Though Hudnut usually took part in such affairs at the Modern, this time he did not. Tunnard took the part his comrade Hudnut would have played, arguing that something was "lacking" in modern architecture—"dare I mention the word, 'beauty'?" The emphasis on "materials, on form, on clean surfaces" is perhaps not so important, Tunnard contended, and there is too much "sociological emphasis" on the right amount of interior space and parking space and on the idea that buildings are "good for people." Tunnard insisted, just as Hudnut would have, that history could help remedy the situation.

> We have to look at the buildings of the past we have been taught *not* to look at. We have got to look at the buildings that have received the approbation of critics and the buildings which people like, and reconcile public taste and good architectural performance. . . . [I]f we don't make the latest thing in architectural magazines our exclusive diet, perhaps we shall be able to create again buildings which receive the approbation of all good critics.[66]

A similar debate had taken hold in England at roughly the same time, when the British *Architectural Review* lauded modern architects in Sweden for making "man and his habits, reactions and needs" the focus of their work. The Swedish style, dubbed the "New Empiricism," then spread to England, with architects there now turning to local materials and homey aesthetic recalling cottages and modern life. These debates over regionalism shared an underlying theme with the earlier debate over monumentality: in place of machinelike rigorousness, architects needed to emphasize what Mumford called the "'feeling elements' in design," or what Hudnut referred to as "emotional content."[67]

Not only did architects and critics debate these issues, a group of students at the GSD also voiced their discontent with the formalistic direction in which the School seemed to be moving. Led by Bruno Zevi— a student of Gropius's from 1940 to 1942 who went on to become one of Italy's leading architectural polemicists—a group of students in 1941 took part in creating a manifesto of some twenty-five pages that was largely critical of the GSD. Zevi recalled years later that "An Opinion on Architecture" originally had a more "violent critical title" and a more "violent" text than its final draft. He himself had authored the original manifesto, and in "some 8–10 meetings full of students," every sentence of the document got discussed and modified. The final result was a much more "generic and weak" manifesto than Zevi had intended, but he "accepted [the changes] because I wanted the signatures of students who were afraid of everything."[68] "An Opinion on Architecture," which the students dedicated to Dean Hudnut, argued that "our life in the school is not fundamentally different from that of any Beaux-Arts school." Along similar lines to Wagner, the students protested that "instead of having a conception of architecture based on common ideas, able to answer the new collective needs of society—to find something new (not something good) has largely become our aim."[69] A "drive towards originality" prevailed at the School, and it faced "the danger of becoming a workshop of mannerism, or a playhouse of individualistic preference." In what seemed an echo of Wagner's words to Gropius, the students queried: "Have we substituted for the 'art for art's sake' of the [Beaux-Arts] 'rendered project' the 'art for art's sake' of the abstract model?"

Although the students noted that Gropius's work in partnership with Breuer in the United States was "of basic importance in the present stage of architecture," they held up the recent Frank House in Pittsburgh as an example of Gropius's turn away from the social principles he had once championed. The Frank House was an "an example of

Walter Gropius and Marcel Breuer, Frank House, illuminated at night, with reflecting pool in foreground, Pittsburgh, Pennsylvania. (Ezra Stoller, Esto)

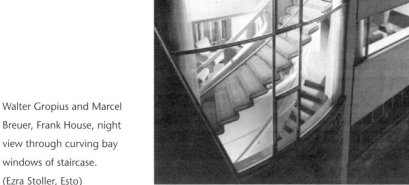

Walter Gropius and Marcel Breuer, Frank House, night view through curving bay windows of staircase. (Ezra Stoller, Esto)

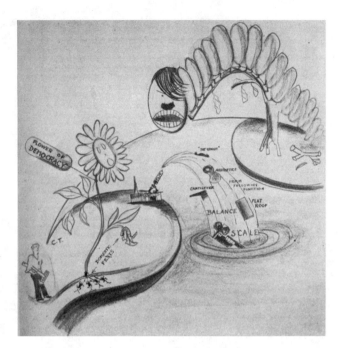

Cartoon from *Task: A Magazine for the Younger Generation in Architecture* (1941, 9). (Courtesy of the Frances Loeb Library, Harvard Design School)

gentleman's architecture," with "extravagant formality" and complete "disregard for the relation between design and industry," the students wrote. Ultimately, the manifesto stated that its goal was "to change the mild course of modern fashion architecture into a struggle for a revolution in the architectural field." To do so required "collective work between all the branches connected with the building industry." Since architecture demanded a knowledge of materials, structure, and site, and an understanding of the people who will use it, the students declared in bold letters that *"COLLABORATION IS THE CREDO AND THE FAITH OF ARCHITECTURE TODAY."*[70]

Not all students participated in this protest. One who did not recalled that those who were involved tended to be the more "verbal students as opposed to people who were trying to express their ideas through design."[71] Indeed, Zevi and his group appealed to Hudnut in their manifesto for the creation of a quarterly magazine with "DEFINITE PRINCIPLES OF CRITICISM" that aimed to make Americans aware of modern architecture. Such a proposal likely appealed to Hudnut, who was himself a literary architect by now, with a strong bent toward propaganda. The first issue of *Task: A Magazine for the Younger Generation in Architecture* appeared just a few months after the student manifesto,

IN THIS ISSUE: Wartime Planning in Britain . . . Washington Letter on Post War Planning . . . The Men Who Are Planning America . . . Editorials . . . Housing and the Production Drive . . . 30 Plans, Maps and Photographs . . . Book Review: On Being An Architect . . . Unity in the Planning Profession . . .

Cover of *Task*, published by GSD students; issue 3 was devoted to contemporary Soviet architecture and city planning. (Courtesy of the Frances Loeb Library, Harvard Design School)

TASK MAGAZINE, Robinson Hall, Cambridge, Massachusetts. Fifty cents a copy

From *Task*, the Soviet issue (3); this is clearly *not* Robinson Hall. (Courtesy of the Frances Loeb Library, Harvard Design School)

CONFLICTING VIEWS OF HOUSE AND TOWN   179

funded by subscriptions and donations. The editorial page of the first issue read much like "An Opinion on Architecture":

> We believe that the architectural schools and the profession do not sufficiently reflect society's needs; to train the student and the young architect in the principle of collective work. This is why we are publishing this magazine. Together with conferences and correspondence it will be a means of achieving clarity of ideas, and forms of organized action, so that our work in building and planning will answer the requirements of society.[72]

Task continued publishing until 1948—albeit in an "improvised" fashion, put together by a group of students and architects: Garrett Eckbo, Richard Stein, Ezra Stoller, Henry Hope Reed Jr., Willo von Moltke, I. M. Pei, and Edward Larrabee Barnes among them. A number of GSD faculty and others in the field also contributed articles during its seven-year run, including Hudnut, Gropius, Christopher Tunnard, Catherine Bauer Wurster, and Martin Wagner.[73] The name of the magazine, *Task,* seems to have derived from that of the Soviet news agency, *Tass,* a connection that the magazine never made explicit but with its collectivist agenda, and even some of the imagery it included, the implication was clear.[74] The magazine came out at a time when the Communist Party in the United States had legitimacy and counted among its members a number professors on academic campuses—neither Hudnut nor Gropius among them.

Bucolic Paradise

The subject of housing design engaged GSD students not just because of their own studio work nor simply because of the prominence of housing issues in contemporary political discourse. One way in which students had learned about modern architecture in the first place was through the housing designs depicted in current architecture magazines and books and in the exhibitions of modern architecture at the Museum of Modern Art. Significantly, students also had the chance to experience firsthand the modern houses their professors were designing in the Boston area. While designing houses had always been a staple exercise in architecture schools, during the Hudnut/Gropius years at the GSD it took on a particular significance; it offered the most accessible route for students to become bona fide modernists themselves.

On numerous occasions, students visited both Gropius's and

Walter Gropius and Marcel Breuer, Gropius House, in Lincoln, Massachusetts, shortly after it was built, 1940. (Courtesy of the Pritchard Papers, University of East Anglia)

Breuer's homes in Lincoln, and they likely saw Walter Bogner's house nearby. Holmes Perkins had also built himself a modern house in Brookline, completed six months before Gropius's house was finished.[75] Gropius, Breuer, and Bogner had all built their homes on land owned by Helen O. Storrow, a wealthy Boston philanthropist partial to modern art and architecture. Gropius and Breuer also designed a house on the property for the Harvard sociologist James Ford and his wife, Katherine. Storrow had offered the four Harvard faculty members sites on her land on Wood Ends Road, and she also assumed the full cost of building and landscaping their houses, which none of them could have afforded. Her tenants then leased the houses from her at a quite reasonable rate with an option to buy. As Isabelle Hyman has described, by 1939 "the Woods End Road colony was like a miniature Siedlung, an unconscious re-creation of European housing exhibitions."[76]

Even decades later the former GSD students could recall their inspiring first visits to the Lincoln colony. Harry Seidler remembered his trip to Gropius's house as "a revelation, bar none. We all were totally overwhelmed."[77] At Gropius's house, students experienced a kind of modern design that differed markedly from the "postwar house" of the GSD studios. Widely published and regarded as a modern classic, this was Gropius's calling card, a model house with which he successfully lured clients. The students came in groups as invited guests, or they went on their own, sometimes bicycling out to visit Gropius's always hospitable wife, Ise.[78]

Breuer's house, too, was a "revelation of a new world of light and space." Edward L. Barnes recalled the impression it made on him during his first visit:

> I had never seen such fresh details and materials. I remember a great deal of white, mirrors beyond Japanese reed screens, a Scotch plaid bedspread, stone, huge sheets of glass, wicker, and chrome, more white walls, somewhere the first Breuer blue wall, an early Calder mobile, and sheer white curtains. I was dazzled by the sureness of this touch—Breuer's ability to combine totally dissimilar elements and materials and yet not crowd the space. And I felt that his architecture was somehow like the Paul Klee paintings in which disparate objects float in space . . . all unrelated yet held together by their exact placement. This quality of tension and contrast seemed to be a true expression of our lives at that time.[79]

The students were also familiar with the other houses that Gropius and Breuer were designing in their Harvard Square office. On weekends, groups of students would troop out to other Gropius-Breuer houses near Boston, sometimes meeting owners intent on their privacy, while others, as at the Chamberlain House in Wayland, received them with delight.[80] Even the 1941 "Opinion on Architecture" praised the "high quality" of these first houses that Gropius and Breuer had designed (except for the Frank House), though the authors did register one complaint—that the work "is done on a strictly individual basis, and not in the light of a school or movement."[81]

This was not a complaint they would have leveled at Martin Wagner's house design of the same era. Though Wagner never designed his own home, he did design one for mass production in 1941, a thirteen-sided, insulated steel "igloo." Wagner planned the low-cost, expandable and contractible, portable igloo to be "proof against almost everything"—earthquakes, fires, wartime bombing, cold weather, even termites. With its floor area of 200 feet and 1,500 cubic foot capacity, Wagner's invention resembled, according to one journalist, an "up-to-date trailer caravan in everything except form." Even its pull-down beds, which unfolded into the living room, could be tipped outward for sleeping outdoors.[82] The British *Architect's Journal* predicted (incorrectly) that Wagner's "ingenious" domed-roof igloo, which would sell for approximately six hundred dollars, would likely become a permanent feature in the landscape for its ability to follow the cycle of family maturation. As the journal noted, "when the young couple inhabiting the basic unit acquire a family, their house can expand accordingly. . . . Finally, when the by now middle-aged parents lose their offspring, their house can contract again and provide a nice windfall for wedding presents by the sale of its unneeded components."[83]

With the exception of Wagner's igloo, the faculty houses shared a number of characteristics that students at the GSD brought to their own work. The buildings all used similar materials—wood, fieldstone, and large areas of glass, the latter to allow the flow of space between indoors and out. The houses were generally light in weight, and they shared an

Marcel Breuer, Breuer House, Lincoln, Massachusetts; the Breuers are shown in the living room of their house, ca. 1940. (Ezra Stoller, Esto)

Martin Wagner's proposed community of "MW" houses, thirteen-sided, steel, pre-fabricated igloolike houses that protect against "most everything," including air raids. (*Architectural Forum* 74 [February 1941]: 91)

emphasis on functionality and economy of means. They generally included terraces that extended living space to the outdoors, flat roofs, open space plans, and all were single-family houses built outside the city. Even Wagner's igloo shared this last characteristic: illustrations of the igloo showed it set in a nonurban environment, usually among trees in a mountain landscape with animals grazing, or sometimes in a decentralized subdivision.[84] Without a doubt, the GSD faculty teaching housing all had a definite preference for living outside the city. Much to Hudnut's dismay, they made this preference well known to students not just by the example of their own work but in a more explicit way in their housing design problems.

The GSD housing problems during the Hudnut/Gropius years assured students, in the vein of New Deal rhetoric, that people instinctively preferred to live in a suburban or rural setting rather than in the dense city. In several housing problems, Gropius and Wagner made the claim that single-story "sprawling dwelling quarters of low density . . . hidden below an optimum of tree cover" offered the ideal form of residence for a healthy, happy, family life, and ultimately for a better world.[85] Engineers had already devoted themselves to satisfying "people's longing for more freedom in space and time," their design problems insisted. By inventing "our space and time-bridging machines [engineers] were nothing but the exponents of millions of freedom-seeking human beings." Therefore architects should "blaze a trail" for greater freedom.[86] Gropius and Wagner especially took pains to distinguish the "de-concentrated" pattern of housing they favored from "the plan-less decentralizing pattern of our recent town development." Though they claimed they could not "cure the 'decentralization disease' by suppressing the people's longing for more freedom," they insisted that this compelling need for freedom would ensure the development of "a constructive pattern of deliberate de-concentration." Not surprisingly, the two architects cited the Greenbelt settlements as the closest in the history of American building to the kinds of "garden-cities embedded in regional city-gardens" that they had in mind for housing Americans.[87]

While some GSD housing problems made specific recommendations for settlement patterns, others simply stressed the need for ample sunlight, fresh air, outdoor living space, and natural scenic views "for the rearing of healthy and happy children and for the pleasures of adults."[88] The problems advanced the notion that people's physical and mental health in fact depended on their living in "greener pastures" and escaping from the mean, congested American city. Some problems took a subtle approach by including fictitious clients "compelled" to live in city apartments with the "consequent difficulty of providing fresh air for their children," or they depicted clients who had grown "tired of the inefficiencies" of the city. For those who believed "strongly in the value of neighborliness, tolerance, and friendly intercourse," the problems pointed to the small community as an "ideal way of living."[89] Several housing design problems, especially those with wealthy clients, simply required students to design homes for nonurban sites without explanation. There was no question for those working on GSD problems during the Hudnut/Gropius years: those who could, lived outside the city.

Lest students had any doubt of this, Gropius and Wagner railed against the city in a number of their different housing problems. In one problem, they described the city as a "crime against the soul of the 20th century man who remonstrates vigorously against congestion." Another housing problem that they coauthored with Newton, Stubbins, and Tunnard proclaimed: "All our cities and settlements are machine-sick! . . . They are not designed and built for the social, economical and technical functioning of the machine age."[90] Some housing problems flatly rejected the idea of "rehabilitating" the existing city: "Why 'rehabilitate' our old cities by building up new dwelling quarters which often house more people on the same site than did the slums which they replace?"[91]

The problems asserted that living outside the city in widely spaced, tree-covered, single-story houses meant living not only a healthier life but also a safer and quieter life. Overshadowing trees protected residents from hurricanes, gales, dust storms, and smoke pollution while keeping noise from air and ground traffic to a minimum. In addition, with ample trees and shrubs to attract them, birds protected residents from the "plagues of insects." The housing problems also noted that a single-story residence ensured more quiet indoor space while also allowing for the best fire escape. Gropius further recommended single-story living for the easy connections that it allowed between interior space and outdoor living space, including "the garden, its sun and air-bath, outdoor sitting and sleeping places, playing and working places."[92]

Gropius and Wagner moreover claimed in a 1941 housing problem that during wartime, tree-covered, single-story housing would safeguard citizens better than any other form of housing. The "natural camouflage" would obscure houses from the air while the wide spaces between them would assure that they made a poor target for enemy bombers.[93] Important as it was to make housing safe during war in the "power-age," the two architects insisted that their ideas of de-concentration developed not out of wartime concerns but from "facts surrounding our 'peaceful life.'" As they told their students: "Far-sighted town planners and architects did not need the horrible experience of modern warfare to get ideas 'from the wrong reason' for the revision of our present building principles. . . . They knew that almost all our present planning and building principles grew obsolete long ago."[94]

The more he saw it developing in the GSD design studios, the more hostile Hudnut grew toward the "back-to-the-country cult" of modern architects.[95] At a time when urban America was in dire disrepair, the arguments being made at the School, he felt, fostered an indifferent, even escapist attitude toward the city and its problems among the planners and architects who should have cared deeply. Subsequent critics have also condemned the attitude toward the city advanced at the GSD during the Hudnut/Gropius years. Klaus Herdeg, for example, has remarked that one "could hardly expect sympathetic, enlightened treatment of urban architectural problems by architects trained in such an anti-city ethos."[96] Vincent Scully also concurred that modern architecture was taught from the late 1930s through the 1940s in an "urbanistically de-structive" manner. That period of architecture and planning, as Scully has said, was filled with "fantasies that hate[d] the city and all pre-existing urban architecture."[97]

Unlike Gropius, Wagner, and others at the GSD, Hudnut loved the dense, lively city. "I am frequently surprised," he wrote, "by the vehemence with which so many of my friends denounce the city and advertise their desire to escape into the country."[98] Given the central role of cities in human civilization, he questioned how there could be any fundamental dissidence between people and the city. Though he recognized the current inhumanity of cities—smoke, congestion, blight—he believed these problems could and must be overcome. Instead of fleeing from cities, Hudnut argued for recovering in them those qualities that throughout history have made cities the "true and congenial homes of mankind." Among those qualities, he identified "the enlargement of personality and of powers; the invigorating contact of mind on mind; the freedom born of city air, the arts which are flourished in cities like flowers in a garden—architecture, the theater, letters, symphonic music; the pageant and adventure . . . and most of all the sweet commerce of a society which is urbane, civilized and polite; words rooted in a word which means *the city*."[99]

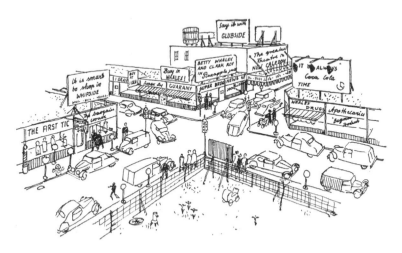

"Shops and markets, with their colored letterings, bright windows, neon lights and the murmur of crowds . . . that is precisely what is needed," sketch by Willo von Moltke for Hudnut's "The Art in Housing." (Reprinted with permission from *Architectural Record* 93 [January 1943]: 62)

Planning Ideas

Hudnut and Gropius had never shared common ideas of the city, but their differences on the subject did not surface until the early 1940s, when Hudnut took issue with the direction in which modern housing seemed to be moving. Despite the growing rift between the GSD's two leaders, students and faculty generally shared a common aim in these years: to prepare for the rebuilding of towns and cities in the postwar world. As part of the broad conversation on city planning for the post-war years, Hudnut, Gropius, Wagner, and faculty from Harvard's School for Public Policy organized the Conference on Urbanism, held at Harvard in March 1942. Though Hudnut did not speak at the conference, Gropius and Wagner did, voicing the same ideas of the city that they would bring to their students, especially in the postwar years.[100] This may have been the first time that Hudnut heard them voice their urbanistic theories at length. If so, it would not have a happy occasion for Hudnut. As planning for the postwar got underway, the city and its future became the subject of a simmering feud between Hudnut and Gropius that would finally escalate into a raging battle. Given the very different ideas of urbanism that Hudnut and Gropius brought with them to the GSD, their coming to blows over the issue of city rebuilding was almost inevitable.

City planning was never taught at the Bauhaus during Gropius's years there, but he had brought with him to Harvard a definite interest in what he called this "most burning and baffling problem of all." His architectural work had led him, he wrote in 1935, "inevitably . . . from study of the function of the house to that of the street; from the street to the town; and finally to the still vaster implications of regional and national planning."[101] At the time Hudnut hired him, Gropius was also an active participant in the CIAM and a promoter of the basic principles identified with that avant-garde organization. He believed that the tra-ditional city was incompatible with modern life, and he argued instead for functionally zoned cities with mass-produced houses that looked out onto vast, open green spaces.

Though Hudnut was familiar with Gropius's basic views on the city when he arrived at Harvard, Gropius knew little, if anything, of Hudnut's work with Hegemann or his long-term interest in city planning. Unlike Gropius, Hudnut had never promoted any particular brand of urbanism, nor had he aligned himself with the CIAM or any other organization promoting a particular planning approach. Hudnut was not interested in advocating a specific type of city; rather, he wanted to advance a new method of approach to urban design. Hudnut wanted to engage architects, landscape architects, and city planners as a team that would work collectively to shape modern cities in a way that satisfied the material and spiritual needs of modern communities and individuals.

Late in 1941, Hudnut at last got the chance to appoint a new faculty member to take Henry Hubbard's place as chair of the Planning Department. With Hubbard gone, Hudnut was finally free to shape the direction of planning studies at the GSD, and he needed a like-minded planner to help him. Hudnut considered only one person for the post, John Gaus, a prominent figure in the planning community who taught political science, with a focus on American regional development and public administration, at the University of Wisconsin.[102] Unwilling to leave that job permanently, Gaus accepted the GSD position as a two-year visiting professor.

Gaus seemed a curious choice for the GSD when compared to Hudnut's other faculty appointments: Gropius, Breuer, Wagner, and Tunnard. Yet precisely because he was neither an architect nor a designer of any sort, Hudnut considered Gaus an ideal addition to the School. When one remembers the kind of broadly educated planner that Hegemann was, Hudnut's bringing Gaus makes perfect sense. Gaus came to the GSD with a vast knowledge of American institutions, culture, and geography—which none of the Europeans on the faculty could match—and a wealth of experience in the administrative side of planning. Whereas the modernists taught *design* (even in their planning courses), Gaus would teach his students to "facilitate better decision making" (his definition of planning) by thinking contextually, with regard to specific social, physical, and political circumstances.[103]

Gaus viewed himself as a "regional" rather than city planner, much more like Lewis Mumford than like his new colleague Martin Wagner. Gaus defined the region as an area delimited by the ecology of its natural setting, by geographic and economic interests, and by a particular administrative apparatus, set of ideals, psychology, and intellectual tradition, akin to what Hegemann had called the "idea pattern" that directed civic life. Although Gaus and Hudnut both believed that the GSD should play to its strengths and focus on *urban* planning, they wanted students to learn from the regional approach to consider the relationships between physical design and social analysis.[104]

Joseph Hudnut (*right*) and John M. Gaus, May 1942. (Courtesy of the Harvard University Archives, call no. HUP Hudnut [2])

During his two years at the GSD, Gaus authored a much-touted, fifty-page report that made concrete suggestions for educating regional and city planners at the School. That report, aptly entitled *The Graduate School of Design and the Education of Planners,* contained the guidelines that Hudnut followed as he tried to shape the curriculum of the GSD during his last decade there.[105] Hudnut sent out some two thousand copies of the report to alumni and members of the planning community, hoping that it would persuade people toward the broad view of planning that he and Gaus shared.

In his report, Gaus argued for a planning education that explored the nature of American life and the problems of communities. He wanted students to understand the kinds of civic tasks and settings they would find in the field and to understand the role of government in the processes of planning and formulating policy. Although he believed that there were many ways to approach the education of planners, Gaus defended the idea of a department of regional planning in the School of Design as one valid path for doing so.[106] Given that planners had to render social and economic policy into physical change, Gaus argued that the design school offered students a substantive base for a future in planning. At the same time, he wanted planning students to branch out and take courses in a number of different departments, such as anthropology, law, or economics. Ideally, he wrote, "a school of planning [should include] the entire resources of a university."[107] Gaus also made an important curricular proposal in his report—that the GSD create a new common first-year program that introduced all beginning students to the basic techniques and principles of the School's three fields. An avid proponent of this idea, Hudnut may even have urged Gaus to include this proposal in his report.

Hudnut embraced a grand view of planning education, as Gaus did. As he informed his readers, tongue-in-cheek, in his 1946 article "What a Planner Has to Know," he had spoken with the chairs of the "seven score departments" at Harvard ("we live here in separate cells like doves in their dove-cot") to see what university courses they considered indispensable to the education of a planner. What he had in mind in asking them this question, he deadpanned,

> was not so much the knowledge which pertains to a planner's trade—the tools by which he makes a living—as that range and depth of understanding which makes a planner truly serviceable to the forward march of humanity. One hundred and twenty courses of study were described by at least one of my colleagues as essential to this end; seventy-five others as "desirable." . . . Thirty-three years would be required by this program for the general education of a planner—I mean by this the cultural disciplines which properly precede or accompany professional courses.[108]

Besides the requisite courses in history, sociology, economics, politics, and the physical sciences, Hudnut also described the key part that "art" must play in educating planners. Essentially he extended the argument he made in "The Post-Modern House" to encompass the entire city, as he worried that planners had lost sight of the real goal of planning: "The town functions; there is light; air and proper exposure; traffic moves smoothly; and the children live at the proper distances from school; but there is oftentimes neither grace nor dignity nor meaning in the city pattern. There is no *architecture*—a term which implies proportion and balance in the buildings, in streets and open places, and form and sequence in their collective whole."[109]

Hudnut tried hard to keep Gaus at the GSD, but he returned to the University of Wisconsin after only two years. Leaving Harvard "must appear demented," Gaus told Hudnut, but Wisconsin seemed to fit him better than the Design School, given his interests in rural-urban relationships and his philosophy of regionalism that required sinking roots, that is, staying long enough in one region to do "intensive, cumulative" work.[110] In 1947, Gaus nonetheless reemerged at Harvard as professor of government in the Littauer School. He renewed his affiliation with the GSD at that time as a member of a council that advised the Department of Regional Planning. The council—which also included sociologist Talcott Parsons, political theorist Carl Friedrich, and others eminent in the fields of government and economics—ensured that planning remain a broadly defined field at the GSD, embracing many disciplines beyond design.[111] From his council seat, Gaus then served as guardian of the planning idea that he had helped institute and that remained at the core of planning studies at the GSD throughout Hudnut's tenure as dean.

Gaus had left the GSD in 1944 with the stage set for the start of a vibrant postwar era. To replace him, Hudnut made an unconventional and revealing appointment, G. Holmes Perkins, who was then one of the GSD's younger tenured faculty members and a practicing architect. Perkins was an unusual choice to head the Department of Planning since he had no training in planning and minimal experience in the field. What Perkins knew of city planning he had learned during the war with the National Housing Administration in Washington. Hudnut anticipated correctly that Perkins's appointment would rile members of the planning profession, who wanted one of their own for the prestigious post.[112] The question, then, is, Why did Hudnut choose an architect with almost no planning experience to head the department at this crucial moment—a time when postwar planning was the School's central concern?

One reason was to appease Gropius, who wanted a designer in that position and not a public administrator like Gaus, with whom he had shared no common ground. More significantly, Perkins was a close friend to both Gropius and Hudnut and may have been the one person who could help mediate the growing power struggle between the two men. Along with the various duties that went along with the Planning Department chair, Perkins found himself acting as the conciliator between Hudnut and Gropius. Shortly after he assumed his post in 1945, he began to bear the brunt of soured relations between the two: "There were petty exasperations toward each other all the time. They came into my office complaining about each other constantly. Gropius was always pushing for what he believed was right. And I guess there finally comes a time when the power struggle gets personal. It was a very unhappy business."[113]

Gropius and Hudnut managed to keep their feuding within the confines of Harvard for at least a few more years and to keep up the image of a unified GSD. When, in 1944, Robert Moses singled out Gropius in a diatribe against the revolutionary "long-haired planners," published in the *New York Times* Sunday magazine, it was Hudnut who fired back in defense.[114] In his "Mr. Moses Dissects the 'Long-Haired' Planners," the powerful New York City parks commissioner condemned the "subsidized lamas in their remote mountain temples" (university professors) for planning the postwar American city in un-American, "modernistic" ways. Mostly Moses maligned the planners—naming Gropius as one—for bringing foreign ideas to the American city and for slighting the country that gave them a new home. Moses accused the planners of viewing Americans as "backward" and "primitive" and of "believing that they ordered things better in the old country."[115] Moses feared that, through "familiar subsurface activities"—teaching, lecturing, and publishing books and essays—planners like Gropius and others following the modern path (among whom, strangely, he included Rexford Tugwell) might seriously impact the shaping of the American city. Moses later claimed that he had lashed out at Gropius after he had heard "one of his characteristic outbursts." According to Moses, Gropius had taken him to task for "myopic vision, stereotypes, failure to take advantage of new materials and methods, and just plain dumbness."[116]

A few weeks after Moses's article appeared, Hudnut responded in the same space in the *Times*.[117] In "A 'Long-Haired' Reply to Moses," Hudnut scorned the commissioner's xenophobia and detailed for readers the historic links between American and European city planning. Hudnut further accused Moses of anti-intellectualism, of resenting both theory and those who applied their analytical minds to urban problems. The Harvard dean then maligned Commissioner Moses's brand of planning for its "limited objectives" and "piecemeal attacks on specific urban problems."[118] Hudnut also used his "Reply to Moses" to outline his own ideas of modern city planning for the broad readership of the *New York Times*. He argued that planners must consider the various components of city life simultaneously—communications, housing, neighborhoods, open spaces, public services, and industry among them. Comprehensive planning would prevent "lopsided or maladjusted" cities that focused to the detriment of all else on a single aspect, like traffic movement. Anticipating Moses's reaction, Hudnut allowed that planners must set limited goals rather than reconciling every civic problem before acting. Hudnut distinguished his ideas of planning from the commissioner's by explaining that one must envisage even these limited goals as part of a "general" plan: "A plan capable of continuous development, a plan in no sense rigid, and a plan in which no proposal is incorporated other than those capable of realization."[119]

Toward the end of his essay, Hudnut accused Moses of fearing "social change" (or, to use Moses's word, "revolution"). If Moses were to look beyond his specialties of highway or park development, he might discover the people who lived, worked, and amused themselves in the city. What if these citizens joined the planning process, Hudnut challenged? What if they formed new groups or institutions to help them shape a city suited to their needs? Despite the bridges, highways, and parks that Moses had scattered along the urban landscape, Hudnut reminded his readers that no "community structure" exists. Quoting Moses's harshest critic, Lewis Mumford, Hudnut added that Americans thus far have only "tinkered with the mechanical structure of our cities."[120]

Given their own feuding over issues of urbanism, it is ironic that Hudnut defended Gropius against Moses's "dissection." Hudnut had perhaps replied to Moses partly in self-defense, for he himself had certainly added to the foreign presence in American urban planning and design. He was also acting in self-defense when he took on Moses for his antitheoretical stance since Hudnut spent much of his time theorizing about the modern city without ever drawing up a single plan. Hudnut's role as Gropius's defender seems especially ironic since he would ultimately find Gropius—despite being foreign and philosophical—guilty of ravaging the city in some of the same ways Moses did. Only a few years after he responded to Moses, Hudnut would condemn Gropius for failing to plan comprehensively. He would also charge him, as he had Moses, with creating an unbalanced or maladjusted city and, moreover, for ignoring what people wanted or needed in their cities. Rather than including them in the planning process, Hudnut reproved his Harvard colleague for imposing on citizens what *he* thought they needed, and in the form of an inflexible master plan.[121] Finally, just as Moses had condemned the "long-haired planners" for using their positions to influence others unduly, so would Hudnut speak out against Gropius's indoctrinating students, making his "fixations of judgment" theirs, "entrenched, absolute and devastating."[122]

Interestingly enough, Moses recalled in his memoirs that at the 1953 Harvard commencement, he and Gropius "made up." The two marched together to receive honorary degrees from the university, in Moses's words, "a strange pair showing Harvard's hospitality to all schools."[123]

Postwar Urbanism

As Gropius and his colleagues in the GSD studios (often Wagner or some of Gropius's former students who now served as assistant teachers in his class) fashioned new cities that would "break down the frontiers between town and country," Hudnut sharpened his critique of modernist urban design.[124] While Hudnut became a fervent critic of Gropius's approach to designing cities, Gropius dismissed Hudnut's approach with the ultimate insult, "applied archaeology."[125]

Inside the GSD's postwar design studios, Gropius, his teaching colleagues, and their students designed "new towns," or "satellite towns," what they called "country cities in city countries."[126] The GSD towns were essentially CIAM towns, verdant, healthful, affordable for many, low in density, and functionally zoned. Conceived according to a strict master plan, the model towns would lie beyond existing suburbs though still within easy access of city services, large consumer markets, and highways. Ideally the towns would house thirty thousand in low-slung, modernist, flexible dwellings (movable, expandable, and shrinkable), arranged into clusters of thirty or so. Each town would have its own schools, commerce, industry, as well as an administrative and social center set in its own verdant zone. Even a quick glance at GSD students' designs points to their talent for blurring the distinctions between cities and country towns.[127]

Freedom, safety, economy, healthfulness, convenience, variety, and speed preoccupied the GSD students as they laid out their towns. To protect from the perils of fast-flowing traffic, for example, they assigned people and buildings to green spaces. Pedestrian pathways wound through landscaped and open areas to the backsides of buildings whose doors became primary entrances as street fronts turned into "mere service-fronts."[128] So that automotive traffic could flow ever faster, students eliminated street intersections and on-street parking. Also for the sake of speed, they designated one-way streets and widened main arteries, arranging them so as to "serve by the shortest and most convenient way." And when their economical and convenient streets lacked "visual interest," students curved or bent them, staggered buildings on them, or arranged them in pleasing patterns. To assure that their streets avoided monotony in their quietude, they added "sight-relief"—grass, trees, and other bucolic stuff.[129] In their New Town design problems, students took the lessons they had learned designing modern housing and applied them to far larger schemes.

Gropius and Wagner were not merely utopians, for they insisted that their New Towns offered the key to renewing existing urban areas. "To solve the complicated problem of rehabilitating our existing cities," they explained, "there is no other way . . . but to start courageously and without prejudice new practical tests by building model communities in one stroke and then examining their living value."[130] Theirs, then, was a two-step approach to city planning: first they created model "country cities," and then they transferred the attributes of these to the city proper, much to Hudnut's dismay.

Hudnut recognized the same urban problems that Gropius did— slums, sprawl, human misery, filth, and other vestiges of industries that had evolved in cities unprepared for change. But while these problems *were* the city to Gropius (and having lived most of his life in German cities, the city was also the symbol of a political legacy that Gropius abhorred), to Hudnut they were momentary "dislocations and derangements."[131] Hudnut insisted that the centralized city—a place distinct

G. A. Doyle, J. T. Kelly, W. H. Trogden, and M. Breslaw, functionally zoned, verdant plan for an East Boston Civic Center, GSD student project, 1951. (Courtesy of the Frances Loeb Library, Harvard Design School)

INVENTING AMERICAN MODERNISM

from the country—could be and must be rebuilt. He loved the crowded, dense city, "the invigorating contact of mind on mind; the freedom born of city air," and, unlike Gropius and other modernists, he believed that only in the city could we find profound happiness and lasting satisfaction. Two years after he defended them against Robert Moses, Hudnut now denounced the "long-haired planners, in whose declamatory pages the city is altogether erased, its harsh outlines . . . dissolved into green communities of contented seraphim."[132]

For the postwar era, Hudnut sought a postmodern, humanistic city; for him this meant a city of "tempered modernity," in tune with the inventions and concerns of the times but never acceding to them entirely. He favored "mechanized cities" marked by the "lightness, freedom and grace of steel."[133] Above all, Hudnut considered streets central to the tradition of cities. Streets had always been significant for the places they led to, for bringing people together, for the currents of activity they fostered, as "the oldest theater of democracy." Whereas Gropius and others like-minded made streets into intricate labyrinths, "zigzags in a park," or lanes for rapid transit, all apart from human intercourse, Hudnut wanted to rebuild them as "public thoroughfares" lined with buildings and integral to buildings. He pictured streets and buildings as parts of a shared urban pattern—with buildings drawing their traffic from the streets and then returning it to them, via front doors and back.[134]

Hudnut took issue with numerous attributes of the GSD New Towns while trying to reclaim the qualities that synchronized cities and human life. Rather than the carefully named and measured "units" that segmented New Towns—the residential unit, the neighborship, and the town nucleus—Hudnut wanted neighborhoods of the traditional sort: tightly knit, sociable, each united by its own local history, commerce, customs, space, structure, and especially streets, independent but still indispensable to the far larger, single neighborhood, the city.[135] Hudnut rejected "antiseptic" functional zoning, whereby function determined the character and boundaries of spaces (or "units") and designated their use for a single purpose or single group. And to combat the "functionalism of thought" visible in modern cities—the contempt for anything that deviated from the "business of living"—he exalted fantasy, surprise, and irrational preference as determinants of civic form.[136]

Hudnut had for many years advocated cities that served the collective cause, much like Gropius. He continued to insist that our "need of a

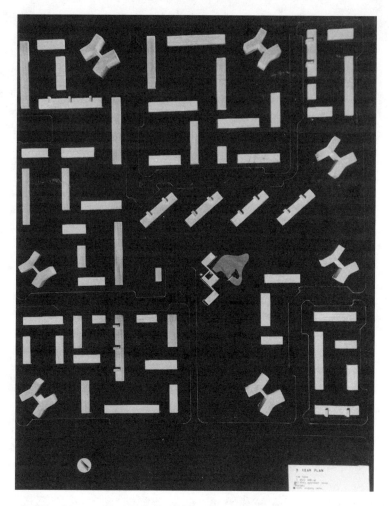

Carlhian, Braxton, Chen-Park, Kornblath, Neer, and Moehlman, plan for the redevelopment of South Boston, with buildings arranged to offer visual variety, GSD
student project, 1947. (Courtesy of the Frances Loeb Library, Harvard Design School)

collective life . . . of belonging and sharing" draws us to cities and holds
us in them.[137] But as Hudnut saw the communal concern outweighing
all other human interests, as it did in the New Towns, marking form,
space, and arrangement with a deadening equality, Hudnut crusaded
for cities also marked by "individual preferences" and "inner experiences, unprofaned by the collective conscience." He wanted cities that
satisfied both the collective life and individual lives.[138] For Gropius, the

INVENTING AMERICAN MODERNISM

collective was everything and "individuum" had always meant only "bourgeois narrow-mindedness and egotism."[139] As Hudnut understood this, he grew ever more opposed to Gropius's ideas of design. It seemed to Hudnut that Gropius could only translate his collectivism into "impersonal, taciturn and universal, endlessly standardized" buildings or planned towns that excluded "every humanist and poetic value—and with these all the joyousness of life."[140]

6 THE BATTLE OVER BASIC DESIGN

Back at the start of the 1939 school year, Hudnut had remarked: "I think it highly probable that we shall think of nothing but war now for the next five or six years. Meanwhile we must keep our shops open and do all we can to keep the nation from entirely forgetting the fact that there is still some art left in the world."[1] Keeping the "shops open" proved to be a challenging task on campuses throughout the nation as the war thinned the ranks of students. At the GSD, it left a mere twenty-six, two-thirds the usual number of students enrolled, along with fewer faculty as Perkins, Stubbins, Newton, and Tunnard all departed to join the war effort. A wartime atmosphere hovered over campus as Harvard—like many other universities and colleges—turned over much of its physical plant to the military. Some three thousand soldiers trained in Harvard's classrooms and dining halls. Robinson and Hunt Halls overflowed with more than three hundred uniformed men in the first several months of 1942 while serving as the campus center for the navy's V-12 training program.[2]

When the new school year began in 1942, the GSD student body expanded once again but with a rather different character than ever before. As one of the old-guard architecture professors, John Humphreys, wrote: "The School is very grim these days. The students we have nowadays are an odd lot—mostly 4-Fs or foreigners—the men that is, and of course the women don't count."[3] The GSD began admitting women to its three departments at the start of the war to take up the places of the absent male students. Although Harvard's governing boards approved their admission only until the end of the war, women remained a permanent fixture at the School. The GSD faculty voted officially to admit women on a permanent basis in 1948 since, in Hudnut's words, nothing more than "convention and custom" had kept the architectural fields and schools male-dominated in the past.[4] By that time, some of the keepers of convention and custom, including John Humphreys, had retired.

The end of the war marked the start of a new, vibrant period at the GSD. Faculty returned from the war, and veterans crowded into the School of Design as into college and university programs across the country, pushing enrollments up to nearly two hundred students in 1945, twice as many as in the previous year. The new students, older and more worldly than those before them, came with a seriousness of purpose unlike any earlier student group. The GI Bill's financial support of veterans also brought the GSD and all of Harvard closer to President Conant's vision of a democratic institution. In the past, many well-qualified prospective students had been unable to finance a professional education, but removing the economic barrier allowed a particularly talented group of students to enroll.

Although absent faculty member returned from the war, the huge influx of students required the addition of several instructors. In the Bauhaus tradition of student becoming teacher, Gropius hired several Master Class graduates to fill the void in Architecture. At various points during the postwar era, he brought in I. M. Pei, John Harkness, Leonard Currie, Chester Nagel, William Lyman, and Charles Burchard to teach in the studios. Hudnut also hired faculty to fill in the gaps during the postwar years, including Hideo Sasaki in Landscape Architecture and Catherine Bauer.[5]

The start of the postwar era at the GSD also marked the beginning of Hudnut's and Gropius's battle over Basic Design. It proved to be a decisive battle for it ended with the dissolution of their partnership. The battle over the first-year course that Gropius had always wanted for the School involved such key issues as the role that history should play in design education and the meaning of tradition in architecture. This final battle also tested the strong wills of both Hudnut and Gropius. While Hudnut took steps to limit the influx of Bauhaus principles into the GSD and to block Gropius's course—which he considered formalistic and irrelevant to architectural design—Gropius used his remarkable lobbying skills to bring his Bauhaus program to Harvard.

The Preliminary Course

The final battle between Hudnut and Gropius began as the GSD set into place a much-anticipated new curriculum for first-year students. The new program required all beginning students in each of the School's three departments to enroll in two core courses, Planning I and Design I. In Planning I, the central course of the first year, students explored the common principles and techniques of each of the GSD's three fields with a team of teachers from each department. The students carried out extensive research on an aspect of a particular city or town, often a part of Boston or an area nearby, studying the actual site, digging through research materials, and conducting interviews with officials and involved citizens. They then worked collaboratively in small groups to design a comprehensive plan for the site and each of the individual elements for the plan. Planning I turned out to be exactly the course that Hudnut had wanted to develop from the time he first founded the GSD. It promoted a "unity of process" among architects, planners, and landscapers and encouraged them to think broadly about the physical, political, and socioeconomic environments as they designed in space and form.[6] Holmes Perkins, who now headed the Department of Planning, played a major part in creating Planning I. He described its method as "the exact reverse of the Beaux-Arts way. We started with the city, and we worked our way down to the individual parts. By hemming the three professions together, the students got accustomed to working together, and they began to respect each other instead of thumbing their nose at each other as they had always done in the past. It really worked."[7]

Most faculty, including Gropius, considered Planning I a strong addition to the GSD curriculum. It was not, however, the course that Gropius had wanted to see as the centerpiece of the first-year program. Design I, the other key component of the new program, did not address the issues Gropius had in mind for GSD students either. Taught by a new instructor, George Le Boutellier, that course introduced students to what the GSD catalogue described as "the fundamental concepts of space, form, and function and the structural relationships by which these are expressed and controlled."[8] Gropius vehemently opposed this course because Hudnut had assigned it in place of the one that he had long championed for the GSD—a Basic Design course modeled after the Bauhaus's famous *Vorkurs*.

Ever since he had arrived at Harvard, Gropius had been determined to institute a Basic Design preliminary course that would serve the same central role it had at Bauhaus—that of the "indispensable prerequisite" to all further study. As at the Bauhaus, Gropius wanted all beginning GSD students to take Basic Design exclusively for six months before pursuing studies in their chosen fields. More than any other single course, Basic Design embodied Gropius's design philosophy and embraced his two primary aims in teaching—to foster individual creativity and to establish a "universal language of form" accessible to all people, regardless of their nationality or social status.[9] In bringing Basic Design to the GSD, Gropius hoped to achieve these same goals that he had set for the Bauhaus. Though he had intended to have the course in place years earlier at the GSD, he recognized after arriving at Harvard that he would need to be patient for a time. In his first years at the School, much else had to be done to modernize the curriculum, especially given the stubbornness of the old-guard teachers and alumni. After this initial period, the war prevented Gropius from pursuing Basic Design, for during those tumultuous years, everything was put on hold. Now, with the war over, Gropius was determined to get the course he wanted, and he put forth what he described as a "very vigorous effort to make myself felt."[10] For his part, Hudnut adamantly disagreed with the fundamental aims and methods of Basic Design, and he rejected the idea of a Bauhaus preliminary course for the school. The last and most heated battle that Gropius and Hudnut fought at Harvard would be over Basic Design.

Gropius's effort to bring his preliminary course to the GSD began with his urging Hudnut back in 1937 to hire Josef Albers. To Gropius, Albers seemed to personify the Bauhaus idea. For ten years, after completing his studies at the Bauhaus, Albers had taught the famous first-year Basic Design course that had served as the backbone of the school's education. Once at Harvard, Gropius had envisioned Albers as a "form master" at the GSD, just as he had been in Germany, teaching first-year students about the nature of materials and the fundamental laws of design. In learning about the formal aspects of designing, Harvard students would experiment with textures, surfaces, colors, and the structural qualities of various materials in a new laboratory-workshop specially equipped for the course. They would work wood, paper, stone, and other media with their hands, exploring their intrinsic qualities and discovering for themselves new ways of expressing these qualities in constructed form.[11]

Gropius imagined that Albers would bring the same approach to the course at Harvard as at the Bauhaus. GSD students would explore the plastic properties of paper, sculpting it by cutting without waste from a single sheet. Or Albers might ask them to transform a metal cone by bending, cutting, stretching, or compressing, again without waste. In exercises like these, where he emphasized thriftiness in materials and labor, Albers tried to prepare students to work within the financial constraints of their clients as well as to strive for an economical modern aesthetic in their constructions. It was especially the emphasis on economy and efficiency in both form and labor that drew Gropius to Albers's version of Basic Design over that of other instructors who had taught the course.[12]

Gropius (like Albers and others from the Bauhaus) considered the Basic Design preliminary course essential in the training of all designers, no matter what their field of specialization. Only in Basic Design could students develop their imaginations to the fullest and discover the path to creativity. As Gropius explained, Basic Design allowed for a "personal experience and self-taught knowledge which finally leads to a creative attitude." He insisted that Basic Design would "develop and ripen intelligence, feeling and ideas, with the general object of evolving 'the complete being' who, from his biological center, can approach his problems with instinctive certainty."[13]

Gropius not only saw Basic Design as the way to creativity, he considered the course essential to establishing what he called a "common language of visual communication" appropriate for the new machine age. Gropius described this new "language" as an "optical key," the visual equivalent of a musical key, the familiar twelve-note framework composers used to make their compositions understood. Starting with Basic Design, Gropius wanted to teach modern visual artists to make their designs accessible (or "international") in an analogous way, by working within a visual framework or key that all people could grasp. Making designs that reached all people remained a crucial aspect of Gropius's democratic Bauhaus philosophy. At the Bauhaus, and now at the GSD, Gropius was seeking to end the "individualistic" era of "l'art pour l'art," so "utterly unrelated to the collective life of man." With the new language providing the "common key for understanding the visual arts," he claimed that people could "believe again in the basic importance of art and architecture for their daily lives." Gropius's new language would not only guide architectural expression but would serve as a "common denominator" for *all* visual arts.[14]

In order to integrate art and architecture into modern life—to make them intelligible and useful to all people—Gropius argued that the new visual language must be "objectively valid," or derived from "scientific visual facts"—"biological, physical, and psychological"—and not from individual "taste and feeling." He insisted that basing the arts on such subjective criteria had forced the artist and his work into "sad isolation." Now, with a new "objective approach" toward a language of vision—representing the "impersonal cumulative experience of successive generations"—designers could finally meet the "spiritual and material needs of human life." Gropius's new language would be based on "visual facts" pertaining to optical illusions, the relation of solids and voids in space, light and shade, color and scale; "scientific facts instead of arbitrary, subjective interpretations or formulae long since stale."[15] Only in Basic Design, Gropius argued, could students could begin to discover these facts for themselves and, at the same time, expand the vocabulary of the new modern language. To guide them, however, they needed an able instructor like Albers and not a figure like Le Boutellier, who had no understanding of the Bauhaus version of design's fundamentals. It did not matter to Gropius that Albers was a painter and printmaker primarily and not an architect. Since he believed that all modern arts—including the three fields at the GSD—should share the same language of design, he considered Albers a fine addition to the School. For his part, Hudnut had definite misgivings about the approach to design that Albers, as a nonarchitect, might bring to Harvard's architects, planners, and landscape architects.

Gropius considered the two goals of Basic Design—fostering creativity and developing a new language of vision—to be integrally related. While students would learn in the course to approach their designs "creatively," they would not do so in an unbridled fashion. Rather, they would work within the parameters of the new visual language, or "optical key." Gropius insisted that keeping within the boundaries of a "supra-individual" objective language would assure students a "foundation of solidarity for [their] spontaneous expression in art." In addition, he offered that "limitation obviously makes the creative mind inventive."[16]

Despite Gropius's relentless efforts to bring Albers to Harvard, he never joined the faculty. Hudnut once offered him a position in 1940, but with a lower salary than he was making at Black Mountain, and Albers did not accept it. Albers did come to the GSD for a few short visiting appointments during the 1940s, and he also gave several lectures to Fine Arts and GSD students. When he finally left Black Mountain in 1949, he settled at Yale rather than Harvard, as the chairman of its Department of Design.[17] Hudnut did not admit it to Gropius, but he had been reluctant from the start to bring Albers to Harvard, partly because he was neither an architect nor planner, but also because Hudnut did not want Basic Design to play a seminal role in the curriculum. Added to that, by the early 1940s, he did not want Gropius to bring any more of his Bauhaus colleagues to the faculty.

Gropius may have been unable to establish a Basic Design course before the war, but in an informal way he had already managed to bring many of its tenets into the curriculum. Since the late 1930s, he and soon a few of the American GSD instructors who were intrigued by the Bauhaus approach—especially Norman Newton in Landscape Architecture—had been incorporating Basic Design principles and exercises into their classes. In 1946, Hudnut took steps to limit the influx of Bauhaus principles in the design studios by hiring Le Boutellier to teach the first-year Design I course. In 1948, Le Boutellier retitled and slightly retooled his course into one called Basic Design. It drew on Bauhaus principles in only the vaguest way, especially given that Le Boutellier had no experience of the Bauhaus.[18] A few former students remembered the course as quite weak, and one related that during much of it "we had to manipulate materials and play with plaster of paris and cut sheet metal and so forth" without any understanding of why they did so.[19] Not surprisingly, Le Boutellier and his version of Basic Design infuriated Gropius. Gropius regarded him as "a half-baked teacher [who] was called in above my head" and whose course "has never been sound." More than Le Boutellier, Gropius blamed Hudnut for thwarting his efforts to establish the Bauhaus course at the GSD. As Gropius related early in 1950, "since [sic] more than twelve years I have fought like the dickens in favor of a decent Basic Design Course in our School; and, on account of non-understanding on the side of Dean Hudnut, I have never succeeded."[20]

By 1950, the tension between Hudnut and Gropius over Basic Design had reached the point that President Conant began to attend GSD faculty meetings as peacekeeper.[21]

Hudnut opposed the idea of instituting a Basic Design preliminary course modeled on the Bauhaus's for a number of reasons. To begin with, he took issue with Basic Design's schismatic approach to designing—the fact that students studied only formal/artistic problems in the course and that technical/construction issues came separately and only in later courses. As Gropius himself had described, the whole Bauhaus curriculum had been based on a "twofold system," on "the duality of the form master and craft master."[22] In his Bauhaus days, Gropius had explained that he employed this two-part system because he could not find teachers "competent in craft" who were also "powerful artists." Given his deep, lifelong interest in forging a "new unity" between art and technology and his "alarm" at the "complete separation of design from the execution of buildings," it is curious that Gropius ever conceived the idea to divide artistic and technical studies, even if he could not find the perfect teacher. It is especially curious that Gropius brought this dual system of training over from the other Bauhaus arts—weaving, woodworking, ceramics, sculpture, glass work, and painting—into architecture. Perhaps more than any other medium, architecture unites these two spheres of form and technique from the very outset.[23] It is particularly surprising that Gropius still wanted to perpetuate the division between artistic and technical studies decades later at the GSD. When he tried to bring this two-part pedagogical scheme to the GSD, however, Hudnut strongly objected.

Gropius's dual system of educating designers conflicted with Hudnut's definition of design as the "single process" of "imagining and making." Unlike Gropius, Hudnut sought a way of educating that forged an essential unity between the various phases of the design process. Hudnut did not view these phases or steps as belonging to two distinct spheres of "craft" and "form." Rather, he argued that technique or construction (craft) "*is* design" and "not a necessary painful adjunct to 'creative design.'"[24] Hudnut feared that if Gropius got his course at the GSD, students would learn—to an extent even greater than they were already—to treat form as something distinct from construction or making. Hudnut strongly believed that form must "lie at the heart of a student's endeavor" and that it was not "something to be added on to functional shapes at an appropriate moment."[25] Albers especially, since he had never made a building or city plan, would surely isolate form from all other aspects of designing architecture.

Hudnut not only objected to the formalistic nature of Basic Design, he opposed the idea of a "common language of visual communication" for all the arts. While Gropius wanted modern architecture to share a new machine aesthetic with other arts (which, in his view, made the painter Albers an appropriate "form master" for architects), Hudnut absolutely did not. Hudnut continued to insist that architects must be content "to capture only those things which architecture can capture." Conveying a unique "architectural idea," as he called it, was more important now—in an era governed by excessive mechanization, mass production, and standardization—than ever before.[26] In Hudnut's view, architecture could achieve real human relevance or reach people on an emotional or spiritual plane only if it spoke its own language in an eloquent way. In the late 1930s, Hudnut had identified space, community, and human values as the qualities that offered architects "peculiar opportunities" for expression. By the mid-1940s, he had added to his list "proportion, relativity, rhythmic disposition," and above all else, the idea of "civic form." By this last phrase, Hudnut was referring to the comprehensive pattern first advanced by Hegemann, and now advanced by the GSD's Planning I.[27]

. . . we are in the midst of a building boom which is crowding our cities with tedious uniformities . . .

Hudnut remarks on the architecture of the moment. (Reprinted with permission from "Architecture and the Individual," *Architectural Record* 124 [October 1958]: 170)

Hudnut and History

Hudnut also resisted Basic Design because Gropius wanted it to take the place of architectural history in the GSD curriculum and, moreover, in the minds of modern architects. Rather than learning from past architectures, Gropius wanted students to learn the fundamental principles of design solely from "practical experience." Gropius had abolished history courses at the Bauhaus, and he had wanted to do the same at the GSD, arguing that "so long as we flounder about in a limitless welter of borrowed artistic expression, we shall not succeed in giving form and substance to our own culture." In Gropius's view, history not only inhibited the making of a modern expression, it stifled individual creativity. Gropius warned that "innocent" beginning students especially must avoid history because "the awe of the masters of the past is so great that frustration may develop from timidity." For Gropius, Basic Design was the antithesis of history for it helped to "liberate the student's individuality from the dead-weight of conventions." In Basic Design, students were freed from the past and worked toward achieving the "perception and knowledge that are really [their] own." In Gropius's view, the past bore no relation to "present creation in design."[28]

Gropius did not quite succeed in eliminating history from the GSD, though he did succeed in demoting it to a minor status.[29] Hudnut had likely been pressured into allowing this diminished role for history after World War II since, by that time, he had become a great defender of the subject. Indeed, in describing an ideal design curriculum for the postwar era—which he published for a wide readership—Hudnut suggested that even "ten courses in history" would serve students well: "These are not too numerous or too arduous to create that sense of continuity, that awareness of past crises and conflicts, of the march of peoples and empires, of the impact of great renowns and ideas, which ought to furnish the mind of [the student] and illumine his forward path."[30]

Hudnut's defense of history here and in many public pronouncements made him seem to his critics—including Gropius—a traitor to the cause of modern architecture. In a typical comment, one critic wrote that, "once a strong champion of modern architecture" but grown "increasingly squeamish" on the subject, Dean Hudnut now "speaks with fond rotundity of his favorite Georgian age and architecture."[31] In fact, Hudnut's ideas of modern architecture and education included an emphasis on history from the very start. What did change markedly was his way of formulating his position. Hudnut never would have described history as a cornerstone of the new education at the time that he founded the GSD, when he was removing history books from Robinson Hall's library. The academy was the enemy to counter then, with its "excessive urgencies of romance" and rigid "dogmatism" steeped in the Beaux-Arts tradition. But by the start of postwar era, Hudnut had a different enemy, the "narrower tyrannies" of the antihistorical modernism that Gropius promoted to such great effect.[32]

Hudnut's appreciation of architectural history remained an important component of his modernism. Studying its history, he maintained, afforded students an essential "experience of architecture." Through history, students learned to see architecture not as an assemblage of individual elements but as a unified and inseparable whole. Seeing buildings or plans with their parts fused together allowed students to "feel" them with an "immediate" and "intuitive" sense and to experience what he called their "emotional content."[33] Hudnut further claimed that in the modern age, students come to us "already engineers," with a far too developed "pragmatical habit of thought." For these students, who plan to be architects without having learned the "meaning of architecture," history would play a significant role. It would "court them into aesthetic experiences, startle them into observation and new impressions, awaken them to the splendor of the art they have so fortuitously embraced."[34] Hudnut argued that history also taught students the critical lesson of viewing time as a "continuous flow." Students learn from history that they and their work belong to a grand continuity. The cities and places they design for are "not static things" but "things in process," with a momentum generated by events that lie far back in time. From history, students learn to think contextually and to make their own designs into elements of a larger, harmonious pattern.[35] Finally, because he viewed history as an endeavor that encouraged intuition, excellence, art, and continuity, Hudnut included contemporary architecture in his history courses, seeing it as part of the continuum of architectural history.

Hudnut not only defended history, but, starting in 1942, he also returned to the classroom to teach a new series of three courses on the history of civic design, a subject getting almost no attention in the 1940s. In his lectures, Hudnut traced architecture's role in the formation of cities and towns rather than offering a history of styles found in all schools of architecture. He analyzed plans from ancient times to the end of the nineteenth century by focusing on certain key moments of the past—like Periclean Athens or London in the days of Nash—instead of following a linear, historical narrative. Hudnut was broadly humanistic in his lectures, including not only buildings but paintings, sculpture, literature, technological developments, social customs, and politics as he tried to demonstrate that cities were not just "great machines for production and consumption." He emphasized the importance of design in the arrangement of cities and also the notion that buildings were elements of a greater, complex fabric.[36] In retrospect, Hudnut got mixed reviews on his teaching. The Chicago architect and GSD alumnus Ben Weese recalled that Hudnut "wasn't totally inspiring. He was very technical and dry." But Weese also noted: "The interesting thing was that Hudnut was a great humanist. I feel embarrassed that as a student, I didn't support or understand this more." Harry Cobb instead remembered Hudnut's courses as "the most affecting single learning experience . . . for many of us." And yet, he also added, "beyond this course, [Hudnut's] was not an effective view in the school."[37] For the most part, students and even faculty found Gropius and his antitraditional Bauhaus ideas far more compelling

As the feuding between Hudnut and Gropius worsened in the late 1940s, with Gropius maneuvering to get his Basic Design course into the curriculum, history took on an increasingly important and sometimes bizarre role. Perhaps Hudnut placed ever more emphasis on history's importance to architects and planners for the reason that Holmes Perkins later suggested—in order to provoke Gropius. The most dramatic example of this, according to Perkins, concerned a design that Hudnut produced for the music building on the Harvard campus. Hudnut had done virtually nothing in the way of design since the early 1920s, although on occasion he was consulted on projects. An exception occurred, however, around 1950, when someone in the Harvard administration asked him to design an extension to the university's music building, Paine Hall, an intricately detailed Federal Revival building designed by John Mead Howells in 1913. What Hudnut came up with, apparently, was nothing like the modern architecture coming out of the GSD studios. Although Hudnut's drawings are now lost and his design was never adopted, Perkins described it as similar in style to Paine Hall and not unlike Hudnut's designs of the 1920s. From Perkins's description, Hudnut's proposal resembled the streamlined Georgian addition that the Boston architect Stanley B. Parker finally got built in 1955. Whether Hudnut designed his addition as mere provocation or out of frustration with the direction in which the GSD had moved, it is hard to reconcile with his nearly lifelong argument against soulless buildings, be they empty revivals or tyrannical, formalistic modern designs.[38]

Ironically, even as he was working on Paine Hall, Hudnut caused a mild uproar in the architectural press for criticizing the stage-set Georgian architecture of Williamsburg in his keynote speech at a symposium there. His comments on Williamsburg were quite in keeping with his earlier critique of the Jeffersonian "pantheons" of Washington. They also bring to mind Ada Louise Huxtable's charge decades later that at Williamsburg "history and place as themed artifact hit the big time."[39] Hudnut began his speech, entitled "We Are No Longer Colonials," by remarking:

> I am never long in Williamsburg without feeling a strong impulse to appear in costume. A handsome blue satin waistcoat fancifully flowered would, I am sure, become me: muslin ruffles *bien brodées,* a pair of gold garters for my breeches' knees. . . . It seems to me when I look about in Williamsburg that the buildings share my mood. They too, desire a fancy dress and a quaintness of prattle and, more fortunate than I am, are indulged most delightfully in these caprices by those high couturiers, Messrs. Perry, Shaw & Hepburn.[40]

Huxtable has similarly written of her bemusement when a costumed Leon Krier and Robert A. M. Stern appeared on a television program about architecture riding though Williamsburg in an eighteenth-century carriage as they blithely admired the buildings and setting before moving on to praise a "vaguely Williamsburged" postmodern suburban shopping center.[41] Hudnut, like Huxtable years later, did not consider faux-historicism the antidote to formalistic modernism.

Gropius and Tradition

Hudnut's invitation to design an addition to Paine Hall may well have been offered to allow him a chance to respond architecturally to Gropius's newly completed project for Harvard, the Harkness Graduate Center. More than a decade after he arrived there, Harvard finally, in 1948, gave the GSD's own world-famous architect a commission to design a building for its campus. Gropius and TAC got the commission for the new Graduate Center at the urging of a few Harvard administrators who had fought hard against skeptics and critics to allow him to build on campus. Surprisingly, Hudnut was among those who spoke out in favor of Gropius.[42] Hudnut had always thought it important that Harvard demonstrate its support of Gropius, and despite their differences now, he still lobbied on Gropius's behalf. Bainbridge Bunting has pointed out, in his architectural history of Harvard, "the irony of Gropius's unexploited presence at Harvard," after the building of the "retardetaire" *moderne* Lamont Library in 1947 by Shepley, Bulfinch, and Abbott, a firm known more for its old Harvard connections than for its modern architecture.[43] It is perhaps doubly ironic that Alvar Aalto, who then held the position of professor of architecture at MIT, designed the poetry room on the second floor of Lamont, rather than Gropius. Perhaps even more ironic, Philip Johnson noted a strange juxtaposition of architectural events at Harvard in 1942: the neo-Georgian Houghton Library went up on campus the same year that President Conant boasted to the overseers in his annual report that Harvard's was "the leading school of modern architecture on this continent and perhaps in the entire world."[44]

Not only was the Graduate Center Gropius's first project for Harvard, it was also one of TAC's first major commissions. The complex housed some six hundred graduate students, a dining room for one

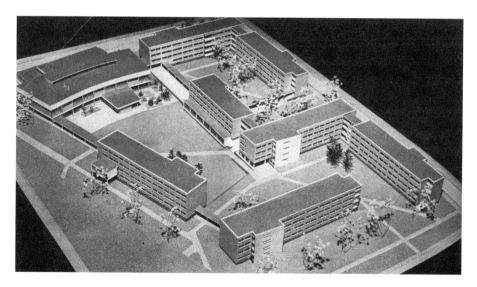

The Architects Collaborative, model of Harvard's Graduate Center. (Reprinted with permission from *Architectural Record* 104 [November 1948]: 118)

The Harvard Graduate Center, Cambridge, Mass., 1949, exterior of Commons Building. Photograph by Bernard Newman. (Courtesy of the Busch-Reisinger Museum, Harvard University Art Museums, Gift of The Architects Collaborative, BRGA.121.13)

thousand, as well as meeting rooms and recreational facilities. Perhaps in part because of the battle over history at the GSD, and surely because he designed it for venerable Harvard, Gropius preferred to speak of the Graduate Center almost solely in terms of its relation to tradition. In an article entitled "Tradition and the Center," to cite one example of his newfound appreciation for history, Gropius explained that Harvard Yard's historic pattern of "quadrangles, varying in size and confined by individually different buildings," served as the starting point for the new center. Not only did its spatial theme "fulfill an ancient requirement of the art of architecture," but Gropius extended the center's tie to tradition by portraying it as "a vital link between the historic mission of a great educational institution and the restless, inquisitive minds of the young men and women of today."[45]

Supporters of the new center also praised it for adhering to tradition, albeit the tradition of innovation. The *Architectural Record* published a model of the project under the title "Harvard Reaffirms an Old Tradition," by which it meant a Harvard tradition of supporting "contemporary innovation," citing H. H. Richardson's Sever Hall as an example. *Time* magazine wrote of the project in a similar light. "The buildings are true to an old Harvard tradition. From colonial to Bulfinch Federal, to Victorian Gothic, to nineteenth-century Romanesque, Harvard has moved with the tides of U.S. architecture."[46]

Not everyone took kindly to setting a strictly geometric, low-slung, unornamented group of buildings, with strip windows, iron and concrete columns, and buff-colored brick on the Harvard campus. Those critical of the center, especially older alumni, protested that "these new buildings show not a gleam of interest in Harvard's past nor any sense of the value of beauty." Ada Louise Huxtable called it "disappointingly pedestrian," while the description "barracks, or rather garage" and "inhuman pile" appeared in Harvard's alumni magazine.[47] In a show of solidarity with Gropius, President Conant displayed the new Graduate Center on his annual Christmas card in 1950.[48] There is no record of Hudnut commenting on the finished buildings.

In many ways, the Graduate Center worked as a manifesto of Gropius's architectural ideas. He might well have described the project as a statement of good design made at an affordable cost. Or he might have explained it as an exemplar of collaboration, first among TAC members, who then worked with Josef Albers, Herbert Bayer, Joan Miró, Jean Arp, and Richard Lippold to coordinate artworks for the buildings. Even students, in the context of a collaborative design problem, suggested features that Gropius used in the actual project.[49] Gropius did not, however, champion the Graduate Center project in terms of collaboration or affordability, preferring instead the cachet of tradition.

Gropius referred to architectural history not just in his work on the Graduate Center but also occasionally inside his GSD studio. He did so generally to make a point about his own theories rather than discussing the formal values or merits of a historical project. For example, he described the Piazza San Marco as a demonstration of his credo "unity in diversity" since a number of different architects had collaborated on its design. The base of the Parthenon verified the "scientific fact" that very long horizontal lines appear to bend inward, and a Palladian theater proved that, to give the illusion of a very axis road that ends in a building, the edges of that road must diverge away from the building. Westminster Cathedral and the Palazzo Riccardi in Florence verified some of his other "visual facts" and optical illusions. Since Gropius had a limited knowledge of architectural history, he relied on others, like

Hudnut or Giedion, to help him with historical references.[50] Gropius's "use" of history might in some ways even be compared to Sigfried Giedion's, though he certainly lacked Giedion's magisterial command of the subject. Like Giedion, however, he used the history of architecture and technology to trace the roots of modern architecture, in particular, to create for himself a place within the greater tradition. It would be interesting to know if Giedion and Gropius ever discussed Gropius's views on the place of history in the education of architects. Alas, there is no record of any such conversation.

Gropius has been condemned for his views on history by a number of critics and architects, including some of his own students. Bruno Zevi, who became a prominent architectural critic in Italy, perhaps offered the most damning commentary in the context of his 1959 essay entitled "Architecture" in the *Encyclopedia of World Art*. Zevi wrote that although many people regard Gropius "as one of the most cultivated and thoughtful" masters of modern architecture, in fact, no one had a "more reactionary and biased concept of history" than Gropius. Zevi's critique of his former teacher drew in particular from comments on history that Gropius made in a 1950 essay, "Blueprint for an Architect's Training." In that essay, as in several others, Gropius wrote that at its best, when history transcended the "intellectual collecting of facts," it explored "the conditions and reasons which have brought about the visual expression of the different periods: i.e. the changes in philosophy, in politics, and in means of production caused by new inventions."[51] Such studies, Gropius continued, "can verify principles found by the student through his own previous exercises in surface, volume, space and color; they cannot by themselves, however, develop a code of principles to be valid for present creation in design. Principles have to be established for each period from new creative work. History studies are therefore best offered to older students who have already found self expression."[52]

Zevi began his attack by considering Gropius's premise that the history of architecture meant a history of "inventions" that determined philosophical, productive, and political changes and that these, in turn, went on to shape the nature of visual expression. Zevi considered this a "brutally positivist concept" that completely ignored the "creative personality" and the "artistic process." He also scoffed at the idea that history could be used to "verify" current taste and, furthermore, that such taste had resulted from "exercises" in surface or volume. Zevi further dismissed Gropius's often repeated warning that only advanced students should study history. Zevi argued that this proved that Gropius saw history much as the academy always had and as it was viewed in the nineteenth-century battle of styles, with the only difference that Gropius regarded the modern style in opposition to the variety of the past.[53] Zevi's attack proved effective enough that Gropius blamed him for a widespread and misguided interpretation of his views on history.

Zevi's essay must have further irked Gropius by claiming Hudnut as a true progressive in the field of architecture. Describing Hudnut as "a quiet man of broad learning," Zevi wrote that Hudnut was "the first to attempt to find a mode of coexistence for modern architecture and the modern history of architecture." In doing so, Zevi contended that Hudnut offered a sound criticism of contemporary practice as well a direction for its future. Although Zevi claimed that the times were not yet propitious for this coexistence, Hudnut had anticipated one of the "most vigorous cultural battles of the 1950s."[54] It was rare in 1959 to find even a mention of Hudnut in a historical or critical account, and it was unheard of to see him hailed as a significant figure in the history of architecture.

Though well known as the great promoter of Frank Lloyd Wright and organic architecture in Italy, Zevi had proved to be quite a supporter of Hudnut's even before 1959. Zevi's concept of organic architecture included more than his hero, Wright; it included whatever he deemed "humanistic" and "democratic" in architecture—Aalto's work, for example, and Hudnut's criticism.[55] During the mid-1940s, Zevi had seen to it that two different Hudnut essays appeared in the pages of the first issues of the Italian architectural magazine *Metron,* which was published between 1945 and 1954. Hudnut's "La Casa Postmoderna," which had debuted in English only few months earlier in the *Architectural Record,* appeared in the fall of 1945, and the following year, Zevi published an Italian version of "The Political Art of Planning." Zevi had founded *Metron* as an organ for promoting the Associazione per l'Architettura Organica (APAO), which functioned as both an architectural and a political group in a country recently liberated from fascism. APAO members believed that in the same way that an "organic" (humanistic and democratic) approach would liberate modern architecture from a rigid, authoritarian modern architecture, so would humanism and democracy serve as liberating forces in Italian society. Though he genuinely sympathized with Hudnut's ideas, Zevi's enthusiasm for the dean may have also been spurred on by his disdain for Gropius and the Bauhaus master's "skeptical teaching."[56]

Design Fundamentals

Despite Hudnut's vigorous opposition to Basic Design, Gropius finally got his course in 1950, and he gave it a new name, Design Fundamentals. Hudnut had little choice but to approve the course since Gropius had persuaded both the GSD faculty to vote in favor of it and President Conant to fund it with $25,000 from his discretionary account. Design Fundamentals got approved on a two-year trial basis only. When two years were up, Hudnut would evaluate it and determine if he wanted the course to continue.

Once Gropius had his course, he had to find the right person to teach it. Hudnut had remained set against Albers, and now the Harvard administration refused to bring on a senior professor for a course that might last only two years. Gropius considered others with Bauhaus affiliations—Herbert Bayer, Naum Gabo, and Gyorgy Kepes—but because he could offer only a small salary, he had to content himself with a less renowned figure. The person he finally hired, Richard Filipowski, did not come from the circle of European modernists but had studied under Moholy-Nagy at the Institute of Design and was teaching there when Gropius came upon him. With a strong recommendation from Gropius's friend Serge Chermayeff, then head of the ID, and with examples of his work, Filipowski persuaded Gropius that he understood the principles and methods of the Bauhaus Basic Design course. He had received a higher salary at his post in Chicago, but Filipowski went to Harvard because "the founder of the Bauhaus asked me to.[57]

Filipowski indeed seemed a true disciple of the Bauhaus. Having studied with Moholy-Nagy, he had come to believe that only in a course like Basic Design could beginning architecture students learn "the elements through which architecture is given form." He claimed that students in the preliminary course could discover for themselves the "aesthetic values of our era" that stem from an "organic attitude to life, contemporary space-time understanding, new materials and industrial techniques." Much like Gropius, he opposed having history in the architecture curriculum, and once at Harvard, he quickly joined ranks with him against Hudnut's view. Filipowski seemed to dig directly at Hudnut when, in the context of an exhibition of GSD students' work

Design I. Design Fundamentals
(a total of 18 class and outside hours weekly)

Tuesday and Thursday, 2-5 (a total of 18 class and outside hours weekly). Throughout the Year. Mr. Filipowski and Mr. Kessler.

By means of comprehensive studio experiments and discussion, the student discovers the *fundamental concepts of space,* function, scale, slight and color, by which these are expressed and controlled to give form.

Sensory perception is developed by working with graphic media as well as with hand and power tools.

Through experiments involving structural, kinetic and visual mans, the student learns to *organize and interpret space.*

By using various materials the student evolves *a plastic understanding* and discovers the structural, visual and spatial qualities of each material. His growing knowledge of materials is then assimilated by building three-dimensional constructions which simultaneously serve as models to learn *the master of graphic projection and descriptive geometry.*

Techniques in draftsmanship are developed organically as a result of graphic experiments in texture variations, in speed of line, in linear weights, tone volume and transparency

(Course description taken from the *Harvard University Official Register, 1951,* 28)

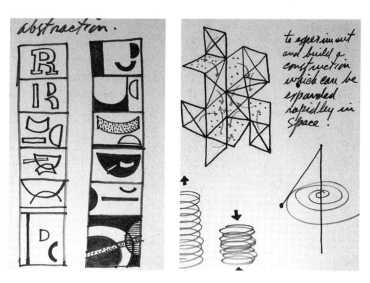

Richard Filipowski, "Abstraction" (*left*) and "A Construction That Can Be Rapidly Expanded in Space" (*right*). These were among a group of drawings that Filipowski used to persuade Gropius that he was the right person to teach Design Fundamentals at Harvard, which was modeled on the Bauhaus's preliminary course, Basic Design (*Vorkurs*). (Courtesy of Richard Filipowski)

Two-dimensional design exercises by GSD students in Design Fundamentals. (Courtesy of Richard Filipowski)

in Design Fundamentals, he claimed that "pedantic lectures on aesthetics, spiced with delicious historical anecdotes and full of well-turned phrases are obsolete as instruments of architectural education." Filipowski instead wanted his students to combine the "intuitive method of the arts, the logic of the engineer and the system of the scientist."[58]

In its first year, some seventy students took Filipowski's Design Fundamentals, both graduate students and undergraduates majoring in architectural sciences. They attended two hours of lecture six days a week and spent twenty hours weekly in the new workshop in Robinson Hall's basement, experimenting with power and hand tools.[59] Much to Hudnut's dismay, with all the time it required of students, Design Fundamentals took the place of Planning I as the major course of the common first year, shifting the GSD's emphasis away from urban design and toward the laws of abstract design.[60]

Filipowski modeled his course directly on the Bauhaus preliminary course. In Design Fundamentals as in the *Vorkurs,* students worked to "enlarge [their] experiences of space and scale perception, explore concepts of process and form, and master control of the resulting techniques." By the end of the year, Filipowski intended them to have discovered a "common denominator of design" that assured sound judgment in any problem they encountered.[61] The students worked in both two and three dimensions, preparing themselves for the drafting board and for designing buildings. In order to develop a sense of form and control in three dimensions, they studied the inherent qualities of materials— wood, paper, plaster, wire, sheet metal—by cutting, bending, scoring, or expanding. Using power tools on these same materials, they looked for structural, aesthetic, and volume changes in them, and they created moving sculptures that defined space or, as Filipowski described it, how "actual motion generates time-space."[62] The students' two-dimensional exercises focused on the tactile, structural, and spatial properties of various surfaces. They used a number of different media—charcoal, crayon, water, or pastels—to produce a range of color variations, to show the emotional nature of color, and to produce warmth, coldness, or inten-

Three-dimensional design exercise by GSD students in Design Fundamentals. (Courtesy of Richard Filipowski)

sity. They also described objects with line, sometimes working at great speed.[63]

Design Fundamentals proved to be tremendously popular, and it converted a number of students to Gropius's way of thinking and the Bauhaus idea.[64] As one devoted student commented in the *Harvard Crimson,* Design Fundamentals "is invaluable because it supplies the architect with his basic tools. Without a knowledge of the fundamentals of space, form and color, the architect's education is incomplete." Another student, claiming to speak for the class as a whole, found Design Fundamentals so powerful that it "can change a student's entire approach to creative activity and, indeed, to life." He argued, much as Gropius did, that "no amount of specialized training will do any good unless it is founded upon the solidity of such an approach and unless people are prepared for life in their own generation."[65]

Several members of the GSD faculty also came to view Design Fundamentals as an essential course in educating architects and urban designers. The course's popularity among the architects was not surprising since the faculty of that department in 1950 included three graduates of Gropius's Master Class and one of his partners at TAC.[66] The landscape architect Norman Newton, a product of the Beaux-Arts era who had undergone a conversion to modernism since joining the faculty in 1939, supported Filipowski's course most enthusiastically. For several years, Newton had been holding weekly discussions with first-year students

GSD student work from Design Fundamentals. (Courtesy of Richard Filipowski)

promoting design "as an integral part of modern life and as an approach to positive creative action." Newton now considered Design Fundamentals vital to this cause, claiming "the work [in the course] has had a most salutary effect in heightening the students' perceptional awareness and in developing a type of creative power not dealt with in other areas of study." Newton believed that the course could open the eyes of all undergraduates no matter what their area of study, and he wanted to make it available to all Harvard students.[67] A memo found among Filipowski's papers indicates that other members of the GSD faculty also wanted Design Fundamentals among the required core courses in Harvard's General Education Program. That program, widely discussed on campuses throughout the United States, grew out of a Harvard committee appointed during the war years to study the "Objectives of a General Education in a Free Society." Led by President Conant, the committee issued the famous *Redbook* in 1946, in which it recommended six year-long courses that would encourage students to communicate clearly and to make sound judgments. According to Filipowski's memo, Design Fundamental's proponents argued that the course fit well into the General Education scheme since it provided a "blueprint for the synthesis of art, science and technology."[68]

Not everyone on the faculty supported the Design Fundamentals course. Some felt, as Hudnut did, that the course was not necessary, that it took up too much of the students' schedule, and that it did not leave enough time for their "professional training." Hugh Stubbins took issue with his colleagues in the Architecture Department by arguing that the course "would be better placed [in] a high school" because it lacked any "theory of architectural design." He questioned the idea that cutting out paper shapes might help in designing architecture. Stubbins also considered Design Fundamentals outdated since it was based on a course taught almost three decades earlier at the Bauhaus. He insisted that "we should be able to improve on that now."[69]

For Gropius, not only had the Bauhaus course remained an absolutely valid model for educating modern architects, but his belief in the power of Basic Design had grown even stronger because he found its essential principles upheld by new research. Along with artists and architects like himself, the late Moholy-Nagy, Albers, or Gyorgy Kepes who promoted the ideas of Design Fundamentals, Gropius pointed to new research in the fields of cultural criticism, education, and psychology, most importantly by the English critic Herbert Read and by Earl C. Kelley, a somewhat obscure professor of education at Wayne University in Detroit.

Gropius knew Read from his time in London, where Read, like Gropius, had belonged to the circle of intellectuals and modern artists living in Hampstead. He and Read had talked at length during the nearly three years Gropius spent in London, and Gropius even claimed that their discussions had inspired Read to write his book *Education through Art,* a study of creative education for children. Gropius considered Read's work essential to developing a modern design language, and he found it wholly sympathetic to his own pedagogical approach.[70] The argument of the book was one that Gropius often reiterated, that "art should be the basis of education" for all students. Much like Gropius, Read blamed social ills on the "suppression of spontaneous creative abilities in the individual." If art were made the center of education, replacing "conformity and imitation," children would develop independence and strength of character. In Read's proposed curriculum, as in Gropius's, art would "foster the growth of what is individual in each human being" while assuring that the student also belonged to a larger collective group. Read believed that learning thrived in a workshop setting and not in a formal classroom, and he promoted the idea of school as a "center of creative activity."[71] Because Read came to similar conclusions from a different route than the one he had taken, Gropius found his own ideas endowed with new authority.

Four years after Read published *Education through Art,* Gropius came upon Earl C. Kelley's new book, *Education for What Is Real* (1947). He quickly made that book required reading for GSD students. Kelley wrote about the significance to education of new findings in the nature of perception and knowing by researchers at the Dartmouth Eye Institute in New Hampshire.[72] For a number of years, the institute had been designing and constructing demonstrations that helped explain the origin and nature of visual perception. In one example, the institute built a distorted room that had two optical illusions associated with it: people or objects in the room appeared to grow or shrink when moving from one corner to another, and the trapezoidal-shaped room also appeared cubic when viewed from certain points.[73] This and many other projects at the institute proved to Kelley that each human being perceives differently and that one's perception derives from one's prior experience. What is "real" is what the individual makes of the objects around him.[74]

Kelley ultimately argued in his book that "perception is a directive for action." By understanding how people perceive—how perception is induced and where it comes from—one can better understand the nature of human beings and can thereby plan for education. Kelley's book elicited a laudatory preface by John Dewey, who claimed that the book filled an important gap in our understanding of the relation between humans and their environment and that it offered a new point of departure for educating children.[75]

After 1947, Gropius referred to Kelley's book and to the experiments at Dartmouth in many of his lectures and essays, and the subject took on great importance in his classroom. In fact, Kelley's book may well have been the sole text that Gropius ever required students to read. Most GSD courses did not require any particular texts since, as one faculty member explained, "we are stimulating inventiveness and imagination with the students and feel their minds should not be frozen on any set patterns."[76] According to William Lyman, an alumnus of Gropius's class and later an assistant in it, students treasured their copies of Kelley's book.[77] Gropius was so smitten with the book and its objective approach that he sent off a copy to Jack Pritchard in London, explaining that it "has intrigued me very much for the statements made in it are not an individual opinion but backed up with the newest scientific research by the Dartmouth Eye Institute."[78]

Gropius's use of the Dartmouth studies differed slightly from Kelley's. While Kelley saw in them the basis for formulating an educational

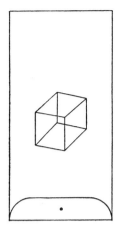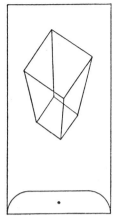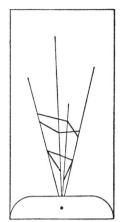

SIDE VIEW

FIGURE B. This is what we see when we look behind the scenes. The one at the left is a cube made of wires. The center one is a drawing on a flat surface. The third is a set of wires with strings on them. This latter one is also shown in a side view. The second and third ones do not resemble cubes in any regard. They lack rectilinear sides and one of them lacks three dimensions.

Figure B from Earl Kelley, *Education for What Is Real* (New York: Harper, 1947), 27.

(Copyright 1947 by Earl C. Kelley, renewed (c) by Kate Winifred Gilmore, reprinted by permission of HarperCollins Publishers)

scheme for children, Gropius focused on the possibilities the studies offered designers who were trying to elicit certain thoughts and feelings from those experiencing their work. In particular, Gropius liked to cite an experiment that showed that quite different materials could cause the same pattern on the retina and result in the same sensation. A viewer looked through three different peepholes, each the size of the pupil of an eye, and well lit at the back. In each case, the viewer saw a cube that looked substantially like the others. In actuality, the peepholes contained very different objects. The first contained a wire cube, the second a drawing on a plane with a series of parallel lines, and the third contained a series of strings stretched between wires. The three had looked alike to the viewer because the peephole had limited vision to one eye and also had established a point of view. Without the peepholes, the viewer easily distinguished the three objects. Gropius found in this and in other such experiments, ideas for controlling the viewer's response to design. Kelley's book explored issues relating to something that Gropius had long been interested in understanding—"what influences the psyche of man in terms of light, scale, form and color."[79]

The Bitter End

Design Fundamentals gained wide acceptance not only at Harvard but also in the larger architectural community. Within a few years, versions of the course were taught at several different schools, and by 1960 almost every architecture program offered a course in basic design. The fact that many of Gropius's former students were teaching at these schools surely helped spread the gospel of a Basic Design course. That gospel was not held quite so sacred at Harvard. Two years after Gropius and Filipowski began Design Fundamentals, Hudnut canceled the course. President Conant's funding had expired, and Hudnut neither wanted the course nor wanted to pay for it out his already strapped GSD budget.[80] Hudnut loathed what he called the "psychological pedagogics" of Gropius's course, and he refused to "exalt such education, even when it includes an experience with newspaper pulp, with the name *Design;* or dissemble its insignificance with such terms as *basic* or *fundamental.*" The abilities to question, observe, analyze, and feel the power of buildings should precede all other processes in architecture schools, Hudnut argued, including "exercises in paper-cutting and the making of abstractions in wire, important as these are."[81] Ultimately, he considered that the course was "not a necessary one" and that it did not "leave enough time for the students' professional training."[82]

Gropius resigned from the GSD in protest against Hudnut's decision in the summer of 1952, one year ahead of his mandatory retirement. Before he did so, he pleaded his case for Design Fundamentals before a universitywide audience in the *Harvard Crimson,* arguing that "my whole faculty is in favor of Design Fundamentals" and that it was being dropped solely because "the dean is against it."[83] The simmering feud between Hudnut and Gropius burst into the open, with the *Crimson* offering a juicy account. The student paper blared in bold headlines that the "Gropius-Hudnut Feud Dominated Last Years," and it sided openly with Gropius, who, it claimed, had "wielded enormous influence over the entire student body, even over those he did not teach directly."[84] According to the *Crimson:* "Walter Gropius became almost a spiritual leader of the Graduate School of Design. To the outside world he was the school; to much of the faculty, he, not Dean Joseph Hudnut, set the policy; and to the students, he was the ideal architect, the master mold into which they poured their talents. . . . When Gropius resigned this fall, many felt the school had lost its heart."[85] As for Hudnut, he had his supporters among the faculty, students, and alumni, though they were far fewer in number and far less vociferous than those favoring Gropius. Essentially they held the position that Gropius had done everything to "thwart the efforts of Hudnut to create a comprehensive curriculum in environmental design."[86] The more common view depicted Hudnut as "reactionary" usually found "skulking behind lantern slides of the past." The *Crimson* also imputed to Hudnut "completely personal" reasons for feuding with Gropius. He was envious of Gropius's popularity, according to the paper, and eager to "pry him from his perch of preeminence."[87]

There was some truth in this portrayal. Gropius, who was sixty-eight at the time he resigned from the GSD, had been due to retire three years earlier at the age of sixty-six, in accord with Harvard policy.[88] The university made only rare exception to the retirement rule for the most eminent of its scholars. Back in 1949, Gropius had argued that he belonged in this distinguished group, and he petitioned President Conant to extend his tenure. In the meantime, Hudnut had urged Conant to enforce Gropius's retirement. Conant did grant Gropius an extension until 1953, and that extension effectively ended Hudnut's working relationship with Gropius. As Holmes Perkins has described, "from that time on, it was impossible between the two of them."[89]

Hudnut may not have known that back in 1950, Gropius had no interest in retiring in three years' time. Rather, Gropius began to hope that when Hudnut retired from the GSD, as he was due to in 1952, he might be able to continue teaching at the School. Gropius let this hope be known to some of his friends with influence at Harvard and in the architectural field. In turn, they joined forces and contacted President Conant, asking him to consider letting Gropius continue his teaching. As Serge Chermayeff, then head of the ID, wrote to Conant:

> The GSD, under the leadership of Professor Gropius, has set the standard in architectural education which is being emulated by schools everywhere. Everything that the GSD has achieved is identified directly with Gropius himself. We feel that the break in the continued development of this work would be not only tragic for Harvard, but would be a tremendous loss to architects and prospective architects everywhere. . . . Gropius's premature withdrawal from education would be deeply felt all over the world. I and my colleagues most respectfully ask for your intervention to prevent this disaster from occurring.[90]

Gropius's eventual biographer and GSD alumnus, Reginald Isaacs, took the occasion to suggest to Conant not only that Gropius stay at Harvard, but that he take over the dean's position when Hudnut retired. Isaacs was speaking not only for himself, he told Conant, but he was "familiar with the attitudes of your faculty members, students, and alumni." As he made his case for Gropius, Isaacs offered backhanded praise to Hudnut for having brought the great master to Harvard, for his "able rebuilding of the GSD, and his distinguished writing." However, Isaacs added, "it seems to many of us that Mr. Hudnut's contribution has been made and is recognized and that he has no cause to envy the still-growing reputation of Mr. Gropius."

> Some of us are led to believe that Mr. Hudnut's attitude toward Mr. Gropius is motivated by fear of possible challenge to the development of the GSD as he has outlined it. Although none of us has assumed that Mr. Gropius wishes to succeed Mr. Hudnut . . . should the Board of Overseers and the Administration recognize that Mr. Gropius has the physical and mental vitality to continue indefinitely and decide to extend his tenure, they may wisely choose to select him as Dean Hudnut's successor.[91]

Having long supported both Gropius and Hudnut, Conant considered their estrangement "almost tragic," and he would not agree to extend Gropius's tenure this second time. It was perhaps for this reason that Gropius came to be, in Conant's words, "less than enthusiastic about the support he received from the Harvard administration" by the time he left the university.[92]

Shortly after Gropius's resignation, the *Crimson* painted the GSD as "a school without direction," a place "hardly worth retaining." In addition to Gropius, several other faculty had left the School: Holmes Perkins, glad to leave his feuding colleagues behind, took on the deanship at the University of Pennsylvania's School of Fine Arts in 1951, where he put together a remarkable program of his own with a faculty that included Louis I. Kahn, Robert Venturi, and Ian McHarg, among others. Richard Filipowski went to MIT, and a number of nontenured planning faculty lost their jobs at the GSD. Hudnut made several temporary appointments to fill the vacant positions and to keep costs down. Meanwhile, Hugh Stubbins took over Gropius's post as acting chairman of the Architecture Department. As a result of these changes, the GSD offered a "poor atmosphere for academic development," according to the *Crimson*. The professors who did stay feared their programs might fall victim to the budget; equipment in the studios had worn out, and the library operated with inadequate funds. At the same time, faculty meetings were filled with tension, and "everything said by a professor or instructor [was] tainted with the bitter feelings of the quarrel."[93]

Hudnut reached retirement age in 1952, but President Conant asked him to remain at the GSD one more year as they chose his successor. Appointing a new dean of the School would be one of President Conant's final acts at Harvard. Conant had submitted his resignation and would assume his new job as U.S. high commissioner in Germany effective January 1953.[94] As he left Harvard, Conant took note in his final annual report of the changes that had taken place at Harvard during his twenty-year tenure, singling out the GSD above all else:

> The most drastic change in any school or department has occurred in what was the School of Architecture and is now the School of Design. A new dean appointed a few years after I took office soon introduced new professors and a totally new outlook. This radical departure from traditional architecture and architectural instruction had first to maintain itself against heavy conservative pressures from outside. But before long others followed our lead; what eighteen years ago was a startling novelty is now accepted as basic doctrine in all architectural schools in the United States.[95]

On a more personal note, after Giedion sent Conant a copy of his new book, *Walter Gropius: Work and Teamwork* in 1954, Conant thanked him for acknowledging in it that as president of Harvard he had a played a part in revolutionizing the course of architectural history. Moreover, Conant noted how rare it was for a "static cultural tradition" to undergo such radical transformation within the context of a university. He added, the "real credit goes to Dean Hudnut."[96]

Although Hudnut retired from the GSD without fanfare, he did not quite depart in silence. Before leaving his post, he clarified in writing and in a series of public lectures some important differences between his concept of modern architecture and that which had emanated from the GSD during his final decade at the School. He did so in part by republishing a number of his essays that had appeared in assorted journals over the last fifteen years in a book entitled *Architecture and the Spirit of Man.* Issued by Harvard University Press in 1949, the book was reviewed in nearly every architectural journal, most often favorably but without much depth. The German critic and architect Paul Zucker offered the most interesting commentary on Hudnut's published campaign for a humanistic modern architecture and urbanism. Zucker admired the book's "emotional and intellectual approach to modern architecture" and claimed that it pointed to the right direction for the further development of modern architectural theory. The interesting part came when Zucker noted that "a whole generation of young American architects led by groups in California, by pupils of Mies van der Rohe, George Howe," and a few nameless others, "have shown in their work that the theories of Dean Hudnut are already in the process of being realized." Zucker's mention of Howe and his allusion to Wurster (the leader in California to whom he was likely referring), both close friends of Hudnut and openly sympathetic to his views on architecture, were far less surprising than the mention of Mies. Zucker was right, however, in relating Hudnut's theories to Mies's work. Hudnut rarely paid tribute to individual architects, and yet, a few years after leaving Harvard, he confirmed that Mies's work did point in the direction that he, too, wanted for modern architecture: "The magic in the work of Mies van der Rohe is an exposition of a human dignity discovered in the technologies of modern structure. This art is not, as many suppose, doctrinaire, but intimate and personal—and I shall dare, considering its life and consistency over the years, to call it, as I might call the art of Cezanne, impassioned."[97] Hudnut had long admired Mies's architecture, and one can only imagine what might have happened had the Harvard professorship gone to Mies, as it almost did back in 1936, rather than to Gropius.

Hudnut's real swan song before leaving Harvard came in the midst of the crisis over Design Fundamentals. In May 1952, he delivered a series of three lectures, "The Three Lamps of Modern Architecture," at his alma mater, the University of Michigan. In essence, Hudnut argued in the lectures that modern architects had taken a wrong turn by allowing three concepts "alien" to their art to dominate it during the last few decades. While these concepts, or "lamps," may have illuminated architecture by throwing into "sudden brilliance" some single aspect of it, like a tower or a facade, they also threw the rest of the building into shadow. The lamp of progress, the lamp of nature, and the lamp of democracy each ultimately obscured what Hudnut considered the real purpose of modern architecture: to express the "spiritual life of our time" in constructed forms, shapes, and spaces unique to the medium of architecture.

Hudnut first took on the idea of progress, explaining that modern architects had accepted that the machine would create a new world order, a glorious technological utopia. They not only accepted it, they grew preoccupied with the promise of spangling new technologies and failed to look below the surface for the ideas, feelings, and values that guided the "spirit of man" in modern times. Moreover, Hudnut argued that the methods by which modern architects expressed their fascination with progress were not the methods of the architect. Rather than making the idea of progress integral to constructed form, they merely "associated" their work with modernity, flaunting structure, utility, and severity with exaggerated cantilevers, unshadowed walls, and immense quantities of plate glass. As they brought their techniques to the surface, these modern architects may have believed that they were expressing the "inward nature" from which they had sprung.[98] Hudnut's point was that they had not.

In the "Lamp of Nature," Hudnut argued that the modernists had also been equating the principles of their art with those of nature and especially of "organic order." They believed that "organic order," like that present in nature, should govern the arrangement and form of their structures, with every element operating in harmony with all others to

"That mighty cantilever which projects my house over a kitchen yard or a waterfall, the lacustrian vertiginious Lally column, the 'stressed skin' and the flexible wall . . . these strike my eyes but not my heart." (Reprinted with permission from Hudnut, "The Post-Modern House," *Architectural Record* 97 [May 1945]: 72)

Buildings are playthings to entertain us
. . . astonish us like acrobats . . .

Illustration from Hudnut's essay "Architecture and the Individual." (Reprinted with
permission from *Architectural Record* 124
[October 1958]: 165)

maintain the life of the whole. As nature's lamp cast its glaring light on their work, they surrendered their art to strict calculation and neglected their own ideas and feelings in the process of design.[99]

The lamp of democracy also distracted modern architects from the real purpose of their art. In the final lecture, Hudnut reproached those who mistook "social purpose" and "scientific efficiency" for architecture. While Hudnut also favored buildings with a democratic purpose—public housing and public schools—he did not favor buildings that associated themselves with democracy by merely "describing" it. By this he meant those plain buildings, overtly economical, oozing with equality or sameness. The lamp of democracy, like those of nature and progress, had also cast its blinding light into the eyes of modern architects and obscured the real significance of architecture, the expression of idea or feeling in architectural form.

Hudnut ended his lectures, which were published as a booklet in 1952, by explaining that he had never intended to "defeat" modern architecture but always to "exalt" it "by bringing it within the channel of a greater tradition."[100] Rather than asking, "Is it progressive? Is it organic? Is it democratic?" he proposed that form, expression, invention and resourcefulness serve as the basis for excellence in modern architecture. By form, he meant the well-tried expedients of rhythmic disposition, proportion, massing, and also those "irrational preferences" that bring individuality and vigor into design. Finally, Hudnut argued that invention, drama, fantasy, color, art, and surprise are essential to architecture, even modern architecture.[101]

Hudnut received a few letters about *The Three Lamps,* one of them, interestingly enough, a congratulatory note from the maverick GSD alumnus Philip Johnson. Hudnut responded gratefully to Johnson, writing that "it is a great satisfaction to me to know that you are in agreement with me on the things that I said because, as you know, I value your judgment in these matters very highly indeed."[102] It may well be that Johnson's famous lecture "The Seven Crutches of Modern Architecture," delivered the following year at Harvard, took its cue from

Hudnut's *Three Lamps*. Much as Hudnut had, Johnson used the Ruskinian trope to get across some similar points—that architects had for too long confused their art with mere technology, utility, and economy. As obituaries marking Johnson's death in 2005 have reaffirmed, this was among the most celebrated speeches of Johnson's long career. Far more irreverent than Hudnut, Johnson had lambasted the design "crutches" he had learned to use at Harvard under Gropius—structure, pretty plan making, utility, and cheapness among them. In an oft-quoted line from another speech, Johnson went where the diplomatic Hudnut would never go: "I would rather sleep in Chartres Cathedral with the nearest toilet two blocks away than in a Harvard house with back-to-back bathrooms."[103]

Aftermath

In what the *Crimson* called "a clear-cut victory for those favoring the policies of Walter Gropius," in 1953 President Conant appointed the Spanish modernist José Luis Sert as the new dean of the GSD as Hudnut stepped down.[104] Gropius and Sert knew each other well, and the Spanish modernist had been on Gropius's short list of people he wanted to head the GSD. Sert not only took over Hudnut's position but also Gropius's role as head of the Architecture Department. By putting one person in the GSD's two most important posts, the School intended to avoid the power struggle of the previous years and advance a single point of view—presumably one akin to Gropius's.

True to expectation, Sert quickly brought back and injected new life into Gropius's Bauhaus-like preliminary course, Design Fundamentals. He also hired a number of Gropius's close allies to teach at the GSD, among them Sigfried Giedion, Naum Gabo, Serge Chermayeff, and Reginald Isaacs, Gropius's former student and future adulatory biographer. It seemed clear to everyone that Gropius's legacy would continue on during the Sert years. In addition to reviving Gropius's course and to his new hires, Sert, then the president of CIAM, also brought to Harvard his interest in "urban design." Sert had assumed his new post at a time of grave crisis for the city—with ever-increasing numbers of slums, deteriorating environmental conditions, and myriad unmet human needs. The problems he had addressed in *Can Our Cities Survive?* had worsened, and as head now of the world's leading School of Design, he determined to act by making urban design his greatest priority. In doing so, Sert built on the groundwork that Hudnut had laid during his seventeen years at the GSD. The commonalities between Sert's ideas of "urban" design and Hudnut's "civic" design are striking.

Hudnut would certainly have agreed with Sert's definition of urban design as "the most creative phase of city planning and that in which imagination and artistic capacities can play a more important part."[105] Moreover, Hudnut and Sert shared ideas of educating students to take part in the process of city design. Like Hudnut, Sert regarded city design as an endeavor that required the engagement of all three of the GSD fields. While the disciplines still vigilantly guarded their precious boundaries, Sert argued for a "synthesis" or "integration" among an array fields for the cause of urban design. Though we are living through "a period of a cult to the individual and the genius," he wrote, "with all due respect to genius, it is not to them that we owe our best cities."[106] Hudnut might well have written these same words.

In 1956, Sert took his first important step in promoting his cause by initiating a series of conferences on the city and its design, not unlike the 1942 Conference on Urbanism that Hudnut and Gropius had run. Hudnut had also organized a second such conference in 1949, entitled "Debunk: A Critical Review of Accepted Planning Principles."[107] The first several of Sert's Urban Design Conferences—which met on an almost annual basis until 1970—drew many practitioners and critics in all three of the GSD's fields to discuss the fundamental nature and meaning of urban design as well as the role of the planner, architect, and landscape architect in its practice.[108] Partly in response to these conferences, in 1960 Sert took another important step in advancing the cause of the city: he created a new interdisciplinary GSD program in "Urban Design," the first of its kind at an American university. The GSD would now turn out students educated to give shape to cities and towns, much as Hudnut had always wanted. Not only is that program still active and lively today, but in recent years it has served as the model for numerous others now in place at many other universities. As he built up the new Urban Design program at Harvard, Sert relied on the foundation that Hudnut had laid of an interdisciplinary and humanistic approach to city design.

Almost no one noticed the debt that Sert owed to the former dean, who remained deep in the shadow of Gropius. In 1968, to mark the occasion of Hudnut's death, and in praise of Sert's urbanistic efforts a year shy of his expected retirement from the GSD, an interesting letter appeared in the *Harvard Alumni Bulletin,* written by Robert Weinberg, a city planner and architect in New York and a Harvard architecture alumnus from the 1920s. Weinberg had remained active at the GSD since his own time there and had been a rare supporter of Hudnut in his dispute with Gropius. Printed under the caption "Dean Hudnut's Dream," Weinberg's letter claimed that "it was only through the fortunate resignation of Gropius in 1953 that Dean Sert was able to carry Dean Hudnut's great dream to its present state of fruition." Sert, he argued, understood not only the "urban crisis" of the 1960s but also "the contribution Harvard must be prepared to make to its solutions by further strengthening the all-inclusive program in the field of design initiated by Dean Hudnut."[109]

With the exception of Weinberg, the assumption has remained that with Sert's appointment as head of the GSD, Gropius had scored yet another victory over Hudnut. He had not only overshadowed Hudnut during their fifteen years together at the GSD, advancing his Bauhaus-like program with far greater success than Hudnut had done in advancing the cause of civic design, but now the Gropius legacy would carry on with Sert. That has long been the accepted view. In some ways, given the faculty that Sert brought to the School and the revival of Design Fundamentals, the accepted view has merit. However, if the creation of the Urban Design program is Sert's greatest contribution to the GSD, as many historians have argued, then it is Hudnut who scored the real victory.[110] In his years at the GSD, Sert carried on and developed the tradition of educating for the activity of city design that Hudnut had first brought to Harvard in 1936.

Years after his retirement, Gropius remained a heroic figure at the GSD, with celebrations, symposia, lectures, and exhibitions held in his honor there. Hudnut, in contrast, ended his association with the school abruptly after he retired. He and his wife, Claire, moved out of Cambridge to Dover, Massachusetts, where they lived, ironically, in their first modern house, a modest, economical, postwar, international style house, in a calm rural setting. Even more ironically, George Le Boutellier, who had taught the version of Basic Design that had so angered Gropius, had designed that house in Dover for himself and sold it to the Hudnuts when he left Harvard.[111] Hudnut continued to teach the history of architecture and urbanism after he left Harvard, first at Colby College in Maine as a distinguished fellow for one year, and then at MIT, where he taught his civic design courses until the early 1960s. He also

Vote for Grope, celebration of Gropius's eightieth birth-day at Harvard. (Courtesy of the Pritchard Papers, University of East Anglia)

held several major advisory positions overseeing architectural and ur-ban design projects, and he continued publishing his critical essays in a range of different journals.[112]

Unlike Gropius, who still lived in Lincoln and practiced with TAC in projects from Baghdad to New York, Hudnut led a reclusive life in his final years, especially after his wife's death in 1963. His first contact with the GSD came thirteen years after he left, when he was invited by Rob-ert Weinberg in 1966 to address an alumni meeting and fund-raising event for the School. Hudnut accepted with some misgivings because of "'the old dispute between Hudnut and Gropius'—that has long been ended and (I hope) forgotten."[113] By then, Hudnut and Gropius, who were in their eighties, had established an amiable, though occasional, correspondence. In accepting his invitation Hudnut told Weinberg:

> It is true that I differed from Gropius in respect to a principle (and prac-tice) of teaching. I still differ from him. But I felt that he had a right to in-troduce his method and principle in whatever instruction was considered by him to be essential. Gropius is a great man but he does not always know how things are done. He does not always know his friends. Please be sure that I shall make no reference to these considerations when, and if, I am present at any alumni gathering. If I make any reference to Gropius it will be to speak of his great value to the School of Design.[114]

When Hudnut addressed the alumni meeting in 1966, he found a far more receptive audience than he had fifteen years earlier at Harvard. In the years since he had been at the GSD, the concept of modern architecture and urbanism that Gropius had promoted at the school had indeed flourished, but it had also been subject to careful scrutiny and criticism by the likes of Jane Jacobs, Robert Venturi, and others, including a number of GSD alumni. After the completion of the Pan Am Building in 1963, Gropius's critics multiplied. In that project, as Ada Louise Huxtable explained, we saw "the betrayal of his own teachings of social and urban responsibility."[115] Three years later, Hudnut's call for a humanistic modern architecture and city no longer sounded "squeamish" or anachronistic, even to Gropius's devoted former students. Many of them now recognized the failings of universally valid forms, emphatic functionalism, untouchable perfection, and technological utopianism.

Before leaving the dean's post at the GSD, in the midst of their bitter feud, Hudnut had paid a huge compliment to Gropius for his contribution to the architectural field. In 1951, before the advent of the Pritzker Prize, Serge Chermayeff circulated a petition among members of the architectural community to recommend Le Corbusier for the Nobel Peace Prize. When asked to sign, Hudnut told him, "I cannot join with you in recommending Le Corbusier . . . if any architect should be recommended for such an honor, it ought to be Gropius." Hudnut's response made a great enough impression on Chermayeff that he recounted it twenty years later to Ise Gropius, who had not heard the story before.[116]

Gropius was one of the few people to attend Hudnut's funeral in 1968. A year later, thousands responded to Gropius's death. Newspapers and magazines throughout the world carried extensive obituaries as friends, former students, and associates all paid tribute. Yet despite these homages, by 1969 the world that Gropius had done so much to create was no longer held in high regard. As Ada Louise Huxtable wrote in her *New York Times* obituary of Gropius, "The death of Walter Gropius did not mark the end of an era: the era was already over." Huxtable felt compelled to remind her readers, in the title of her obituary, that "he was not irrelevant."[117]

Hudnut had long been forgotten by the time of his death, even though the fate of his "post-modern" architecture and urbanism had also changed. By 1968, Hudnut's call for buildings and cities marked by history, spontaneity, contextualism, symbols, and individual concerns was being echoed by architects and urbanists throughout the world. Although Hudnut may have had no direct bearing on this turn of fortune, he surely had tremendous foresight. While later critics attacked modernists for what they had done to the postwar landscape—with decentralization, standardization, and abstract design—as early as the 1940s, Hudnut challenged them for what they were about to do. Though not always heard, in a clear and often ironic voice, Hudnut offered compelling ideas for an alternative kind of modern architecture, urbanism, and design education at a difficult time and from an unexpected place. For these reasons, his part in the history of modern architecture is relevant.

NOTES

ABBREVIATIONS
AAA   Archives of American Art, Smithsonian Institution
       Alfred Barr Papers; Marcel Breuer Papers; Edward Bruce Papers; Walter Gropius
          Papers; Reginald Isaacs Papers
ACSA Association of Collegiate Schools of Architecture
       Minutes
AIA   American Institute of Architects
       Convention Proceedings; Membership Records
Avery   Avery Library Archive, Columbia University
       Alumni Records; Serge Chermayeff Papers; Committee on Administration,
          Minutes
BHL   Bentley Historical Library, University of Michigan
       Emil Lorch Papers
CF-CU Central Files, Columbia University
CUAC Columbia University Architecture Centennial Papers
CWF   Colonial Williamsburg Foundation
       A. Lawrence Kocher Collection
GARL George Arents Research Library, Syracuse University
       Marcel Breuer Papers; Ralph Walker Papers
HL   Houghton Library, Harvard University
       Walter Gropius Papers
HUA   Harvard University Archives
       James B. Conant Papers; Graduate School of Design (GSD) Papers; Special Stu-
          dents Papers
ID   Institute of Design Papers, University of Illinois, Chicago
LC   Library of Congress
       David Finley Papers; Mies van der Rohe Papers; Henry Richardson Shepley
          Papers
LIU   Long Island University Library, Brooklyn Center
       Robert Weinberg Papers
Loeb   Frances Loeb Library, Harvard University
MOMA Museum of Modern Art

NA   National Archives
        Edward Bruce Papers; Commission of Fine Arts Papers
PMA   Philadelphia Museum of Art Archives
        Fiske Kimball Papers
RF   Richard Filipowski Papers, Private Collection
SIA   Smithsonian Institution Archives
UEA   University of East Anglia
        Jack Pritchard Papers
UIC   Institute of Design Papers, University of Illinois, Chicago
UVA   University of Virginia Library, Manuscripts and Archives
        Fayerweather Hall; Minutes, Rector and Visitors; President's Papers, 1919–25
Yale   Yale University Library, Manuscripts and Archives
        Joseph Albers Papers; Christopher Tunnard Papers

INTRODUCTION

1. George Edgell to J. B. Conant, 9 May 1935, Conant Papers, 1934–35, UA I 5.168, HUA.

2. Gropius to *Architectural Forum* editor Walter Saunders, 4 May 1938, HL.

3. "Retrospect in Boston," *Time* 59 (21 January 1952): 58.

4. Michael Maccoby, "Design—A School without Direction," *Harvard Crimson,* 11 December 1952, 3.

5. Arthur Woltersdorf and William Wurster, in "Views," *Pencil Points* 26 (May 1945): 14

6. Joseph Hudnut, "The Post-Modern House," *Architectural Record* 97 (May 1945): 70–75.

7. Sigfried Giedion, J. L. Sert, and Ferdinand Léger, "Nine Points on Monumentality," quoted in Joan Ockman, ed., *Architecture Culture 1943–1968* (NY: Rizzoli, 1993), 29.

8. See Stanford Anderson, "The New Empiricism—Bay Region Axis: Kay Fisker and Postwar Debates on Functionalism, Regionalism, and Monumentality," *Journal of Architectural Education* 50 (February 1997): 197–207.

9. Hudnut made the "woodshed" reference in a letter to Gropius, 3 July 1946, Gropius Papers, HL. See also Hudnut's "The Post-Modern House" for his skeptical view of the Bay Region style, 70.

10. Klaus Herdeg, *The Decorated Diagram: Harvard Architecture and the Failure of the Bauhaus Legacy* (Cambridge: MIT Press, 1983), vii.

11. Anthony Alofsin, *The Struggle for Modernism: Architecture, Landscape Architecture, and City Planning at Harvard* (New York: Norton, 2002).

12. Ibid., 51.

13. Ada Louise Huxtable, "He Was Not Irrelevant," *New York Times,* 20 July 1969.

14. Alofsin, *The Struggle for Modernism,* 13.

15. A few other books deserve mention here. Melanie Simo, *A Coalescing of Different Forces and Ideas: A History of Landscape Architecture at Harvard 1900–1999* (Cambridge: Harvard University Graduate School of Design, 2000), offers a substantive discussion of the figures who loomed large in the landscape architecture field during the Hudnut/Gropius era, including Christopher Tunnard and the famous trio of student rebels, Dan Kiley, Garrett Eckbo, and James Rose. Alexander Caragonne's *The Texas Rangers* (Cambridge: MIT Press, 1995) offers an excellent discussion of postwar architectural education, particularly at Cornell and Texas.

1 HUDNUT

The complete source for the epigraph to chapter 1 is as follows: John Gaus to Hudnut, 19 October 1944, GSD Paper, UAV 322.7.4, HUA.

1. Leopold Arnaud to James Stewart Polshek, 8 June 1980, Centennial Papers, Avery. I am very grateful to the late Walter Creese for the wonderfully descriptive letter he sent me. Creese to author, 28 September 1987; Creese served as a teaching assistant in Hud-

nut's history class. John Coolidge, in Margaret Henderson Floyd, ed., *Architectural Educa-tion and Boston* (Boston: Boston Architectural Center, 1989), 62.

2. "Profile," *Harvard Foundation News* 1 (February 1950): 3; Walter Creese to author; Lawrence Kocher to Hudnut, 17 July 1937, GSD Papers, UAV 322.7.4, subseries III, HUA.

3. Hudnut's few remaining effects were left with Elizabeth Deviney, of Dover, Massa-chusetts, who shared them with me in July 1987.

4. G. Holmes Perkins, interview by author, 31 December 1990, Philadelphia. For men-tion of the Hudnut Building, see "Art in Review," *New York Times,* 19 April 1932.

5. Reginald Isaacs, *Gropius: An Illustrated Biography of the Creator of the Bauhaus* (Boston: Little, Brown, 1991), 238; G. Holmes Perkins, interview by author, 31 December 1990, Philadelphia; John Harkness, interview by author, 14 December 1990, Cambridge, Mass.

6. G. Holmes Perkins, interview by author, 31 December 1990, Philadelphia.

7. Sam Hurst, "Introduction of Walter Gropius," Gropius Papers, HL; Frederic Day Jr., interview by author, 30 November 1990, Concord, Mass. Reginald Isaacs's Papers at the Archives of American Art, Smithsonian Institution, contain more than one hundred wonderfully descriptive questionnaires filled out by Gropius's former students about the influence of his teaching on their subsequent careers.

8. Winfried Nerdinger's *Walter Gropius* (Berlin: Mann, 1985) remains the indispensable source on the architect. Reginald Isaacs's *Gropius: An Illustrated Biography of the Creator of the Bauhaus* offers an uncritical view of the author's beloved teacher.

9. Elizabeth Deviney, interview by author, July 1986, Dover, Mass.

10. Walter Creese to author, 28 September 1987.

11. Hudnut, "Foundations," *Line Magazine* 1 (1952): 1; *Portrait and Biographical Album, Mecosta County, Michigan* (Chicago: Chapman Brothers, 1883), 247–48, 262–63, 234–54.

12. Joseph Hudnut, Student Records, Special Students Papers, 1901–7, HUA. Hudnut was placed on academic probation after receiving two *C*'s and a *D.*

13. James Phinney to Hudnut, 31 August 1936, Isaacs Papers, AAA. On Patterson and Davidson, the engineering firm employing Hudnut as a draftsman, see Albert Nelson Marquis, ed., *The Book of Chicagoans* (Chicago: Marquis, 1911), 175, 527.

14. Emil Lorch to Charles Thatch, 10 August 1912, Lorch Papers, BHL.

15. "The College of Architecture, University of Michigan Memo," 29 April 1936, Emil Lorch Papers, BHL; "Department of Architecture, General Statement," *University of Michi-gan Bulletin,* 1911.

16. Arthur C. Weatherhead, *A History of Collegiate Education in Architecture in the United States* (self-published, 1941), 120.

17. On Lorch, see Marie Frank, "Emil Lorch: Pure Design and American Architec-tural Education," *Journal of Architectural Education* 57 (May 2004): 28–40, and "Platonic Thought in American Design Theory c. 1900," in Liana De Girolami Cheney and John Hendrix, eds., *Neoplatonic Aesthetics* (New York: Peter Lang, 2004), 251–58. Ross published *A Theory of Pure Design: Harmony, Balance Rhythm* (Boston: Houghton, Mifflin) in 1907. A student of Charles Eliot Norton, Ross taught design theory at Harvard from 1899 until 1935; he also painted and was an important art collector who donated more than eleven thousand objects to the Boston Museum of Fine Arts. Dow, also a painter, taught at Co-lumbia's Teacher's College, among other institutions. His most famous students, Georgia O'Keefe and Max Weber, developed his ideas of abstraction in their work. Dow was also an important figure in the American arts and crafts movement.

18. Ross, *A Theory of Pure Design,* 58, 110.

19. Frank, "Emil Lorch: Pure Design and American Architectural Education," 30, 35; Ross, preface to *A Theory of Pure Design.*

20. Frank, "Emil Lorch: Pure Design and American Architectural Education," 30. Frank addresses some of the differences between Dow's and Ross's views of Pure Design.

21. Ross, *A Theory of Pure Design,* 193.

22. Frank, "Emil Lorch: Pure Design and American Architectural Education," 30, 35.

23. Program of *The Awakened Ramses,* Michigan Union Opera, 1911; and *Michiganen-sian,* 1912, 101, BHL.

24. *Boyd's Co-Partnership and Residence Business Directory of Philadelphia City* (Philadelphia: Boyd's Directory Office, 1906); Thomas Owen, *History of Alabama and Dictionary of Alabama Biography*, 859.

25. Emil Lorch to Charles Thatch, 10 August 1912, Lorch Papers, BHL.

26. *The Bulletin of the Alabama Polytechnic Institute, 1912–1913*, 131.

27. Hudnut to Turpin Bannister, 21 February 1945, GSD Papers, UAV 322.7.4, subseries I, HUA. Many thanks to Gene Geiger of Special Collections, Auburn University, for the photograph and information on the President's House, still extant and used as campus offices. The church building no longer exists. A description of it and a poor-quality photograph of it are contained in Carolyn Ellis Lipscomb, *Auburn United Methodist Church, 1837–1987: A History of a Great Church and the People Who Made It That Way* (Auburn: 1987), 12, 13.

28. Hudnut to Charles Maginnis, 14 February 1936, GSD Papers, UAV 322.7.4, subseries I, HUA.

29. Joseph Hudnut, "Confessions of an Architect," *Tomorrow*, February 1950, 12; and Joseph Hudnut, "Statement on Werner Hegemann," 29 July 1936, GSD Papers, UAV 322.7, subseries I, HUA.

30. Hudnut reflected on his early architectural ideas in his "Statement on Werner Hegemann."

31. The 1910 memo is translated in "Gropius at Twenty-Six," *Architectural Review* (July 1961): 49–51.

32. Gropius to his mother, 21 October 1907, quoted in Reginald Isaacs, *Walter Gropius: Der Mensch und sein Werk*, translated by Georg G. Meerwein (Berlin: Mann, 1984), 91.

33. According to his TAC partner, John Harkness (Harkness, interview by author, 14 December 1990, Cambridge, Mass.).

34. Nerdinger, *Walter Gropius*, 2.

35. For a broad portrait of architectural schools before World War II, see Weatherhead, *A History of Collegiate Education in Architecture*.

36. "School of Architecture," *Annual Report of the President and Treasurer to the Trustees, for the Year Ending June 30, 1926*, 162.

37. Richard Snow (Boring's nephew and Columbia architecture alumnus, 1931), interview by Richard Oliver, February 1981, CUAC Papers, Avery.

38. Hudnut, "Statement on Werner Hegemann."

39. Werner Hegemann wrote to Erich Stern about his personal situation and about conditions in Germany on 11 October 1922, 4 October 1925, 10 January 1928, and 19 January 1935. Stern Papers, University of Wisconsin Milwaukee Library. On Hegemann, see Christiane Crasemann Collins, *Werner Hegemann and the Search for Universal Urbanism* (New York: Norton, 2005).

40. Hudnut, "Statement on Werner Hegemann." There is no mention in Hudnut's or Hegemann's papers as to where their meeting took place.

41. Joseph Hudnut, "Neighborhood Centers in Chicago," *Journal of the American Institute of Architects* 4 (February 1916): 68–70.

42. Christiane Collins, "A Visionary Discipline: Werner Hegemann and the Quest for the Pragmatic Idea," *Center: A Journal for Architecture in America* 5 (January/February 1989): 79; Christiane Collins, "Hegemann and Peets: Cartographers of an Imaginary Atlas," in Werner Hegemann and Elbert Peets, *The American Vitruvius* (New York: Princeton Architectural Press, 1988).

43. See Kevin Mattson, *Creating a Democratic Public* (University Park: Pennsylvania State University, 1998), 40–43.

44. Werner Hegemann, *Report on a City Plan for the Municipalities of Oakland and Berkeley* (Oakland/Berkeley: Municipal Governments of Oakland and Berkeley, 1915).

45. Werner Hegemann and Elbert Peets, *Washington Highlands* (Milwaukee, 1919); Hegemann, *Wyomissing Park* (Wyomissing, 1919), found in Elbert Peets Papers, #2772, Cornell University Archives.

46. Hudnut, "Statement on Werner Hegemann." This statement—a memorial tribute to Hegemann—was to serve as a preface for Hegemann's posthumous book, *City Planning, Housing* (New York, 1937), but Hudnut felt it was too personal for this purpose.

47. Hudnut, "Statement on Werner Hegemann."

48. Ibid.

49. Hudnut, preface for Werner Hegemann, *City Planning Housing,* vii, viii.

50. Hudnut, "Statement on Werner Hegemann."

51. On Hegemann's career, see Ruth Nanda Anshen, introduction to *City Planning, Housing,* 2: xiii–xxii; Collins, "A Visionary Discipline; Christiane Collins, "Werner Hegemann (1881–1936): Formative Years in America," *Planning Perspectives* 11 (1996): 1–21; Donatella Calabi, "Werner Hegemann, o dell'ambiguita borghese urbanistica," *Casabella* 428 (1977): 54–60.

52. George R. Collins and Christiane C. Collins, *Camillo Sitte: The Birth of Modern City Planning* (New York: Rizzoli, 1986), 364. Hegemann's books include *Der gerettete Christus* (Potsdam: Kiepenheuer, 1928); *Fridericus; oder, Das Königsopfer* (Hellerau: Hegner, 1926); *Napoleon, oder Kniefall vor dem Heros* (Hellerau: Hegner, 1927); *Entlarvte Geschichte* (Leipzig: Hegner, 1933).

53. Anthony Sutcliffe, *Towards the Planned City* (New York: St. Martin's, 1981), 174.

54. Hegemann praised the park movement and Chicago's comprehensive planning to German audiences in such publications as *Amerikanische Parkanlagen: Zierparks, Nutzparks, Aussen- und Innenparks, Nationalparks, Park-Zwickverbände. Ein Parkbuch zur Wanderausstellung von Bildern und Plänen amerikanischer Parkanlagen* (Berlin: Wasmuths, 1911) and *Der neue Bebauungsplan für Chicago* (Berlin: Wasmuth, 1911).

55. W. Oechslin, "Between America and Germany: Werner Hegemann's Approach to Urban Planning," in J. P. Kleihues and C. Rathgeber, eds., *Berlin/New York, Like and Unlike* (New York: Rizzoli, 1993), 285.

56. Ibid., 285, 287.

57. Ibid, 292.

58. Collins, *Camillo Sitte,* 365, uses the phrase "open forum." Hegemann consolidated the two magazines in 1930.

59. Hegemann was forced to retract this statement in a court settlement. Oechslin, "Between America and Germany," 292.

60. See his remarks on Le Corbusier's "ghastly" skyscrapers, *City Planning, Housing,* 2: 274; see also Hegemann, "Kritik des Großstadt-Sanierungs-Planes Le Corbusiers," *Der Städtebau,* 1927, 69ff. Hegemann had once before been considered for the same job as Wagner, as Berlin's *Stadtbaurat* in the 1920s (see Oechslin, "Between America and Germany," 285).

61. Werner Hegemann, *Das steinerne Berlin: Geschichte der grössten Mietskasernenstadt der Welt* (1930; Braunschweig: Vieweg, 1988).

62. Hegemann, introduction to *Das steinerne Berlin.*

63. Hegemann and Peets, *American Vitruvius,* 2. Hudnut's drawings are on page 283.

64. Ibid., 1.

65. The book was also republished in 1972 by Benjamin Blom, on behalf of the Society of Classical America (see *Classical America* 4 [1977]), but it got virtually no notice at that point. Leon Krier, preface to Werner Hegemann and Elbert Peets, *The American Vitruvius* (New York: Princeton Architectural Press, 1988).

66. Hudnut to Ralph Adams Cram, 10 December 1938, GSD Papers, UAV 322.7, subseries I, 1b, HUA.

67. Hudnut, "Confessions of an Architect," 112.

68. Ibid.

69. For a time, the office letterhead read "Hudnut and Montgomery," and it later changed to "Joseph Hudnut" with "W. E. Manhart, Associate." Peets File, GSD Papers, UAV 322.148, subseries II, HUA.

70. "Joseph (Fairman) Hudnut," *Harvard Class of 1910, 25th Anniversary Report,* 377;

Hudnut, "Confessions of an Architect," 11; Hudnut to William Hudnut, 14 October 1948, GSD Papers, UAV 322.7.4, HUA. Hudnut's published buildings include: "New York House of Mr. and Mrs. William O. Hubbard," *Arts and Decoration* 17 (July 1922): 172–73; "Institutional Churches," and "Jamaica, N.Y., First Baptist Church Plan," *Architectural Forum* 40 (April 1924): 141–44; "Town and Parlor Wing, The First Baptist Church, Jamaica, L.I., N.Y.," *American Architect* 125 (February 1924); and "First Methodist Episcopal Church, Jamaica L.I." *Architectural Record* 60 (July 1926): 39–44.

71. Hudnut to Ralph Adams Cram, 10 December 1938, GSD Papers, UAV 322.7, subseries I, Ib, HUA; Joseph Hudnut, "Picture, Sentiment, and Symbol: Some Comments on Modern Church Architecture," *Architectural Record* 96 (September 1944): 84.

72. Robert A. M. Stern, *New York: 1930* (New York: Rizzoli, 1987), 167.

73. Hudnut, "We Are No Longer Colonials," *House and Garden* 97 (May 1950): 166.

74. Hudnut, "Picture, Sentiment, and Symbol," 84.

75. Hudnut, "Confessions of an Architect," 14

76. Mumford biographer Donald Miller has told me that many people he interviewed made this charge against Mumford, including Philip Johnson, though no one made it in print, or even in a letter to Mumford, with the "grand exception" of Catherine Bauer. Donald Miller to author, 23 February 2000.

77. Arthur Woltersdorf and William Wurster, in "Views," *Pencil Points,* 26 (May 1945): 14.

78. Hudnut and Kimball often mention Hegemann in their correspondence, contained in the Kimball Papers, PMA.

79. ACSA, Minutes, 1927, 2.

80. UVA, Minutes, Rector and Visitors, vol. 9, pt. 3, 1924–28, 363.

81. It is unclear just what Hudnut meant here by "modern." Hudnut to President Alderman, 16 April 1925, President's Papers, RRG2/1/2.472, subseries VI, 1919–25, and Academic Faculty Minutes, Roll 1–4, 1899–1932, RG 19/2/1, pp. 164–65, UVA.

82. Richard Snow interview by Richard Oliver, February 1981, CUAC Papers, Avery.

83. *Harvard Class of 1910,* 378; Joseph Hudnut, *Modern Sculpture* (New York: Norton, 1929).

84. Hudnut, *Modern Sculpture,* 90, 5.

85. Joseph Hudnut, "The Romantic Architecture of Morningside Heights," *Columbia University Quarterly* 22 (1930): 404.

86. Hudnut to Frederick Allen (author and critic for *Harper's Magazine*), 4 August 1941, GSD Papers, UAV 322.7.4, subseries I, HUA.

87. Hudnut, "The Romantic Architecture of Morningside Heights," 406.

88. Henry-Russell Hitchcock, "Modern Architecture—A Memoir," *Journal of the Society of Architectural Historians* 27 (December 1968): 229.

89. Typescript of Max Abramovitz interview by Richard Oliver, 19 March 1981, CUAC Papers, Avery.

90. Coolidge, in Floyd, *Architectural Education and Boston,* 61.

91. Joseph Hudnut, preface to Walter Gropius, *The New Architecture and the Bauhaus* (New York, 1936).

92. Ibid.; Jill Pearlman, "Joseph Hudnut's Other Modernism at the 'Harvard Bauhaus,'" *Journal of the Society of Architectural Historians* 56 (December 1997): 457–58; Hudnut, "The Post-Modern House," 74.

93. Joseph Hudnut, "On Teaching the History of Architecture," *Journal of Architectural Education* 122 (Summer 1957): 6; and Hudnut, "Humanism and the Teaching of Architecture," 14.

94. Hudnut, "On Teaching the History of Architecture," 6.

95. Joseph Hudnut, "What a Planner Has to Know," *American Society of Planning Officials Journal* (1946): 159; Hudnut, "Humanism and the Teaching of Architecture," 14.

96. The Beaux-Arts Institute of Design (BAID), headquartered in New York, dominated design teaching by distributing and judging design programs to various schools from 1916 until the 1930s. Thirty-one of the forty-eight U.S. architecture schools still competed

in BAID competitions while additional schools used BAID design programs. Bannister, *The Architect at Mid-Century* (New York: Reinhold, 1954), 190.

97. "Meeting of the Patrons of the Ateliers with the Trustees of the Beaux-Arts Institute of Design, Held at the Century Club, New York, March 29, 1927," 9, 10, 21, 32. Transcript found in the Avery Library.

98. Quoted in Rosemarie Haag Bletter, "Modernism Rears Its Head—The Twenties and Thirties," in Richard Oliver, ed., *The Making of an Architect, 1881–1981, Columbia University in the City of New York* (New York, 1981), 103.

99. Ibid., 2.

100. See the "Meeting of the Patrons" for the numerous complaints against the BAID.

101. Henry-Russell Hitchcock, "Architectural Education Again," *Architectural Record* 67 (April 1930): 446.

102. On Hudnut at Columbia, see Oliver, *The Making of an Architect, 1881–1981.*

103. He was actually appointed acting dean in 1933 and dean in 1934. See Oliver, *The Making of an Architect, 1881–1981,* and Theodor Rohdenberg, *A History of the School of Architecture, Columbia University* (New York: Columbia University Press, 1954), for the history of architecture at Columbia. "School of Architecture, Report of the Dean," *Columbia University, Annual Report of the President and Treasurer to the Trustees, 1934,* 190.

104. The relevance of Dewey's ideas to architectural education had also been recognized at this time. See Frederick Ackerman, "The Relation of Art to Education," *Journal of the American Institute of Architects* 4 (May, June, July, November 1916): 190–93, 234–38, 281–84, 455–57.

105. *Columbia Spectator,* 25 October 1933, 3, 6, and October 1930, 4.

106. Hudnut, "Round Table Discussion, The Teaching of Architectural History," ACSA, Minutes, 1929, 29.

107. *Columbia Spectator,* 14 February 1933, 1.

108. "School of Architecture, Report of the Dean," *Columbia University, Annual Report of the President and Treasurer to the Trustees, 1934,* 180–90; "Columbia University School of Architecture, Design Problems and Sketches, 1926–1927," CF-CU. For discussion of the "project method" and for an overview of American progressive education, see Lawrence Cremin, *The Transformation of the School: Progressivism in American Education, 1876–1957* (New York: Knopf, 1961).

109. "School of Architecture, Report of the Dean," *Columbia University, Annual Report of the President and Treasurer to the Trustees, 1935,* 184; see also "School of Architecture," 1934, 180.

110. Hudnut, "Statement on Werner Hegemann"; Walter Creese to author, 28 September 1987.

111. Hudnut, "Notes on Educational Policy in the School of Architecture," June 1935, CF-CU.

112. Hudnut to Frank Fackenthal, 31 January 1935, and Hudnut to Fackenthal, 22 March 1935, CF-CU. Hudnut solicited funds from sympathetic individuals and from the Emergency Committee in Aid of Displaced German Scholars, which also helped fund Hegemann's position. For a list of the individual funders, see "Dedication and Acknowledgments," in Hegemann, *City Planning, Housing,* 1: v. Hegemann dedicated this book to Hudnut and Alvin Johnson, head of the New School.

113. On the Town Planning studio, see Hudnut to Nicholas Murray Butler, 19 November 1934 and 21 January 1935; Hudnut to the President and Trustees of the Carnegie Corporation, 16 November 1934, CF-CU; and "School of Architecture, Report of the Dean," 1935, 183–84.

114. "New Dean, New Institute," *Architectural Forum* (June 1934): 36; see also "Columbia Plans Urban Institute," *New York Times,* 24 April 1934. The term "urbanism" was introduced by Louis Wirth in his "Urbanism as a Way of Life" (1938) and came into common usage in the 1960s with Serge Chermayeff, Christopher Alexander, and Vincent Scully. See Nan Ellin, *Postmodern Urbanism* (New York: Princeton Architectural Press, 1999), 250.

115. Harmon Goldstone, transcript of interview with Richard Oliver, 1980? CUAC Papers, Avery; and Hudnut to President Nicholas Murray Butler, 12 June 1934, CF-CU. Born in Riga, Latvia, to Swedish parents, Ruhtenberg came to the United States in 1933.

116. Harmon Goldstone, transcript of interview with Richard Oliver, 1980? CUAC Papers, Avery.

117. Johnson to Oud, 23 November 1933, and Oud to Johnson, 11 December 1933, Papers in Registrar's Office, MOMA.

118. Lawrence Kocher to Walter Gropius, 29 May 1934, and Gropius to Kocher, 7 July 1934, A. Lawrence Kocher Collection, Colonial Williamsburg Foundation Library, Williamsburg, Va., CWF. Many thanks to Mrs. Margaret Kocher for making her husband's papers available to me.

119. In 1934, the administration turned down almost any request that required an outlay of money. Also, Hudnut later alluded to the fact that there were limitations on the changes he could make at the Columbia School of Architecture. Hudnut to Ronald Bradbury, 17 February 1936, GSD Papers, UAV 322.7, subseries I, Ib, HUA. Similarly, in 1935, trying to convince Hudnut to stay at Columbia, President Butler felt compelled to claim he would support Hudnut's independent actions in developing the Columbia school. Butler to Frank Fackenthal, 6 June 1935, CF-CU.

120. Alfred Barr to A. Conger Goodyear, 8 January 1935, Barr Papers, AAA.

121. Russell Lynes, *Good Old Modern; An Intimate Portrait of the Museum of Modern Art* (New York: Atheneum, 1973), 177.

122. Richard Norton Smith, *The Harvard Century* (New York: Simon and Schuster, 1986), 109; James Hershberg, *James B. Conant, Harvard to Hiroshima and the Making of the Nuclear Age* (New York, 1993), 79; and James B. Conant, "Harvard, Present and Future," *School and Society* 43 (4 April 1936): 454.

123. Conant fit within the tradition described by Morton White, *Social Thought in America: The Revolt against Formalism* (New York: Viking, 1949). For a bibliography of Conant's writings, see the *Journal of General Education* 5 (October 1950): 48–56. On Conant's life and career, see his autobiography, *My Several Lives, Memoirs of a Social Inventor* (New York: Harper and Row, 1970).

124. See Conant, "President's Report," *Official Register of Harvard University,* for the years 1933–52, and Smith, *The Harvard Century,* 116.

125. James B. Conant, "The University Tradition in America—Yesterday and Tomorrow," *School and Society* 44 (September 1936): 389.

126. Ibid., 108.

127. George Edgell to Conant, 9 May 1935, Conant Papers, 1934–35, UA I 5.168, HUA.

128. Discussion of the various candidates is found in the Conant Papers, 1934–35, UA I 5.168, HUA; see, in particular, Edgell to Conant, 9 May 1935, and "Petition for Hubbard as Dean," 8 May 1935; Robert L. Duffus, "Architects and Educators," *Architectural Record* 80 (September 1936): 191. Discussion of the various candidates is found in the Conant Papers, 1934–35, UA I 5.168, HUA.

129. James B. Conant to Harold Bush-Brown, 2 May 1935, Conant Papers, UA I 5.168, HUA.

130. Hudnut to Ronald Bradbury, 17 February 1936, GSD Papers, UAV 322.7, subseries I, Ib, HUA.

131. Hudnut to Frederic Delano, 5 July 1940, GSD Papers, UAV 322.138, HUA.

132. On Butler's conservatism, see Laurence Vesey, *The Emergence of the American University* (Chicago: University of Chicago Press, 1965), 363–67. Dorothy Dunbar Bromley expresses a more extreme view in "Nicholas Murray Butler, Portrait of a Reactionary," *American Mercury* 34 (March 1935): 286–98.

133. See Conant, "President's Report," *Official Register of Harvard University,* for the years 1933–52.

134. Ibid.; and "Mr. Conant and Germany: A Presidential Autobiography," *Harvard Alumni Bulletin* 38 (10 April 1936): 812–19.

2 MODERN MOVEMENTS IN THE IVY

1. G. Holmes Perkins, interview by author, 31 December 1990, Philadelphia.

2. "A Queen Anne Front . . . A Mary Ann Back," *Architectural Record* 70 (August 1931): 126. One of those students, Richard M. Bennett, later a prominent Chicago architect, worked on the addition with faculty member John Humphreys.

3. Edgell to Conant, 9 May 1935, Conant Papers, UA I 5. 168, HUA.

4. On the collaborative problems, see Simo, *The Coalescing of Different Forces and Ideas,* 25. In *The Struggle for Modernism,* Anthony Alofsin has argued that collaboration had long been the ethos at the three Harvard schools. I am unpersuaded by his argument, as I have written in my review of his book in the *Harvard Design Magazine* (Fall 2002/Winter 2003): 82–84.

5. "French Medal to Harvard," *Architectural Record* 74 (January 1933): 26. See "School of Architecture" in the *Official Register of Harvard University* for course changes after the Depression. G. H. Edgell, "School History," 3, 5, GSD Papers, UAV.322.8, HUA; Haffner to Conant, 20 May 1935, Conant Papers, UA I 5.168, HUA; Walter Bogner, "The Education of Architects in Relation to the Future of Architects," 1933, TMs 1–8, Vertical File, Loeb.

6. G. Holmes Perkins, interview by author, 31 December 1990, Philadelphia.

7. Ibid.

8. Simo, *The Coalescing of Different Forces,* 26; G. Holmes Perkins, interview by author, 31 December 1990, Philadelphia.

9. Haffner to Conant, 20 May 1935, Conant Papers, UA I 5.168 HUA; G. Holmes Perkins, interview by author, 31 December 1990, Philadelphia.

10. "Report of the Overseers' Committee," 13 May 1935, UA II.10.7.5.158, HUA; Henry R. Shepley, "Autobiography for Harvard Class of 1910 Reunion," Shepley Papers, LC; Gilmore Clarke File, Commission of Fine Arts Papers, RG 66, NA. Members of this group included Shepley, Clarke (a landscape architect), and Otto Teegan, head of the BAID.

11. G. Holmes Perkins, interview by author, 31 December 1990, Philadelphia.

12. Hudnut to Ronald Bradbury, 17 February 1936, GSD Papers, subseries I, Ib, 1932–42, HUA.

13. On Robinson Hall renovations, see Hudnut and J. W. Lowes correspondence, 1936, GSD Papers, UAV 322.7, subseries II, IIa; and Hudnut to R. B. Johnson, 26 October 1935, and 12 February 1936, UAV 322.7, subseries VII, VIIb, HUA.

14. For blueprints of Hudnut's restructuring of Robinson Hall, see Vertical File, VF NA6602, Camb-Harv, 1935, Loeb; and Hudnut to J.W. Lowes, 24 January 1936, GSD Papers, HUA.

15. Hudnut to R. B. Johnson, 28 April 1937, GSD Papers, UAV 322.7, subseries II, IIa, HUA. On Hunt Hall, see Bainbridge Bunting, *Harvard: An Architectural History* (Cambridge: Harvard University Press, 1985), 75–76.

16. "Hudnut Whirlwind Comes to Climax," *Boston Evening Transcript,* undated clipping (December 1938?) found in Bruce Papers, Box 11, NA.

17. On Robinson Hall renovations, see Hudnut and J. W. Lowes correspondence, 1936, GSD Papers, UAV 322.7, subseries II, IIa; and Hudnut to R. B. Johnson, 26 October 1935 and 12 February 1936, UAV 322.7, subseries VII, VIIb, HUA. See, for example, Winfried Nerdinger, who claims that Robinson Hall was modernized "on Gropius's initiative" ("From Bauhaus to Harvard: Walter Gropius and the Use of History," in *The History of History in American Schools of Architecture 1865–1975* [New York, 1990], 94).

18. Hudnut to Eric Arthur, 14 January 1948, GSD Papers, UAV 322.7.4, subseries IV, HUA; and Hudnut, "Memorandum for the Visiting Committees of the Graduate School of Design," CF-CU.

19. William Perry, interview by Richard Chafee, 29 September 1971, AIA Archives.

20. Ibid.

21. See Hudnut to J. W. Lowes, 24 January 1936, in which he briefly describes his plans for the "complete reorganization" of the library. GSD Papers, UAV 322.7, subseries II, IIa, HUA.

22. Katherine McNamara, "The Library of the Graduate School of Design," 19 May 1961, GSD Papers, UAV 322.7, subseries II, IIa, HUA.

23. Hudnut to R. B. Johnson, 12 February 1936, GSD Papers, UAV 322.7, subseries II, IIa, HUA. See "School of Architecture" and the "Graduate School of Design" in various *Addenda to the Official Register of Harvard University*, 1935–50, for Robinson Hall photographs.

24. Hudnut, "Minutes of Conference on Industrial Design," Museum of Modern Art, 11–14 November 1946, MOMA Library; Hudnut and Gropius, *Minority Report of the Harvard Committee on Regional Planning*, 1940, GSD Papers, UAV 322.138, HUA.

25. Hudnut, "Minutes of Conference on Industrial Design."

26. Hudnut to Frederic Delano, 5 July 1940, and Hudnut to John Coolidge, 12 November 1940, UAV 322.7, subseries I, HUA.

27. Hudnut to Frederic Delano, 5 July 1940.

28. Ibid.

29. "Professor H. V. Hubbard," *Harvard Alumni Bulletin* 42 (15 March 1940): 756; see also the *Official Register of Harvard University* for 1909, 1923, 1929.

30. Harvey S. Perloff, *Education for Planning: City, State, and Regional* (Baltimore: Johns Hopkins University Press, 1957), 11, 20, 57–60.

31. Werner Hegemann to Erich Stern, 4 October 1925, Erich Stern Papers, Milwaukee Urban Archives, University of Wisconsin, Milwaukee.

32. Hudnut to Conant, 4 December 1935, Conant Papers, UA I 5.168, HUA.

33. On the Harvard City Planning Studies, see "Department of Regional Planning," *Official Register of Harvard University, 1936–37,* 33–34; see also the "Dean's Report," *Official Register of Harvard University* for the various years; Hubbard, "To Former Students in City and Regional Planning," memo, 22 April 1941, Vertical File, Loeb.

34. Henry V. Hubbard and Theodora Kimball, *An Introduction to the Study of Landscape Design* (New York: Macmillan, 1917), 323.

35. Jon A. Peterson, "Frederick Law Olmsted Sr. and Frederick Law Olmsted Jr.: The Visionary and the Professional," in Mary Corbin Sies and C. Silver, eds., *Planning the Twentieth-Century American City* (Baltimore: Johns Hopkins University Press, 1996).

36. Henry V. Hubbard and Theodora Kimball Hubbard, *Our Cities To-day and To-morrow* (Cambridge: Harvard University Press, 1929).

37. Melanie Simo devotes many pages to the split between landscape architecture and city planning in *The Coalescing of Different Forces and Ideas,* 17ff.

38. Ibid., 18.

39. Henry Hubbard, fiftieth anniversary, "Harvard Class Record, 1897," 1947, cited in Simo, *The Coalescing of Different Forces and Ideas,* 33; and Hudnut and Gropius, *Report of the Harvard Committee on Regional Planning,* 17.

40. Mary Daniels, "Bremer Pond," in Charles Birnbaum and Robin Karons, eds., *Pioneers of American Landscape Design* (New York: McGraw Hill, 2000), 300.

41. Pond letter, quoted in Daniels, "Bremer Pond," 302.

42. Elbert Peets, "The Landscape Priesthood," *American Mercury* 37 (January 1927): 94.

43. Ibid., 99.

44. G. Holmes Perkins, interview by author, 31 December 1990, Philadelphia; and Jean-Paul Carlhian, interview by author, 12 May 1988, Boston.

45. "Memorandum: Proposed Appointment of a Professor of Design in the Graduate School of Design, Harvard University," undated, ca. May 1936, Barr Papers, AAA.

46. Conant, *My Several Lives,* 67–72; "Mr. Conant and Germany: A Presidential Autobiography," *Harvard Alumni Bulletin* 38 (10 April 1936): 812–19.

47. Hudnut to Barr, 18 May 1936, Barr Papers, AAA; Barr to Mrs. Nelson Rockefeller, 2 July 1936, cited in Rona Roob, "1936: The Museum Selects an Architect," *Archives of American Art Journal* 23 (1983): 24; Barr to Philip Goodwin, 6 July 1936, Barr Papers, AAA.

48. Hudnut to Barr, 18 May 1936; Hudnut to Barr, undated cable; Hudnut to Barr, 10 June 1936, Barr Papers, AAA.

49. Barr to Philip Goodwin, 6 July 1936, and Barr to Conger Goodyear, 6 July 1936, Barr Papers, AAA.

50. Ibid.

51. Barr to Philip Goodwin, 6 July 1936, Barr Papers, AAA.

52. Hudnut to Barr, 1 July 1936, and Barr to Hudnut, 26 August 1936, Barr Papers, AAA; Edward Durrell Stone, *The Evolution of an Architect* (New York: Horizon Press, 1962), 35–36.

53. Hudnut to Barr, 9 September 1936, Barr Papers, AAA.

54. Ibid. Although several authors have discussed Hudnut's attempt to bring Mies to Harvard, none of them has consulted the archives at Harvard University: Franz Schulze, *Mies van der Rohe, A Critical Biography* (Chicago: University of Chicago Press, 1985); Elaine S. Hochman, *Architects of Fortune, Mies van der Rohe and the Third Reich* (New York: Weidenfeld and Nicholson, 1989); Kevin Harrington, "Mies's Curriculum at IIT," in *Mies van der Rohe: Architect as Educator* (Chicago: Illinois Institute of Technology, 1986); Margaret Kentgens-Craig, *Bauhaus and America First Contacts, 1919–1936* (Cambridge: MIT Press, 1999).

55. Hudnut, *Memorandum, September 1936,* Conant Papers, UA I 5.168, HUA.

56. Ibid.

57. Ibid.

58. Ibid.

59. Ibid.

60. Smith, *The Harvard Century,* 87–88, 113

61. Hudnut, *Memorandum, September 1936.*

62. Hudnut to Mies, 3 September 1936, Mies Papers, LC.

63. Hudnut to Mies, 6 November 1936, Mies Papers, LC; Hudnut to G. Holmes Perkins, 7 December 1936, GSD Papers, UAV 322.7, subseries III, IIIa, HUA.

64. Hudnut to Mies, 3 September 1936, Mies Papers, LC; Hudnut to Barr, 29 September 1936, Barr Papers, AAA; Mies to Hudnut, 15 September 1936, Mies Papers, LC; Mies to Willard Hotchkiss, 2 September 1936, Hotchkiss Papers, Illinois Institute of Technology, Chicago, cited in Harrington, "Mies's Curriculum at IIT," 67; Hudnut to Mies, 28 September 1936, Mies Papers, LC.

65. Hudnut to Mies, 16 November 1936, Mies Papers, LC; Hudnut to Gropius, 8 December 1936, Gropius Papers, HL.

66. Hudnut to Gropius, 8 December 1936, Gropius Papers, HL.

67. Ibid.

68. Hudnut to Perkins, 7 December 1936, GSD Papers, UAV 322.7, subseries III, IIIa, HUA; Hudnut to Gropius, 8 December 1936, Gropius Papers, HL.

69. Hudnut to Perkins, 7 December 1936, GSD Papers, UAV 322.7, subseries III, IIIa, HUA.

70. Jack Pritchard, *View from a Long Chair: The Memoirs of Jack Pritchard* (London: Routledge and Kegan Paul, 1984), 103. On MARS, see John Gold, *The Experience of Modernism* (London: E&FN Spon, 1997), 110–12.

71. See Pritchard, *View from a Long Chair.*

72. Quoted in Leslie Cormier, "Walter Gropius: Emigre Architect" (PhD diss., Brown University), 54.

73. Ibid., 48, 75–76. Gropius's and Fry's most prominent buildings in England included the Levy House in Chelsea and the Village College Impington in Cambridgeshire.

74. Anthony Blunt, "Art: The English Home," *Spectator* 158 (15 January 1937): 84.

75. David Elliot, "Gropius in England" (London: Building Center, 1974), 5.

76. Walter Gropius, farewell speech in London, 9 March 1937, Pritchard Papers, UEA, PP/24/5/7.

77. Quoted in Kentgens-Craig, *The Bauhaus and America,* 87.

78. Gropius to Manon Gropius Burchard, 6 November 1934, quoted in Isaacs, *Gropius: An Illustrated Biography,* 192. Isaacs writes of Gropius's impressions of America in 1928 on pages 145–50, 223.

79. Pritchard to Gropius, 1 December 1936, quoted in Isaacs, *Walter Gropius,* 217.

80. On Gropius's relationship to the National Socialists and on the closing of the Bau-

haus in 1933, see Peter Hahn, "Bauhaus and Exile," 211–33, and Kathleen James, "Walter Gropius at Harvard, 1937–45," 242–47, both in Stephanie Barron, ed., *Exiles and Emigrés* (New York: Abrams, 1997).

81. At Harvard (as at the Bauhaus), Gropius's social aspirations still informed his teaching and architectural philosophy in very significant ways. Some historians have recently questioned whether Gropius turned away from his social goals to purely artistic ones after emigrating to America. See Hahn, "Bauhaus and Exile." Thanks to Karen Koehler for making her manuscript on this subject available to me ("The Bauhaus in Exile and the Fear of Reception: The Museum of Modern Art, 1938").

82. Hudnut to Gropius, 24 December 1936, and Gropius to Hudnut, 24 December 1936, Gropius Papers, HL.

83. "Gropius Dinner March 9th 1937," guest list found in the Pritchard Papers, UEA, PP/24/5/7.

84. Gropius, farewell speech, 9 March 1937, Pritchard Papers, UEA, PP/24/5/7.

85. Hudnut to Barr, 16 November 1936, Gropius Papers, AAA; Gropius to Marcel Breuer, 17 April 1937, Hudnut to Gropius, 12 June 1937, and Gropius to Hudnut, 9 June 1937, Gropius Papers, HL; Gropius's sketch for the Caryl Peabody Nursery School is published in Nerdinger, *Walter Gropius,* 193.

86. Ernestine Fantl to Hudnut, 15 February 1937, GSD Papers, subseries I, HUA.

87. Hudnut to Gropius, 23 December 1936, Gropius Papers, HL.

88. Cormier, *Walter Gropius: Emigre Architect,* 74–75. On Frank Pick, see Michael Salter, *The Avant-Garde in Interwar England: Medieval Modernism and the London Underground* (New York: Oxford University Press, 1999).

89. Cormier, *Walter Gropius: Emigre Architect,* 75.

90. Hudnut to Gropius, 23 December 1936, Gropius Papers, HL.

91. Hudnut, preface to Gropius, *The New Architecture and the Bauhaus,* 7.

92. Hudnut, *Memorandum, November 24, 1936,* Conant Papers, UA I 5.168, HUA.

93. Hudnut to Perkins, 7 December 1936, GSD Papers, UAV 322.7, subseries III, HUA.

94. Hubbard to Conant, 27 November 1936, Conant Papers, UA I 5.168, HUA.

95. Reginald Isaacs, "Charles Wilson Killam—A Minute on his Life and Services," 12 December 1961, Loeb; G. Holmes Perkins, interview with author, 31 December 1990, Philadelphia; Killam to Conant, 10 December 1936, Conant Papers, UA I 5.168, HUA.

96. Charles Killam, "School Training for Architects: Some Pertinent Thoughts on Education," *Pencil Points* 18 (July 1937): 441–47; Hudnut to Gropius, 13 April 1937, GSD Papers, UAV 322.7.4, HUA.

97. Charles Killam, "School Training for Architects," 441–47.

98. Gilmore Clarke to Henry Shepley, 19 January 1937, Clarke File, Commission of Fine Arts Papers, NA.

99. Lawrence Kocher to Hudnut, 26 January 1937, GSD Papers, UAV 322.7, subseries I, HUA; Barr to Conant, 20 March 1937, Conant Papers, UA I 5.168, HUA; "Gropius Comes to School of Design as Full Professor," *Harvard Crimson,* 25 January 1937, 1.

100. "Gropius, Eminent Architect, Takes Over New Duties," *Harvard Crimson,* 1 April 1937, 1.

101. Hudnut to Kocher, 29 October 1937, GSD Papers, UAV 322.7.4, subseries 1, HUA.

102. Dewey's phrase, quoted in Robert Westbrook, *John Dewey and American Democracy* (Ithaca: Cornell University Press, 1991), 362.

103. Hudnut to Abraham Garfield, 3 August 1943, GSD Papers, UAV 322.7.4, subseries I, HUA.

104. Hudnut to Coolidge, 27 Dec. 1937, GSD Papers, UAV 322.7 subseries I, box 3, HUA.

105. Gropius to Hudnut, 24 December 1936, Gropius Papers, HL.

106. G. Holmes Perkins, interview by author, 31 December 1990, Philadelphia.

107. Ibid.

108. Herbert Bayer, Walter and Ise Gropius, *Bauhaus, 1919–1928* (New York: Museum of Modern Art, 1938), 34.

109. Gropius, "The Bauhaus Contribution, Letter to the Editor," *Journal of Architectural Education* 18 (June 1963): 14; cf. Gropius, "Lecture in Concord Academy," 1 December 1938, HL.

110. G. Holmes Perkins, interview by author, 31 December 1990, Philadelphia. See Gropius's letters to Marcel Breuer during spring 1937, Gropius Papers, HL and AAA; see also his letters to Joseph Albers, Gropius Papers, HL, and Albers Papers, Yale; Hudnut to Gropius, 23 December 1936, Gropius Papers, HL.

111. Hudnut to Gropius, 23 December 1936, Gropius Papers, HL.

112. Ise Gropius to Jack and Molly Pritchard, 19 April 1937, Pritchard Papers, PP/24/1–9, UEA.

113. Ibid. See also letter to Breuer quoted in Isabelle Hyman, *Marcel Breuer, Architect: The Career and the Buildings* (New York, Abrams, 2001), 88. As Ise Gropius wrote to the Pritchards, 26 May 1937, "we have just been to our 57th party since we've come to the States." Pritchard Papers, PP/24/1–9, UEA.

114. According to a letter written by Ise Gropius to James Marston Fitch, 27 November 1971, Gropius Papers, AAA.

115. Isabelle Hyman's *Marcel Breuer, Architect* fills a large gap in the literature on Breuer. My discussion of Breuer at Harvard owes a debt to Hyman's book, especially chapters 3 and 4.

116. Gropius to Breuer, 17 April 1937, 1 June 1937, and 30 September 1937, Gropius Papers, HL; Hudnut, "Report of Progress Under Grant Made by the Carnegie Corporation," GSD Papers, UAV 322.7, subseries I, HUA.

117. Marcel Breuer to F. R. S. Yorke, 31 August 1937, Breuer Papers, GARL.

118. Ibid.

119. Henry-Russell Hitchcock, *Exhibition of the Work of Marcel Breuer, June–September 1938, Robinson Hall, Harvard University,* Breuer Papers, AAA; Hyman, *Marcel Breuer, Architect,* 99. Hitchcock had already written quite favorably of the "promising" young Breuer, in his earlier catalogue essay for *Modern Architecture in England* (New York: Museum of Modern Art, 1937), 37.

120. Henry-Russell Hitchcock, *Exhibition of Work of Marcel Breuer,* 11, 16, 17. See also Hitchcock, *Modern Architecture: Romanticism and Reintegration* (New York: Payson and Clarke, 1929).

121. Hitchcock, *Exhibition of the Work of Marcel Breuer,* 17–18.

3 MODERNISM TRIUMPHANT

1. Gropius to Conant, 18 December 1949, Isaacs Papers, AAA.

2. "Keep on Planning," *Boston Globe,* editorial, 2 July 1936. See also editorial page of the *Nation* 143 (10 October 1936): 432; *Harvard Crimson,* 3 June 1936, 8 June 1936, and 18 June 1936.

3. Hudnut to Frederic Delano, 8 July 1940, GSD Papers, UAV 322.138, HUA.

4. Holmes Perkins confirmed that Hudnut hoped Wagner's appointment would cause Hubbard to retire.

5. Otto Reichert-Facilides clarified the nature of Wagner's position in a letter responding to my review of Alofsin, *The Struggle for Modernism* in the *Harvard Design Magazine* 17 (Winter 2002–3).

6. Both Gropius's (HL and AAA) and Breuer's papers (GARL) contain numerous appeals for help and letters showing that they did all they could to give it. Martin Wagner to Gropius, 29 June 1937, Gropius Papers, HL; *Official Register of Harvard University, 1938–39,* 294. On Wagner's salary, see Hudnut to Frederic Delano, 8 July 1940, GSD Papers, UAV 322.138, HUA.

7. Otto Reichert-Facilides, letter to *Harvard Design Magazine* 17 (Winter 2002–3).

8. See for example, "Housing, Berlin-Britz: Horseshoe Plan Surrounding Lake," *Architecture* 60 (December 1929): 337.

9. L. Larsson, "Metropolis Architecture," in Anthony Sutcliffe, ed., *Metropolis 1890–1940* (Chicago: University of Chicago Press, 1984), 210.

10. "Dr. Wagner at Harvard," *American Society of Planners Official Newsletter* 4 (December 1938): 100.

11. Ibid. On Wagner's Boston proposal, see Wilhelm Seidensticker, "Aufgaben des Städtebaues," *Die neue Stadt* 5 (1951): 306.

12. Jeffry Diefendorf, *In the Wake of War* (Oxford: Oxford University Press, 1993), 183.

13. Henry Cobb, interview by author, 21 May 2003, New York.

14. Lloyd Rodwin, in "Alumni Meet to Discuss Legacy of Hudnut/Gropius Era," *HGSD News,* November–December 1982, 2. At a similar forum, however—the Landscape Architecture Centennial held at the GSD in April 2000—a few speakers singled out Wagner as having made a profound impact on their professional lives.

15. Gropius, quoted in Diefendorf, *In the Wake of War,* 186.

16. G. Holmes Perkins, interview by author, 31 December 1990, Philadelphia.

17. Henry Cobb, interview by author, 21 May 2003, New York; G. Holmes Perkins, interview by author, 31 December 1990, Philadelphia.

18. Lecture #1, "Site and Shelter," Wagner Papers, Special Collections, Frances Loeb Library, Harvard GSD.

19. Ibid. John Harkness told me of the course's nickname. Harkness, interview by author, 14 December 1990, Cambridge, Mass.

20. Hubbard's coup is discussed in Hudnut's correspondence with Conant, Frederic Delano (an Oversight Committee member), and others, also in the *Minority Report of the Harvard Committee on Regional Planning.* The University of Nebraska and Kansas State taught planning in their engineering schools and regarded the field as a branch of engineering. Chicago's planning program began in 1945; drawing from Charles Merriam's and Robert Park's earlier work there, it emphasized the social sciences and regional studies. Mel Scott, *American City Planning* (Berkeley and Los Angeles: University of California Press, 1969), 366, 468.

21. Hudnut to Wagner, 17 January 1941, GSD Papers, UAV 322.138.5, HUA.

22. Although it was signed by both Hudnut and Gropius, Hudnut clearly wrote the report. *Minority Report of the Harvard Committee on Regional Planning.*

23. Ibid., 9.

24. Mumford to Hudnut, 22 October 1940, GSD Papers, UAV 322.138, HUA.

25. "Dean Hudnut Charged with Ousting Hubbard," *Harvard Crimson,* 22 March 1940.

26. George Howe to Hudnut, 8 April 1953, GSD Papers, UAV 322.7, HUA.

27. Hudnut to James B. Conant, 5 May 1937, GSD Papers, 322.7.4, HUA.

28. See Gropius, *The New Architecture and the Bauhaus* (1935), for a brief discussion of his planning ideas around the time he came to Harvard.

29. Frederick Law Olmsted Jr. to Conant, 13 February 1938, and Hudnut to Conant, 23 February 1938, Conant Papers, UAI.5.168, HUA.

30. Hudnut to Frederic Delano, 5 July 1940, GSD Papers, UAV 322.138, HUA. See Marc Snow, *Modern American Gardens* (New York: Reinhold, 1967).

31. Ibid., 27–28.

32. Simo, *The Coalescing of Different Forces and Ideas,* 31; Garrett Eckbo, "Pilgrim's Progress," in Marc Trieb, ed., *Modern Landscape Architecture: A Critical Review* (Cambridge: MIT Press, 1993), 208.

33. Garrett Eckbo, quoted in Elizabeth Meyer, "The Modern Framework," *Landscape Architecture* (March 1983): 50.

34. Melanie Simo discusses Eckbo's marginalia in "The Education of a Modern Landscape Designer," *Pacific Horticulture* (Summer 1988): 19–30, and in Peter Walker and Melanie Simo, *Invisible Gardens: The Search for Modernism in the American Landscape* (Cambridge: MIT Press, 1994), 123. I am also indebted to Simo's work on landscape architecture at Harvard, especially *The Coalescing of Different Forces and Ideas.*

35. Marc Snow [James Rose], *Modern American Gardens* (New York: Reinhold, 1967).

36. Garrett Eckbo, quoted in Meyer, "The Modern Framework," 52.

37. Walker and Simo, *Invisible Gardens,* 124, 184.

38. Dan Kiley, quoted in Simo, *The Coalescing of Different Forces and Ideas,* 31.

39. This view was widely shared by the numerous alumni present at the conference "One Hundred Years of Landscape Architecture at Harvard," Graduate School of Design, 6–8 April 2000. Dan Kiley, quoted in Simo, *The Coalescing of Different Forces and Ideas,* 31.

40. Garrett Eckbo, quoted in a display at the exhibition One Hundred Years of Landscape Architecture at Harvard, Graduate School of Design, 6–8 April 2000.

41. Eric Kramer, "The Walter Gropius House Landscape: A Collaboration of Modernism and the Vernacular," *Journal of Architectural Education* 57 (February 2004): 9.

42. Gropius and Martin Wagner, "Housing as a Townbuilding Problem," February–March 1942, 42, found in the Avery Library.

43. Christopher Tunnard, "Walter Gropius at Harvard," speech to the Society of Architectural Historians Annual Meeting, Boston, January 1962, Tunnard Papers, Yale.

44. Tunnard, *Gardens in the Modern Landscape,* rev. ed. (New York, Scribner 1948), contains Hudnut's introduction.

45. Hudnut, "Can the Modern House Have a Garden?" lecture presented at Horticultural Society of New York, 15 December 1937, Vertical File, Loeb. See also Joseph Hudnut, "Gardens for Modern Houses," *Bulletin of the Horticultural Society of New York* (January 1938): 6–8; and Joseph Hudnut, "Space and the Modern Garden," *Bulletin of the Garden Club of America* 9 (May 1940): 16–24.

46. Hudnut, "Can the Modern House Have a Garden?"

47. Garrett Eckbo, "Small Gardens in the City," *Pencil Points* 18 (September 1937): 573. See also Garrett Eckbo, "Sculpture and Landscape Design," *Magazine of Art* (April 1938): 202–8; James Rose, "Freedom in the Garden," *Pencil Points* (October 1938): 639–43; and reprints of articles by Eckbo, Kiley, and Rose in Trieb, *Modern Landscape Architecture.*

48. James C. Rose, "Freedom in the Garden," reprinted in Trieb, *Modern Landscape Architecture,* 69.

49. Garrett Eckbo, Dan Kiley, and James Rose, "Landscape Design, The Urban Environment," *Architectural Record* 85 (May 1939): 70–77; "Landscape Design, The Rural Environment," *Architectural Record* 86 (August 1939): 68–74; "Landscape Design, The Primeval Environment," *Architectural Record* 87 (February 1940): 74–79.

50. Christopher Tunnard, "Walter Gropius at Harvard," speech at Annual Meeting of the Society of Architectural Historians, Boston, 27 January 1962, Tunnard Papers, Yale.

51. Christopher Tunnard to Jack Pritchard, 8 February 1939, Pritchard Papers, UEA, PP/16/3/3/46.

52. Hudnut to Mrs. Paul Badger, 29 February 1940, GSD Papers, UAV 322.7, subseries I, HUA.

53. Hudnut to Hubbard, 13 July 1939, GSD Papers, UAV 322.7, subseries I, HUA; John Welsh, "Tunnard: The Modernist with a Memory," *Landscape Design* (October 1987): 20–23.

54. John Dixon Hunt, "The Dialogue of Modern Landscape Architecture with Its Past," in Trieb, *Modern Landscape Architecture,* 135.

55. Tunnard, quoted in Eckbo, Kiley, and Rose, "Landscape Design, The Urban Environment," 71.

56. Ibid.; see also Lance Necker, "Strident Modernism/Ambivalent Reconsiderations: Christopher Tunnard's 'Gardens in the Modern Landscape,'" *Journal of Garden History* 10, 4 (1990): 237–46; Welsh, "Tunnard: The Modernist with a Memory," 20; Walker and Simo, *Invisible Gardens,* 149.

57. Hudnut to Hubbard, 13 July 1939, GSD Papers, UAV 322.7 subseries I, HUA.

58. Lawrence Halprin, quoted in Simo, *The Coalescing of Different Forces and Ideas,* 33.

59. Tunnard, "Walter Gropius at Harvard"; Christopher Tunnard, "What Kind of Landscape for New England?" *Task* 1 (Summer 1941), 39–43.

60. Christopher Tunnard, "Modern Gardens for Modern Houses," *Landscape Architecture* 34 (January 1942): 57–64.

61. Lance Neckar, "Christopher Tunnard," in Trieb, *Modern Landscape Architecture,* 154.

62. Tunnard, quoted on placard at the Landscape Architecture Centennial Exhibition, GSD, April 2000.

63. Tunnard's later books include: *The City of Man* (New York: Scribner, 1970); with Henry Hope Reed, *American Skyline; the Growth and Form of Our Cities and Towns* (Boston: Houghton Mifflin, 1955); with Boris Pushkarev, *Man-Made America: Chaos or Control? An Inquiry into Selected Problems of Design in the Urbanized Landscape* (New Haven: Yale University Press, 1963); *The Modern American City* (Princeton, N.J.: Van Nostrand, 1968); *World with a View: An Inquiry into the Nature of Scenic Values* (New Haven: Yale University Press, 1978).

64. Simo, *The Coalescing of Different Forces and Ideas,* 34.

65. Ibid., 38.

66. Hudnut and Gropius, *Minority Report,* 10. Also quoted in Simo, *The Coalescing of Different Forces and Ideas,* 34.

67. J. B. Conant, "President's Report," *Official Register of Harvard University, 1938–39,* 11.

68. Leonard Currie, "Somewhat Biased Reminiscences of Gropius," *HGSD News,* 5 January 1983, 5.

69. Herdeg, *The Decorated Diagram,* 13, 14.

70. John Parkin, quoted in Huxtable, "He Was Not Irrelevant."

71. Ibid.

72. John Harkness, interview with author, 14 December 1990, Cambridge, Mass.

73. Richard Stein, "The Legacy of Walter Gropius," *Architectural Design* 52 (1982): 60.

74. Questionnaires in Isaacs Papers, AAA.

75. Seymour Howard to Reginald Isaacs, 14 May 1964, Isaacs Papers, AAA.

76. Ibid. Paul Rudolph, comments published in *Perspecta* (Summer 1952), found in Isaacs Papers, AAA. The comments—contained on questionnaires sent to GSD alumni by Reginald Isaacs in 1964 and now housed in the Isaacs Papers—offer a rich source for understanding students' experiences of Gropius as teacher.

77. Stein, "The Legacy of Walter Gropius," 58, 60; Reginald Knight to Reginald Isaacs, 8 April 1964, Isaacs Papers, AAA.

78. Comments from questionnaires in Isaacs Papers, AAA.

79. Franz Schulze, *Philip Johnson: Life and Work* (New York: Knopf, 1994), 150.

80. Ibid., 149.

81. John Morse to Walter Bogner, 28 April 1966, testimonial letters to Walter Bogner, GSD Papers, subseries II, Administrative Records, IIa, HUA.

82. Henry Cobb, interview by author, 21 May 2003, New York. Cobb was chair of the Architecture Department at the GSD from 1980 to 1985.

83. John Morse to Walter Gropius, 20 July 1964, Isaacs Papers, AAA.

84. Stein, "The Legacy of Walter Gropius," 58.

85. G. Holmes Perkins, interview by author, 31 December 1990, Philadelphia; for admissions requirements, see "Faculty of Design," *Official Register of Harvard University* for the various years.

86. Bruno Zevi, "Architecture," *Encyclopedia of World Art* (New York: McGraw-Hill, 1959): 1: 686, 692. See Robert Stern, "Yale 1950–1965," *Oppositions* 4 (October 1974): 35–62.

87. Stein, "The Legacy of Walter Gropius," 58.

88. Schulze, *Philip Johnson: Life and Work,* 150.

89. John Black, interview by author, 27 January 1990, Chicago.

90. Peter Christie, and also William Lyman, 1964 questionnaire, Isaacs Papers, AAA.

91. Garrett Eckbo, quoted in Landscape Architecture Centennial Exhibition, GSD, April 2000.

92. Paul Rudolph interview, in John Cook and Heinrich Klotz, *Conversations with Architects* (New York: Praeger, 1973), 95, 108.

93. Nikolaus Pevsner, "Gropius: A Moral Force in Architecture," clipping in Pritchard Papers, PP/24/11/16, UEA.

94. Huxtable, "He Was Not Irrelevant."

95. John Harkness, interview by author, 14 December 1990, Cambridge, Mass.; Edward Larrabee Barnes, "Remarks on Continuity and Change," *Perspecta* 9/10 (1964–66): 292.

96. Schulze, *Philip Johnson: Life and Work,* 150.

97. John Harkness, interview by author, 14 December 1990, Cambridge, Mass.; Barnes, "Remarks on Continuity and Change," 292.

98. "Marcel Lajos Breuer as He Is Remembered," *Journal of the American Institute of Architects* 70 (August 1981): 11.

99. Hyman, *Marcel Breuer, Architect,* 100.

100. Breuer in Paul Heyer, *Architects on Architecture: New Directions in America* (New York: Penguin, 1966), 267.

101. "Great Teachers," Barnes to William Saunders, 26.

102. Breuer in Heyer, *Architects on Architecture,* 267; Gropius to Serge Chermayeff, 23 March 1950, ID Papers, UIC.

103. On the Gropius and Breuer partnership buildings, see Hyman, *Marcel Breuer, Architect,* and Nerdinger, *Walter Gropius.*

104. Landsberg quoted in Hyman, *Marcel Breuer, Architect,* 108.

105. On the question of authorship, see Hyman, *Marcel Breuer, Architect,* 102–16; see also Joachim Driller, *Breuer Houses* (London: Phaidon, 2000), 102ff.; and Nerdinger, *Walter Gropius,* 198. All three authors refer to D. H. Wright, "The Architecture of Walter Gropius," honors thesis, Harvard College, 1950, in which Gropius commented on authorship in the margins.

106. Serge Chermayeff, Chicago Architects Oral History Project, May 1985, interview by Betty Blum, p. 9, http://www.artic.edu/aic/collections/dept_architecture/chermayeff .html.

107. Breuer to Gropius, 23 May 1941, Gropius Papers, HL.

108. Breuer to Gropius, 23 May 1941, (letter #2), Gropius Papers, HL.

109. Gropius to Breuer, 25 May 1941, Gropius Papers, HL.

110. Gropius to Herbert Bayer, quoted in Reginald Isaacs, *Gropius* (Boston: Bulfinch, 247).

111. See Breuer to James Marston Fitch, 30 December 1960, Breuer Papers, AAA.

112. Moholy-Nagy to Walter Paepke, 31 July 1946, and Sibyl Moholy-Nagy to Paepke, 30 November 1946, ID Papers, UIC.

113. Petition from GSD Students to Breuer, 9 February 1948, Breuer Papers, GARL. Hyman wrote that Breuer had hung the petition in his New York office.

114. "Graduate School of Design," *Official Register of Harvard University, 1940–41,* 267.

115. Dorothy May Anderson, *Women, Design, and the Cambridge School* (West Lafayette, Ind.: PDA, 1980); Hudnut to Gropius, 23 December 1936, Gropius Papers, HL.

116. Quoted in Simo, *The Coalescing of Different Forces and Ideas,* 24.

117. G. Holmes Perkins, interview by author, 31 December 1990, Philadelphia.

118. John Black, interview by author, 27 January 1990, Chicago; G. Holmes Perkins, interview by author, 31 December 1990, Philadelphia; and Henry Cobb, interview by author, 21 May 2003, New York. See also Carter Manny to his family, 27 October 1940, quoted in Schulze, *Philip Johnson,* 149.

119. Hugh Stubbins, *Hugh Stubbins, Architecture: The Design Experience* (New York: Wiley, 1976), 177–78; Hudnut to Arthur Weatherhead, 5 October 1943, GSD Papers, UAV 322.7, subseries I, HUA. Stubbins's buildings at Harvard include the Countway Library, Pusey Library, and Loeb Drama Center.

120. George Birkhoff to Hudnut, 9 November 1937, and Jerome Greene to Hudnut, 15 November 1937, UAV 322.7, GSD subseries II, IIa, HUA. Quoted in Eduard F. Sekler, "Sigfried Giedion at Harvard University," in Elisabeth Blair MacDougall, ed., *The Architectural Historian in America* (Washington: National Gallery of Art, 1990), 265.

121. Quoted in Sekler, "Sigfried Giedion at Harvard University," 266.

122. Ibid., 268.

123. Ibid., 266.

124. Several of the alumni I interviewed recalled their amused reactions to Giedion's lectures. See also Sekler, "Sigfried Giedion at Harvard University."

125. Sigfried Giedion, "To the Editors of *Task*," and H. Seymour Howard Jr., review of *Space, Time and Architecture,* both in *Task* 2, undated (1941?): 37–38.

126. Max Hall, *Harvard University Press: A History* (Cambridge: Harvard University Press, 1986), 80–82. On Giedion, see Spiro Kostof, "Architecture You and Him: The Mark of Sigfried Giedion," *Daedalus* 105 (Winter 1976): 189–204; see also Sokratis Georgiadis, *Sigfried Giedion, eine intellektuelle Biographie* (Zurich: Institute für Geschichte und Theorie der Architektur, 1989).

127. Peter Fergusson, "Medieval Architectural Scholarship in America, 1900–1940: Ralph Adams Cram and Kenneth John Conant," in MacDougall, *The Architectural Historian in America,* 137–38. See also John Coolidge, "Harvard's Teaching of Architecture and of the Fine Arts, 1928–1985," in Floyd, *Architectural Education and Boston,* 60–61.

128. See "Graduate School of Design," in the *Official Register of Harvard University* for the years 1936–52 to trace changes in GSD course requirements.

129. Hudnut, "Graduate School of Design," *Official Register of Harvard University, 1938–39,* 284; "Memorandum: Reorganization of Instruction in Architecture at Harvard University," 7 February 1936, CF-CU; *Memorandum of the Visiting Committees of the Graduate School of Design,* 11 June 1936, Conant Papers, UA I 5.168, HUA.

130. "Arch. Sci. Seeks Creative Effort," *Harvard Crimson,* 23 April 1942, 4; *Official Register of Harvard University, 1939–40,* "GSD, Courses Offered in Harvard College," 52–53.

4 TRUMPET BLASTS
The complete source for the epigraph to chapter 4 is as follows: Nikolaus Pevsner, "Judges VI, 34," *Architectural Review* 106 (August 1949): 77.

1. Hudnut, "Statement on Werner Hegemann."

2. Hudnut to Carroll Meeks, 2 October 1944, GSD Papers, UAV 322.7.4, subseries I, HUA; Joseph Hudnut, "City Planning and the Public Mind: Comment on the Boston Contest," *Architectural Record* 97 (January 1945): 60; Joseph Hudnut, "The Political Art of Architecture," *Journal of the Royal Institute of Canadian Architects* 23 (March 1946): 54.

3. Jean Paul Carlhian described the Love Nest to me. J. P. Carlhian, interview by author, 12 May 1988, Boston.

4. Walter Creese to author.

5. Hudnut to Halsey Munson, 18 September 1951, GSD Papers, UAV 322.7.4, subseries 1, HUA.

6. See the reviews of Hudnut's collection of essays *Architecture and the Spirit of Man* (Cambridge: Harvard University Press, 1949) in *Architectural Forum* 90 (June 1944): 60; and 91 (November 1949): 134.

7. Paul Zucker, "*Architecture and the Spirit of Man,* by Joseph Hudnut," *Journal of Aesthetics* 8 (June 1950): 272.

8. Review of Hudnut's 1949 book, *Architecture and the Spirit of Man,* in the *New Yorker* 26 (4 March 1950).

9. Hudnut, preface to Gropius, *The New Architecture and the Bauhaus,* 7, 8, 9.

10. Joseph Hudnut, "Architecture and the Modern Mind," *Magazine of Art* 33 (May 1940): 314.

11. Ibid., 291; Hudnut, preface to Gropius, *The New Architecture and the Bauhaus,* 10.

12. Hudnut, "Architecture and the Modern Mind," 291.

13. Ibid.

14. Joseph Hudnut, "Architecture Discovers the Present," *American Scholar* 7 (Winter 1939): 114.

15. Joseph Hudnut, "Architecture in a Mechanized World," *Octagon* 10 (August 1938): 6.

16. Hudnut, "Architecture in a Mechanized World," 4, 5; Hudnut, "Can the Modern House Have a Garden?" 13.

17. Hudnut, "Architecture in a Mechanized World," 5, 6.

18. Ibid., 6.

19. Maccoby, "Design–A School without Direction," 3.

20. Gropius made this comment in "How Do Students Become Architects?" survey by John Knox Shear, *Architectural Record* (October 1954): 179.

21. Hudnut to Frederick Allen, 23 July 1941, GSD Papers, UAV 322.7.4, HUA.

22. See the 1937–38 Jefferson Memorial controversy correspondence in GSD Papers, UAV 322.7.4, HUA. Dewey wrote "Presenting Thomas Jefferson" in 1940; it appears in *John Dewey, The Later Works, 1925–1953* (Carbondale: Southern Illinois University Press, 1988), 14: 201–23.

23. On Pope, see Steven Bedford, *John Russell Pope, Architect of Empire* (New York: Rizzoli, 1998). Kay Fanning, "On Kimball and the Jefferson Memorial," paper presented at "Fiske Kimball: Creator of an American Architecture" symposium, University of Virginia, 19 November 1995, http://www.lib.virginia.edu/dic/exhib/fiske/conference/Fanning.html.

24. Hudnut quoted in "Goodbye, Messrs. Chips," *Time* 61 (29 June 1953): 68.

25. See GSD Papers on the controversy; see also Joseph Hudnut, "Twilight of the Gods, Jefferson Memorial, Washington, D.C." *Magazine of Art* 30 (August 1937): 481; "A Temple for Thomas Jefferson," *New Republic* (22 March 1939): 190–91; Joseph Hudnut, "Address to the American Federation of Arts," 4 May 1937, GSD Papers on Jefferson Memorial controversy, UAV 322.7, subseries I, HUA.

26. Hudnut, "Address to the American Federation of Arts."

27. Joseph Hudnut, "Classical Architecture Not Essential," *Architectural Record* 54 (August 1937): 55.

28. Hudnut to the editor of the *Washington Post,* 30 March 1938, in the GSD Papers on the Jefferson Memorial controversy.

29. Hudnut, "Address to the American Federation of Arts," 5.

30. Joseph Hudnut, "The Last of the Romans," *Magazine of Art* 34 (April 1942): 173.

31. Ibid., 7; Hudnut, "Twilight of the Gods."

32. Delano had read Hudnut's "Architecture Discovers the Present," *American Scholar* 7 (Winter 1938): 106–14. Delano to C. G. Abbot, Secretary of the Smithsonian, 13 August 1938, SIA, box 149, folder 4.

33. The competition was for an architect rather than a building: the winner would work with the Commission of Fine Arts to make his building fit in with the rest of the Mall. The story of the Smithsonian Gallery of Art can be pieced together through archives at the Smithsonian Institution, the Edward Bruce Papers at both the National Archives and the Archives of American Art. Travis McDonald has written about the competition in James Kornwolf, ed., *Modernism in America, 1937–1941* (Williamsburg, Va.: Joseph and Margaret Muscarelle Museum of Art, 1985).

34. Ned Bruce to Hudnut, 14 December 1938, Bruce Papers, NA.

35. Quoted in Kornwolf, *Modernism in America,* 182, and Bruce to Hudnut, 23 July 1939, Bruce Papers, NA.

36. Bruce to FDR, and Bruce to Eleanor Roosevelt, 24 April 1941, Bruce Papers, NA.

37. Hudnut to Ned Bruce, 7 December 1939, Bruce Papers, NA.

38. C. L. Borie to Frederic Delano, 3 December 1938, Bruce Papers, NA.

39. Ibid., 184; Hudnut to Ned Bruce, 4 November 1939, Bruce Papers, NA. C. L. Borie, architect with the Philadelphia firm Zantzinger and Borie, was the most vociferous of these critics. Ned Bruce noted that he was "more or less appointed by the AIA as critic-in-chief of the Smithsonian Gallery plan."

40. Clarence Stein, William van Alen, Albert Kahn, William Perry (of the Robinson Hall library incident), Paul Cret, Albert Kahn, Wallace Harrison, Hugh Stubbins, Richard Stein, Holmes Perkins, William Wurster, William Lescaze, Henry Churchill, Emil Lorch (Hudnut's professor at Michigan). The complete list is available at the National Archives, RG 121.

41. Hudnut to Ned Bruce, 7 December 1939, Bruce Papers, NA.

42. Hudnut to Gropius, 23 December 1938, Gropius Papers, HL.

43. Ibid., 11, 14, 15; see also Bulletin Number 5, 12 April 1939. Various "bulletins" or addenda to the program were issued during the competition.

44. Ibid.

45. Mumford quoted in Ockman, *Architecture Culture,* 27.

46. Sigfried Giedion, J. L. Sert, and Ferdinand Léger, "Nine Points on Monumentality," quoted in Ockman, *Architecture Culture,* 29.

47. Ibid., 18.

48. The timing of the competition was as follows: the program was first issued in late January 1939, and architects had until 1 March to signal their intent to register. Entries were due 29 April. Those chosen to submit entries in the second competition were notified on 15 May, and their final drawings were due 21 June.

49. Hudnut, "A National Competition to Select an Architect for the Proposed Smithsonian Gallery of Art, Washington, DC" (Washington: Smithsonian Gallery of Art Commission, 1939), 9.

50. "Report of the Jury Award," 28 June 1939, Bruce Papers, NA. The ten finalists included: Eliel Saarinen; Percival Goodman; James Mitchell and Dahlen K. Ritchey (both Hudnut students at Columbia, and Ritchey also went to the GSD); Holmes Perkins (GSD); Paul Cret; Edward Durrell Stone; Philip Goodwin; Marc Peter and Hugh Stubbins (both of the GSD); Eliot Noyes and Robert Woods Kennedy (both of the GSD); and Harry Manning and David Carlson.

51. Hudnut to Ned Bruce, 7 December 1939, Bruce Papers, NA.

52. Ibid.

53. Ibid.

54. John Holabird quotes a letter sent to him by Ned Bruce. Holabird to Bruce, 29 March 1940, Bruce Papers, NA.

55. Hudnut discusses Clarke's allegations in a letter to Ned Bruce, 4 December 1939, Bruce Papers, NA.

56. The Commission of Fine Arts rejected the Gallery building in an informal way—they never met formally to consider the project. See MacDonald's essay in *Modernism in America* on why the museum was never built. This is also well documented in the Smithsonian Archives, and in the Bruce Papers in the National Archives. Photographs of many of the 408 drawings are housed in the Smithsonian Archives, and the model of the Saarinen building is in storage at the Smithsonian Institution. See also Mina Marefat, "When Modern Was a Cause," *Competitions* (Fall 1991): 36–49.

57. Elizabeth Mock, ed., *Built in the USA, 1932–1934* (New York: Museum of Modern Art, 1944), 25.

58. "Can Modern Architecture Build a Symbol?" *Architectural Forum* 106 (June 1957): 152.

59. "Belluschi, Hudnut appointed to National Commission of Fine Arts," *Architectural Forum* 93 (August 1950): 15.

60. "Truman Shakes up Arts Commission," *New York Times,* 19 June 1950.

61. David De Long, "Eliel Saarinen and the Cranbrook Tradition in Architecture and Urban Design," in Robert Judson Clark et al., *Design in America: The Cranbrook Vision, 1925–1950* (New York: Abrams, 1983), 47.

62. Albert Christ-Janer, *Eliel Saarinen* (Chicago: University of Chicago Press, 1948), xiv.

63. "College Planning," *Architectural Record* 102 (December 1947): 87–106.

64. Christ-Janer, *Eliel Saarinen,* 113.

65. Joseph Hudnut, "Kleinhans Music Hall, Buffalo," *Architectural Forum* 75 (July 1941): 41.

66. Ibid.

67. Joseph Hudnut, "Crow Island School, Winnetka, Ill.," *Architectural Forum* 75 (August 1941): 85.

68. Many thanks to Katherine Taylor for pointing out this correspondence to me. Let-

ter to Jean Block, 28 November 1945?; see also Hudnut to Herbert Zimmerman, 7 March 1945, Correspondence on the Administration Building, University of Chicago Archives; Herbert Zimmerman, "The Administration Building," *University of Chicago Magazine,* January 1947, 10–11.

69. Hudnut to President Colwell, 14 October 1948, GSD Papers, UAV 322.7.4, subseries I, Ib, HUA.

70. Ibid.

71. References to these committees are scattered throughout the GSD Papers, HUA.

72. Hudnut to AIA President, James Edmunds, 10 October 1945, AIA Archives.

73. Joseph Leland to James Edmunds, (undated) October 1945, AIA Archives.

74. Harold Willis to Philip Creer, 27 February 1953, AIA Archives.

75. See Hudnut to Phillip Goodwin, 12 May 1944, American Society of Planners and Architects Papers, Records of External Offices and Organizations, UAV 322.7, subseries X.

76. Gropius to Breuer, 1 June 1937, Gropius Papers, HL.

77. Gropius to Walter Saunders, 4 May 1938, Gropius Papers, HL.

78. Saunders to Gropius, 19 May 1938, Gropius Papers, HL.

79. Hudnut, *Memorandum, September 1936.*

80. Éva Forgács, *The Bauhaus Idea and Bauhaus Politics* (Budapest: Central European University Press, 1995), 116, 26.

81. See any of Gropius's lectures included in the Gropius Papers, e.g., manuscript for 1937 talk at the New York "Architectural League Club," Gropius Papers, HL.

82. See Gropius, MS, "Training the Architect," 1939, Gropius Papers, HL.

83. Alfred Barr to Gropius, 3 March 1939, Gropius Papers, HL.

84. Moholy's school was called the New Bauhaus from 1937 to 1938; from 1939 to 1944, it was known as the School of Design. Known thereafter as the Institute of Design, it became part of the Illinois Institute of Technology in 1949.

85. Gropius to Norma Stahle, 18 May 1937, in Hans Wingler, *Bauhaus* (Cambridge: MIT Press, 1978), 192.

86. Moholy to Hudnut, undated 1937, GSD Papers, UAV 322.7.4, subseries I, HUA.

87. On the Institute of Design, see Wingler, *Bauhaus;* James Sloan Allen, *The Romance of Commerce and Culture* (rev. ed., Boulder: University Press of Colorado, 2002), and David Travis and Elizabeth Siegel, eds., *Taken by Design* (Chicago: University of Chicago Press, 2002).

88. Gropius talk to *CIAM 8,* 12 July 1951, Gropius Papers, HL.

89. Sigfried Giedion, "On CIAM's Unwritten Catalogue," *Journal of the Society of Architectural Historians* 3 (January–April 1943): 46.

90. According to Eric Mumford in "CIAM Urbanism after the Athens Charter," *Planning Perspectives* 7 (1992): 415 n. 20.

91. Foreword to José Luis Sert, *Can Our Cities Survive?* (Cambridge: Harvard University Press, 1942).

92. Eric Mumford, *The CIAM Discourse on Urbanism, 1928–1960* (Cambridge: MIT Press, 2000), 134.

93. Mumford to Sert, 28 December 1940, quoted in Mumford, *The CIAM Discourse on Urbanism,* 132.

94. "Architects Form for World Project," *New York Times,* 3 November 1944.

95. Hudnut to George Fred Keck, 28 June 1944, GSD Papers, Records of External Offices and Organizations, UAV 322.7, subseries X, HUA.

96. Mumford, *The CIAM Discourse on Urbanism,* 147.

97. Hudnut to G. Holmes Perkins, 27 November 1944, GSD Papers, Records of External Offices and Organizations, UAV 322.7, subseries X, HUA.

98. On Telesis, formed in 1939, see "Vernon DeMars," http://sunsite.berkeley.edu:2020/ dynaweb/teiproj/oh/unihist/demars/@Generic__BookTextView/159;pt=181. See also Richard Plunz, *A History of Housing in New York City* (New York: Columbia University Press, 1990), 250.

99. Hudnut to George Fred Keck, 28 June 1944, GSD Papers, HUA.

100. Hudnut to Philip Goodwin, 12 May 1944, GSD Papers, HUA.

101. ASPA, Minutes of the Meeting, 1 April 1944, GSD Papers, Records of External Offices and Organizations, UAV 322.7, subseries X, HUA. On FAECT, see "Planners Network," http://www.plannersnetwork.org/htm/pub/archives/143/heifetz.html; and Plunz, *A History of Housing in New York City,* 249.

102. Hudnut to G. Holmes Perkins, 27 November 1944, GSD Papers, Records of External Offices and Organizations, UAV 322.7, subseries X, HUA.

103. Hudnut to James Edmunds, 10 October 1945, AIA Archives.

104. ASPA, Minutes of the Meeting, 1 April 1944, GSD Papers, Records of External Offices and Organizations, UAV 322.7, subseries X, HUA.

105. "Minutes, Executive Committee," 17 November 1945, GSD Papers, Records of External Offices and Organizations, UAV 322.7, subseries X, HUA.

106. List of ASPA members, and "Constitution, The American Society of Planners and Architects," Loeb, Special Collections. Janet O'Connell to Hudnut, 7 November 1944, GSD Papers, Records of External Offices and Organizations, UAV 322.7, subseries X, HUA.

107. See Joseph Hudnut, "Architecture's Place in City Planning," *Architectural Record* 97 (March 1945): 70–73.

108. "Report of the President, the ASPA, First Annual Meeting, 27 January 1945," UAV 322.7, subseries X, HUA; and Hudnut and Gropius, *Minority Report of the Harvard Committee on Regional Planning.*

109. "Report of the President, the ASPA, First Annual Meeting, 27 January 1945."

110. "Planning Is Politics," *Architectural Forum* 82 (March 1945): 7.

111. Hudnut and Richard Neutra, "Memorandum Submitted to the Secretary General of the United Nations," 1 May 1946, GSD Papers, HUA. It is likely, given the prose style and content of the document, that Hudnut wrote much of the ASPA/CIAM joint documentation without Neutra's help.

112. Hudnut and Richard Neutra, "An Architectural Competition for the Buildings of the United Nations Organization," GSD Papers, Records of External Offices and Organizations, UAV 322.7, subseries X, HUA.

113. "Press Release Concerning the Construction of the UN Headquarters," Truman and the UN Collection, "Establishing Headquarters in NY" folder, Truman Library, http://www.trumanlibrary.org/whistlestop/study_collections/un/large/un_hq/un_hq11-3.htm.

114. Louis Kahn, "An Urban Community," 25 January 1945, GSD Papers, UAV 322.7, subseries X, HUA.

115. Louis Kahn to Hudnut, 15 May 1946, GSD Papers, UAV 322.7.4, subseries I, HUA; David Brownlee and David De Long, *Louis I. Kahn: In the Realm of Architecture* (New York: Rizzoli, 1991), 34, 44.

116. Harold Willis to Philip Creer, 27 February 1953, AIA Archives.

117. G. Holmes Perkins, interview with author, 31 December 1990, Philadelphia.

118. For another view of ASPA, see Andrew Shanken, *Planning Perspectives* 20 (April 2005): 147–75.

119. Among the many in similar positions, Mies and Moholy-Nagy also had FBI files. See Kentgens-Craig, *The Bauhaus and America,* 180–82, 238–44. Hudnut was not the subject of an official investigation as Gropius was (letter to author from FBI).

120. "Gropius, Walter Adolph," FBI files acquired through the Freedom of Information Act, 26 March 1991, communication written on 10 August 1940, #HQ 65–21066.

121. Gropius FBI Files. The Gropiuses' neighbor and fellow Harvard professor James Ford and his wife, Katherine Morrow Ford, wrote *The Modern House in America* (New York: Architectural Book Publishing Co., 1940).

5 CONFLICTING VIEWS OF HOUSE AND TOWN

1. Huxtable, "He Was Not Irrelevant."

2. Joseph Hudnut, "The Invisible City," *Journal of the American Institute of Planners* 15 (Summer 1949): 10.

3. Kenneth Jackson, *Crabgrass Frontier* (New York: Oxford University Press, 1985), 193; Gwendolyn Wright, *Building the Dream* (Cambridge: MIT Press, 1981), 220. Edith Wood, quoted in Mel Scott, *American City Planning* (Berkeley and Los Angeles: University of California Press, 1969), 284.

4. Lawrence Veiller, quoted in Scott, *American City Planning,* 258.

5. Report of the Urbanism Committee to the National Resources Committee, *Our Cities: Their Role in the National Economy,* June 1937, 76.

6. Housing legislation quoted in Scott, *American City Planning,* 329; Bauer, "Now at Last: Housing," *New Republic* 92 (8 September 1947): 119; editorial cited in Jackson, *Crabgrass Frontier,* 244.

7. Catherine Bauer, *Modern Housing* (Boston: Houghton Mifflin, 1934), xvi.

8. Scott, *American City Planning,* 284. See also Edith Elmer Wood, *Recent Trends in American Housing* (New York: Macmillan, 1931).

9. See Gropius and Wagner, "Townlets and Towns, A Study on City Reconstruction Made by the Students of the GSD, Harvard University," 23 August 1946, Loeb.

10. Quoted in Jackson, *Crabgrass Frontier,* 195.

11. Joseph Arnold, *The New Deal in the Suburbs* (Columbus: Ohio State University Press, 1971), 1967.

12. Ibid.; Wright, *Building the Dream,* 223. See also Cathy D. Knepper, *Greenbelt, Maryland: A Living Legacy of the New Deal* (Baltimore: Johns Hopkins, 2001).

13. Scott, *American City Planning,* 342.

14. Jackson, *Crabgrass Frontier,* chap. 11, offers an excellent discussion of the ties between federal subsidies and the growth of suburbia; Plunz, *A History of Housing in New York City,* 280.

15. National Resources Committee, *Our Cities,* 84.

16. Hudnut to Conant, 20 April 1938, Conant Papers, UAI.5.168, HUA.

17. Hudnut, *Memorandum, September 1936.*

18. "Gropius to Harvard," *Architectural Forum* 66 (March 1937): 33.

19. Ibid.

20. Carol Aronovici, ed., *America Can't Have Housing* (New York: Museum of Modern Art, 1934). A description of the exhibition imagery, which focused on New York City, appears on 75–78. See also Richard Pommer, "The Architecture of Urban Housing in the United States during the Early 1930s," *Journal of the Society of Architectural Historians* 37 (December 1978): 261.

21. Walter Gropius, "Minimum Dwellings and Tall Buildings," in Aronovici, *America Can't Have Housing,* 42.

22. Ibid., 42, 43.

23. Quoted in Eric Mumford, *The CIAM Discourse on Urbanism,* 38, 50; Gropius published an English version of this lecture/essay as "Houses, Walk-ups, or High-rise Apartment Blocks?" in *The Scope of Total Architecture* (New York: Collier, 1962), 103–15.

24. Nerdinger, *Walter Gropius,* 136.

25. Ibid., 188.

26. Quoted in Nerdinger, *Walter Gropius,* 156.

27. See Hyman, *Marcel Breuer, Architect,* 302–4.

28. Nerdinger, *Walter Gropius,* 136.

29. Gropius, "Houses, Walk-ups, or High-rise Apartment Blocks?" 114. Gropius also argued for high-rises in numerous GSD student design problems.

30. Nerdinger, *Walter Gropius,* 289.

31. Plunz, *A History of Housing in New York City,* 190.

32. Hudnut, "Housing and the Democratic Process," *Architectural Record* 93 (June 1943): 42–46.

33. Ibid., 43.

34. Ibid.

35. Ibid., 44.

36. Ibid., 45.

37. *Harvard Catalogue 1938,* "GSD Description of Courses," 48. See various design problems held in both the GSD Papers, HUA, and Special Collections, Loeb.

38. Catherine Bauer, "The Housing Seminar: Comments and Recommendations," 29 September 1946, and "Housing Seminar, Purpose and Scope," GSD Papers, UAV 322.7.4, subseries IV, HUA.

39. Joseph Hudnut, "The Art in Housing," *Architectural Record* 93 (January 1943): 57–62.

40. Gropius and Wagner, "Housing as a Townbuilding Problem," February–March 1942, 3; Walter Bogner and Martin Wagner, "A Housing Problem, Small Houses for the Families of Professional Men," April 1940; and Martin Wagner, Walter Gropius, and Marcel Breuer, "Housing Problem," November 1939, GSD Papers, UAV 322.7.4, subseries IV, HUA; Walter Gropius, "A Post-War Dwelling for the Average Family," December 1944, Vertical File, Loeb.

41. Gropius and Wagner, "Housing as a Townbuilding Problem," 30, 33, 34.

42. Both Gropius and his wife, Ise, were remarkably generous in helping refugees from the war. They opened their home to many, including Wachsmann. On his case, see Isaacs, *Gropius,* 243.

43. Gilbert Herbert, *The Dream of the Factory-Made House* (Cambridge: MIT Press, 1984), recounts the story of Gropius and Wachsmann's project and the General Panel Corporation. See "Variety of Houses from Identical Prefabricated Units of General Panel Corporation, Designed by Harvard Students," *Pencil Points* 24 (December 1943): 76–77.

44. See "Exchange Problem, with AA in London," 1938; Gropius, "A Post-War Dwelling for the Average Family"; Gropius, "The Post-War Shelter for the Average Family," design problem, February 1943, GSD Papers, UAV 322.7.4, subseries IV, HUA.

45. Gropius and Wagner, "Housing as a Townbuilding Problem," 44.

46. Ibid.; Gropius, "The Post-War Shelter for the Average Family"; Gropius, "Toward a Living Architecture, Ornament and Modern Architecture," *American Architecture* 19 (January 1938): 22.

47. Gropius, "Toward a Living Architecture, Ornament and Modern Architecture," 22.

48. Ibid.

49. Hubbard, Bogner, (Gropius, Wagner?), "The Small Home," February 1938; Bogner, "An Entrance for a Theatre Building," 18 February 1937; unsigned landscape problems, "A Rose Garden," February 1940; and unsigned and untitled problem, 27 January 1939, GSD Papers, UAV 322.7, subseries VIII, HUA.

50. Gropius, "The Post-War Shelter for the Average Family."

51. Herdeg, *The Decorated Diagram,* 78. Herdeg draws from a Gropius problem entitled "Site Development for Family Residences."

52. Ibid.

53. Gropius, "The Post-War Shelter for the Average Family."

54. Hudnut, "Art in Housing," 58–59.

55. On "sight-relief," see "A Satellite Town for Metropolitan Boston," April 1946, appendix 6, Vertical File, Loeb; Hudnut, "Art in Housing," 59.

56. Hudnut, "The Post-Modern House," 70, 73, 75.

57. Ibid.

58. Ibid.

59. The essay has been anthologized in Joan Ockman's *Architecture Culture 1943–1968.*

60. Wagner to Gropius, 8 September 1940, Gropius Papers, HL.

61. Martin Wagner, lecture notes from "Housing" course, A 6, "Site Planning" lecture, p. 6, undated, Special Collections, Loeb.

62. Wagner to Gropius, 8 September 1940, Gropius Papers, HL.

63. Ibid.

64. Hudnut, "The Post-Modern House," 74.

65. Mumford, "Skyline," *New Yorker,* 11 October 1947, 106, 109.

66. Christopher Tunnard, in "What Is Happening to Modern Architecture?" *Museum of Modern Art Bulletin* 15 (Spring 1948): 14.

67. Lewis Mumford, in "What Is Happening to Modern Architecture?" *Museum of Modern Art Bulletin* 15 (Spring 1948): 2. Hudnut frequently used the phrase "emotional content" in personal letters and in publications. See Anderson, "The New Empiricism—Bay Region Axis."

68. Bruno Zevi to author, 28 January 1994.

69. "Preface to *A Call*," (May 1941), Breuer Papers, GARL. Students made minor editorial changes and retitled the manifesto "An Opinion on Architecture."

70. From the 1941 "An Opinion on Architecture" and an earlier draft, entitled "Preface to *A Call*," in Breuer Papers, GARL.

71. John Harkness, interview by author, 14 December 1990, Cambridge, Mass.

72. *Task* 4 (1943): 1.

73. See the assorted issues of *Task* for the various contributors.

74. John Harkness suggested this connection to me in our interview, 14 December 1990, Cambridge, Mass.

75. Perkins told me that his house was finished before Gropius's (interview by author, 31 December 1990, Philadelphia). On Perkins's house, see "Holmes Perkins, Architect, House in Brookline, Mass.," *Architectural Forum* 71 (July 1939): 25ff.

76. Hyman, *Marcel Breuer, Architect,* 105.

77. "Great Teachers: Marcel Breuer," *GSD News,* Fall 1995, 29.

78. John Black, GSD alumnus, interview by author, 27 January 1990, Chicago.

79. Edward L. Barnes, "Remarks on Continuity and Change," *Perspecta* 9/10 (1964–66): 292.

80. "Great Teachers: Marcel Breuer," 29.

81. "An Opinion on Architecture."

82. "No Traditionalist Is Martin Wagner," *Architect's Journal* 94 (July 1941): 39; Herbert Ripley, "Back to Pithecanthropous Erectus," *Weekly Bulletin, Michigan Society of Architects* 16 (6 January 1942): 1.

83. "No Traditionalist Is Martin Wagner," 39.

84. On Wagner's igloo, see "Building for Defense," *Architectural Forum* 74 (February 1941): 87–90.

85. Gropius and Wagner, "Housing as a Townbuilding Problem."

86. Ibid.

87. Ibid.

88. Walter Bogner, "An Apartment House for Modern Requirements," March–April 1937, GSD Papers, UAV 322.4, subseries IV, HUA.

89. Gropius and Wagner, "Housing as a Townbuilding Problem"; Gropius, Newton, Stubbins, Tunnard, and Wagner, "Housing Problem," April 1941, 1; Gropius and Perkins, "An Apartment House Group", April–June 1937, GSD Papers, UAV 322.7.4, subseries IV, HUA; Walter Bogner, "A Residence," December 1938, and unsigned, "A Group of Four Country Residences," November–December 1939, GSD Papers, UAV 322.7, subseries VIII, HUA.

90. Gropius and Wagner, "Housing as a Townbuilding Problem"; Gropius, Newton, Stubbins, Tunnard, and Wagner, "Housing Problem," April 1941.

91. Gropius and Wagner, "Housing as a Townbuilding Problem."

92. Gropius, Newton, Stubbins, Tunnard, and Wagner, "Housing Problem," April 1941.

93. Ibid.

94. Ibid.

95. Hudnut mocked planners' and architects' "back-to-the-country cult" in numerous articles. See "Housing and the Democratic Process," 42–43, and "New Cities for Old," *Mademoiselle,* January 1945, 91.

96. Herdeg, *The Decorated Diagram,* 81.

97. Vincent Scully, "Doldrums in the Suburbs," *Perspecta* 9–10 (1965): 5.

98. Hudnut, "New Cities for Old," 9.

99. Ibid., 142.

100. See Guy Greer, ed., *The Problem of the Cities and Towns: Report on the Conference on Urbanism, Harvard University, March 1942*.

101. Gropius, *The New Architecture and the Bauhaus*, 98, 99.

102. Hudnut, "Confidential Memo on John Gaus," March 1941, GSD Papers, UAV 322.7.4, subseries I, HUA.

103. Ibid.; John Gaus, curriculum vitae, GSD Papers, UAV 322.7.4, subseries I, HUA; John Gaus, "Education for Regional Planning," *Journal of the American Institute of Planners* 17 (Winter 1951): 3, 6.

104. John Gaus, *The Graduate School of Design and the Education of Planners* (Cambridge: GSD, 1943), 35, 45–46.

105. G. Holmes Perkins, interview by author, 31 December 1990, Philadelphia.

106. Gaus, "Education for Regional Planning," 7, 8; Gaus, *The Graduate School of Design*, 32, 34, 47.

107. Gaus, *The Graduate School of Design*, 20, 38–40.

108. Hudnut, "What a Planner Has to Know," 157–58.

109. Ibid., 162.

110. Gaus to Hudnut, GSD Papers, UAV 322.4, subseries I, Ib, HUA.

111. Hudnut to Talcott Parsons, Carl Friedrich, Morris Lambie, Charles Abbott, Seymour Harris, and D. S. Whittlesey, 6 April 1945, GSD Papers, UAV 322.138, HUA.

112. G. Holmes Perkins, interview by author, 31 December 1990, Philadelphia.

113. Ibid.

114. Robert Moses, "Mr. Moses Dissects the 'Long-Haired' Planners," *New York Times Magazine*, 25 June 1944, 16, 17, 38, 39.

115. Ibid., 16, 17. Moses also included several Americans in his list, including Lewis Mumford, Rexford Guy Tugwell, and Frank Lloyd Wright.

116. Robert Moses, *Public Works: A Dangerous Trade* (New York: McGraw Hill, 1970), 856.

117. Joseph Hudnut, "A 'Long-Haired' Reply to Moses," *New York Times Magazine*, 22 July 1944, 16, 36–37.

118. Ibid., 36.

119. Ibid., 16.

120. Ibid., 36–37.

121. Ibid., 36; Hudnut, "New Cities for Old," 142.

122. Hudnut "On Teaching the History of Architecture," 6.

123. Moses, *Public Works*, 856.

124. Gropius and Wagner, "A Program for City Reconstruction," *Architectural Forum* 79 (July 1943): 75.

125. Richard Filipowski noted that Gropius often described Hudnut's work with this phrase. Interview by author, 9 June 1988, Cambridge, Mass.

126. Gropius and Wagner, "A Program for City Reconstruction," 75.

127. These are the common characteristics of a wide range of GSD planning problems from the Hudnut/Gropius era. GSD Papers, HL and Loeb.

128. "Satellite Town for Metropolitan Boston," April 1946.

129. Ibid. These quotations are drawn from several different South End of Boston Redevelopment design problems and a housing problem for South Cambridge, GSD Papers, UAV 322.272, HUA.

130. Gropius, "Faith in Planning," *Planning 1952: Proceedings of the Annual National Planning Conference,* Boston, October 1952, 14.

131. Hudnut, "New Cities for Old," 142; Hudnut, "The Invisible City," 10.

132. Hudnut, "The Political Art of Architecture," 53.

133. Hudnut, "Confessions of an Architect," 13; Hudnut, "New Cities for Old," 142;

Hudnut, "The Invisible City," 9; Hudnut, "Second Thoughts on the Skyscraper," *Transatlantic,* September 1945.

134. Hudnut, "Housing and the Democratic Process," 44; Hudnut, "Art in Housing," 272; and Hudnut, "Second Thoughts on the Skyscraper," 9.

135. On New Town Units, see collaborative design problem, "A Satellite Town for Metropolitan Boston," 8 April 1946, GSD Papers, UAV 322.7.4, subseries 4, HUA; Hudnut, "Housing and the Democratic Process," 44; Joseph Hudnut, "The New Housing: An Architect's Lament," *Tomorrow* 9 (April 1950): 15.

136. Joseph Hudnut, "On Genuine Education," *Task,* 1948, 80.

137. Hudnut, "The Invisible City," 5.

138. Ibid., 7; and Hudnut, "The Post-Modern House," 75.

139. Forgács, *The Bauhaus Idea and Bauhaus Politics,* 126.

140. Hudnut, "Humanism and the Teaching of Architecture," 15.

6 THE BATTLE OVER BASIC DESIGN

1. Hudnut to Ned Bruce, 11 September 1939, Bruce Papers, NA.

2. Memorandum, Contribution of the GSD to the War Effort, 2 May 1946, GSD Papers, 322.7GSD, subseries VII, VIIb, HUA.

3. John Humphreys to unidentified, 3 February 1944, GSD Papers, UAV 322.7, subseries III, HUA.

4. Hudnut to David Bailey, 30 September 1948, on the faculty's unanimous decision to admit women, GSD Papers, UAV 322.7, subseries II, IIa, HUA.

5. These included William Wheaton and Coleman Woodbury in Planning, and Jean Paul Carlhian in Architecture. Lester Collins took over Bremer Pond's position as chair of the Department of Landscape Architecture. For other appointments, see "Faculty of Design," *Official Register of Harvard University,* 1945–53.

6. Ibid., 27–28; Hudnut, "Architecture Discovers the Present," 106; G. Holmes Perkins, interview by author, 31 December 1990, Philadelphia; and "GSD Final Report, Committee for the Revision of the Curricula," 22 May 1950, GSD Papers, UAV 322.7, subseries II, IIa, HUA.

7. G. Holmes Perkins, interview by author, 31 December 1990, Philadelphia.

8. "Graduate School of Design" *Official Register of Harvard University, 1946–47,* 17.

9. Gillian Naylor, *The Bauhaus Reassessed* (New York: Dutton, 1985), 9.

10. Gropius to Serge Chermayeff, 16 March 1950, ID Papers.

11. Wingler, *The Bauhaus,* 8, 142–43. I have presented these ideas in my article "Joseph Hudnut's Other Modernism at the 'Harvard Bauhaus,'" *Journal of the Society of Architectural Historians* 56 (December 1997): 450–76.

12. Forgács, *The Bauhaus Idea and Bauhaus Politics,* 140; Naylor, *The Bauhaus Reassessed,* 154–55.

13. "Outline of the Course, Design Fundamentals," 23 October 1950, GSD Papers, UAV 322.7, subseries II, IIa, HUA; "Basic Design: A Course Proposed for the First Year of Professional Training in the HGSD," Gropius Papers, AAA.

14. Gropius, "Re: The Education of an Architect," 1939, Gropius Papers, AAA.

15. Ibid.; Gropius described his scientific visual language in numerous essays and speeches. See "Suggestions for the Curriculum of an Architect's Training at Harvard," 1937, and "Address Given by Professor Walter Gropius to the GSD Visiting Committee," 30 March 1937, Gropius Papers, AAA. See also "Tuesday Evening Session," Association of Collegiate Schools of Architecture annual meeting, 9 May 1950, in *ACSA/Journal of Architectural Education Proceedings* (Spring 1951): 81.

16. Gropius, "Re: Education of an Architect," 2; Gropius, letter to the editor, *Journal of Architectural Education* 18 (June 1963): 15.

17. Albers to Gropius, 9 May 1940, Albers Papers, Yale; Hudnut to Gropius, 23 December 1936, Gropius to Hudnut, 14 January 1937, Gropius Papers, HL.

18. Gropius to Serge Chermayeff, 16 March 1950, ID Papers; "Description of Courses," *Official Register of Harvard University 1949–50*, 27.

19. Oral History of Benjamin Horace Weese, Chicago Oral History Project, Art Institute of Chicago, 11; at http://www.artic.edu/aic/collections/dept_architecture/weeseben.pdf; Henry N. Cobb, interview by author, 21 May 2003, New York.

20. Gropius to Chermayeff, 16 March 1950, ID Papers.

21. Ibid.; G. Holmes Perkins, interview by author, 31 December 1990, Philadelphia.

22. Hudnut, "Foundations," *Line Magazine* 1 (1952), unpaginated; and Joseph Hudnut, "The Anticipation of Order," *Journal of Architectural Education* (Autumn 1958): 23. Gropius describes the "twofold" system in Forgács, *The Bauhaus Idea and Bauhaus Politics*, 84.

23. Gropius, quoted in Maccoby, "Design—A School without Direction," 3; Forgács, *The Bauhaus Idea and Bauhaus Politics*, 84–85.

24. Joseph Hudnut, "The Political Art of Planning," *Architectural Record* 94 (October 1943): 45; Hudnut and Gropius, *Minority Report of the Harvard Committee on Regional Planning;* Hudnut, "Foundations."

25. Hudnut, "The Anticipation of Order," 23.

26. Hudnut, *The Three Lamps of Modern Architecture* (Ann Arbor: University of Michigan Press, 1952), 1, 7.

27. Hudnut, "Architectural Values," in Thomas Creighton, ed., *Building for Modern Man* (Princeton, 1949), 93; Hudnut, "Architecture in a Mechanized World," 3; "The Bases of Judgment," memo from Hudnut to David Finley, 29 January 1951, Finley Papers, Library of Congress; Hudnut, "Architecture's Place in City Planning," *Architectural Record* 97 (March 1945): 71.

28. Walter Gropius, "Blueprint for an Architect's Training," *L'architecture d'aujourd'hui* 20 (February 1950): 74.

29. See "Graduate School of Design," in the *Official Register of Harvard University* for the years 1936–52 to trace changes in GSD course requirements.

30. Joseph Hudnut, "What a Young Planner Ought to Know," *Journal of the American Institute of Architects* 7 (February 1947): 60.

31. "People," *Architectural Forum* 97 (July 1952): 59.

32. Hudnut, "Confessions of an Architect," 13.

33. Hudnut, "On Teaching the History of Architecture," 6; Hudnut, "Humanism and the Teaching of Architecture," 14.

34. Hudnut, "On Teaching the History of Architecture," 6.

35. Hudnut, "What a Planner Has to Know," 159; Hudnut, "Humanism and the Teaching of Architecture," 14.

36. Walter Creese, who served as a teaching fellow in Civic Design, described Hudnut and his course in a letter to author, 28 September 1987; G. Holmes Perkins, interview by author, 31 December 1990, Philadelphia; Hudnut to Carol Aronovici, 27 January 1945, GSD Papers, UAV 322.7.4, subseries I, HUA; "Descriptions of Courses," *Official Register of Harvard University 1946–1947*, 37.

37. Oral History of Benjamin Horace Weese, Chicago Oral History Project, Art Institute of Chicago, 10; Henry Cobb, quoted in "Alumni Meet to Discuss Legacy of Hudnut/Gropius Era," *HGSD News* 11 (November–December 1982): 6.

38. G. Holmes Perkins, interview with author, 31 December 1990, Philadelphia. John Harkness also referred to Hudnut's music building (interview by author, 14 December 1990, Cambridge, Mass.). On Stanley B. Parker's design, see Bainbridge Bunting, *Harvard: An Architectural History* (Cambridge: Belknap Press of Harvard University Press, 1985), 248–49.

39. Ada Louise Huxtable, "Inventing American Reality," *New York Review of Books*, December 3, 1992, 24–29.

40. Quoted in Thomas Creighton, "P.S. Harvard Dean Is Critical of Williamsburg, Harvard Dean Praises Williamsburg Influence," *Progressive Architecture* 31 (May 1950): 168. Hudnut's speech "We Are No Longer Colonials" appeared in a slightly different version in *House and Garden* 97 (May 1950): 166ff.

41. Ada Louise Huxtable, *The Unreal America* (New York: New Press, 1990), 17.

42. On the Graduate Center, see Bunting, *Harvard: An Architectural History,* 222–25, 228–29. According to Richard Filipowski, Hudnut encouraged the administration to give Gropius the Graduate Center commission. Richard Filipowski, interview by author, 9 June 1988, Cambridge, Mass.

43. Bunting, *Harvard, An Architectural History,* 216–17.

44. Philip Johnson, "Architecture of Harvard, Revival and Modern: The New Houghton Library," in Philip Johnson, *Writings* (New York: Oxford University Press, 1979), 62; J. B. Conant, "President's Report," *Official Register of Harvard University, 1938–39,* 11.

45. Gropius, "Tradition and the Center," *Harvard Alumni Bulletin* 53 (14 October 1950): 69. Gropius wrote a nearly identical article for a broader audience, "Not Gothic but Modern for Our Colleges," *New York Times Magazine,* 23 October 1949, 16–18.

46. "Harvard Reaffirms an Old Tradition," *Architectural Record* 104 (November 1948): 118–19; "Up to Date," *Time* 56 (25 September 1950): 49

47. Alumni critics include R. Clipston Sturgis, *Harvard Alumni Bulletin* 53 (14 October 1950): 55, and Edward Norman, *Harvard Alumni Bulletin* 53 (21 April 1951): 532. Huxtable, "He Was Not Irrelevant."

48. "Professors Reply to Alumni Blasts at New Modernistic G.E. Building," *Harvard Crimson,* 17 April 1951, 4.

49. "New Grad Center Near Jarvis Court Will Bring End to Housing Project," *Harvard Crimson,* 15 October 1948, 1; Gropius and William Lyman, "A Graduate Center for Harvard University," design problem, June 1948, Vertical File, Loeb.

50. Gropius, "True Architectural Goals Yet to Be Realized," *Architectural Record* 129 (June 1961): 149.

51. Gropius made this point often. See "Blueprint for an Architect's Training," 74.

52. "Blueprint for an Architect's Training" reads, for example, much like part of Gropius's 1937 "Suggestions for the Curriculum of an Architect's Training at Harvard," Gropius Papers, AAA.

53. Zevi, "Architecture," 1: 686, 688.

54. Ibid., 1: 692.

55. Ockman, *Architecture Culture,* 68.

56. Joseph Hudnut, "La Casa Postmoderna," *Metron,* October 1945, 15–23; Joseph Hudnut, "Urbanistica, Arte, Politica," *Metron,* 1946, 50–57; Hudnut, "The Political Art of Planning," 44–48; Bruno Zevi, "Wright and Italy," in Anthony Alofsin, ed., *Frank Lloyd Wright, Europe and Beyond* (Berkeley and Los Angeles: University of California Press, 1999), 66.

57. Quotations are from notes for an exhibition produced in the Design Fundamentals course, fall and spring 1950–51, RF; Richard Filipowski, interview by author, 9 June 1988, Cambridge, Mass.

58. From notes for an exhibition produced in the Design Fundamentals course, fall and spring 1950–51, RF.

59. Gropius, "For the Dean's Annual Report: Outline of the Course, Design Fundamentals," RF.

60. Gropius to Chermayeff, 15 March 1950, ID Papers; Richard Filipowski, interview by author, 9 June 1988, Cambridge, Mass.

61. Filipowski, untitled notes (draft of course outline for Annual Dean's Report, c. autumn 1950), RF.

62. Filipowski, "Three Dimensional Experiments," and "Design Fundamentals Workshop," 2 September 1950, RF.

63. Filipowski, "Design Fundamentals—Fall–Spring Terms, 1951–52, Graphics and Color," FP.

64. Students were polled about their views on the course. "Design School Council Seeks Conant Parley," *Harvard Crimson,* 25 February 1952), 1.

65. "Unbalanced Design," *Harvard Crimson,* 27 February 1952, 2; John Benedict, "Design for Today," *Harvard Crimson,* 28 February 1952, 2.

66. Malcom Rivkin, "Hudnut Drops Design I, Based on Gropius Ideas," *Harvard Crim-*

son, 23 February 1952, 1. Chester Nagel, William Lyman, and Charles Burchard were all graduates of Gropius's class, and Norman Fletcher was a member of TAC.

67. Norman Newton, "Report of the Chairman of Architectural Sciences," *Official Register of Harvard University, 1950–51*, 473; Norman Newton, *Approach to Design* (Cambridge: Addison-Wesley Press, 1951).

68. Unsigned memo, "Thoughts on Design Fundamentals as a Course within a Program of General Education," RF. See the Redbook, *General Education in a Free Society, Report of the Harvard Committee* (Cambridge: Harvard University Press, 1946).

69. Rivkin, "Hudnut Drops Design I," 1. Stubbins is cited in Maccoby, "Design—A School without Direction," 3.

70. Walter Gropius, "On Herbert Read," in Robin Skelton, ed., *Herbert Read, A Memorial Symposium* (London: Methuen, 1970); Walter Gropius, "Design Topics," *Magazine of Art* 40 (December 1947): 299; Herbert Read, *Education through Art* (London: Faber and Faber, 1943).

71. Gropius, "On Herbert Read," 27–28; Read, *Education through Art,* 8.

72. Earl C. Kelley, *Education for What Is Real* (New York: Harper, 1947), preface and 38.

73. The Ames Room can still be seen on the following Web site: http://psylux.psych .tu-dresden.de/i1/kaw/diverses%20Material/www.illusionworks.com/html/ames_room .html

74. On the Dartmouth Eye Institute, later the Hanover Institute, see Adelbert Ames Jr., *Visual Perception and the Rotating Trapezoidal Window* (Washington: American Psychological Association, 1950), 1; Kelley, *Education for What Is Real,* 25.

75. Kelley, *Education for What Is Real,* preface.

76. Walter Bogner to Harald Omsted, 22 January 1947, GSD Papers, UAV 322.7 GSD subseries II, IIa, HUA.

77. William Lyman, interview by author, 10 November 1990, Portsmouth, N.H. Lyman served as Gropius's Master Class assistant from 1947 to 1952.

78. Gropius to Jack Pritchard, 20 April 1948, Pritchard Papers, PP/24/1–9, UEA.

79. Gropius, "Topics of Design," 5–7; Gropius, "Design Topics," 300.

80. Rivkin, "Hudnut Drops Design I." The *Harvard Crimson* reported that the GSD had a $10,000 deficit. Maccoby, "Design—A School without Direction," 1.

81. Hudnut, "Fundamentals."

82. Rivkin, "Hudnut Drops Design I."

83. Ibid.

84. See the *Harvard Crimson* articles: Maccoby, "Design—A School without Direction," "Unbalanced Design," and "Design for Today."

85. Maccoby, "Design—A School without Direction," 3.

86. These are the retrospective words of Robert C. Weinberg in the *Harvard Alumni Bulletin* 70 (3 February 1968).

87. See Maccoby, "Design—A School without Direction," 3.

88. Harvard required faculty members to retire on 30 June of their sixty-sixth year, according to Harvard's Office of Human Resources.

89. G. Holmes Perkins, interview by author, 31 December 1990, Philadelphia.

90. Chermayeff to Conant, 27 May 1950, Gropius Papers, HL.

91. Isaacs to J. B. Conant, 24 May 1950, Gropius Papers, HL.

92. Conant to Giedion, 25 August 1954, Gropius Papers, HL.

93. Maccoby, "Design—A School without Direction," 3, 4; "Decadent Design," *Harvard Crimson,* 26 November 1952, 2; G. Holmes, interview by author, 31 December 1990, Philadelphia; see "Faculty of Design," *Official Register of Harvard University,* 1949–53, for changes in the GSD's faculty.

94. Maccoby, "Design—A School without Direction," 3; "Conant Resigns as President," *Harvard Crimson,* 12 January 1953, 1.

95. Conant, "President's Report," *Official Register of Harvard University, 1951–52,* 33–34.

96. Conant to Giedion, 24 August 1954, Gropius Papers, HL.

97. Hudnut, "L'architect sur Clef," lecture delivered at MIT, summer session 1956. Many thanks to Richard Filipowski for making a text of this lecture available to me.

98. Ibid., 5, 8, 12, 13, 14.

99. Ibid., 20, 22.

100. Hudnut, *The Three Lamps of Modern Architecture* (Ann Arbor: University of Michigan Press, 1952), 57.

101. Hudnut, "The Bases of Judgment in Architecture," memo to the Commission of Fine Arts, 29 January 1951, Finley Papers, LC.

102. Hudnut to Johnson, 12 March 1953, GSD Papers, 322.7.4, subseries I, HUA.

103. First published in *Perspecta* 3 (1955), "The Seven Crutches" has also been reproduced in Johnson, *Writings,* and Ockman, *Architecture Culture.* Vincent Scully, "Doldrums in the Suburbs," *Perspecta* 9 (1965), 290.

104. "Sert Proposes to Introduce New Design I," *Harvard Crimson,* 18 March 1953.

105. Ibid.

106. José Luis Sert, opening remarks to the Urban Design Conference, April 9, 1956, Loeb Library, Graduate School of Design.

107. See "Symposium I, Debunk," held at Harvard's Littauer Center, 7 May 1949, proceedings published by the Council for Planning Action in Boston, 1949.

108. I am indebted to Richard Marshall for his work on the Urban Design Conferences. A version of his paper "Shaping the City of Tomorrow: José Luis Sert's Urban Design Legacy" will appear in a forthcoming volume, *Josep Lluis Sert: The Architect of Urban Design* (Yale University Press). Marshall also delivered a version of this essay at the symposium on Sert held at the GSD in November 2003.

109. Robert Weinberg, "Dean Hudnut's Dream," letter to *Harvard Alumni Bulletin* 70 (3 February 1968).

110. That view of Sert was put forward at the November 2003 conference at the GSD on Sert. It is also the underlying theme in the forthcoming volume, *Josep Lluis Sert: The Architect of Urban Design.*

111. The house in Dover was razed around 1990.

112. "The Gropius Symposium," *Arts and Architecture* 69 (May 1952): 29–33; "Birthday Fete for Gropius," *Architectural Record* 124 (July 1958): 9, 25; "Gropius's 80th Birthday Marked by Old Friends and Students," *Architectural Record* 134 (July 1963): 10. Among other positions, Hudnut served on the National Commission of Fine Arts and on the review board for Baltimore's urban renewal program. He also published some fifteen articles after leaving Harvard. G. Holmes Perkins, interview by author, 31 December 1990, Philadelphia.

113. Hudnut to Robert Weinberg, 25 December 1966, Weinberg Papers, LIU.

114. Ibid.

115. Huxtable, "He Was Not Irrelevant." On the Pan Am Building's critics, see Meredith Clausen, *The Pan Am Building and the Shattering of the Modernist Dream* (Cambridge: MIT Press, 2005).

116. Hudnut to Chermayeff, 30 January 1951, and Chermayeff to Ise Gropius, 23 April 1972, Chermayeff Papers, Avery.

117. See Ockman, *Architecture Culture,* for an excellent overview of the period, which she calls "the interregnum between modernism and what is now called postmodernism." Huxtable, "He Was Not Irrelevant."

INDEX

Italicized page numbers refer to illustrations.

Aalto, Alvar, 6, 105, 213, 217
Alabama Polytechnic University, Auburn, 18
Albers, Josef, 80, *81,* 105, 203–4, 205, 206, 208, 215, 218, 223
Allen, Frederick Lewis, 128
Alofsin, Anthony, 7–8
American Institute of Architects (AIA), 141–42, 148, 149; Hudnut's relationship to, 141
American Scholar, 131
American Society of Planners and Architects (ASPA), 5, 123, 147–53; list of members, *150*
Architects Collaborative, The (TAC), 1, 163, 221, 236; Harkness Graduate Center (Harvard University), 212–15, *213, 214*
Architectural Forum, 138, 143, 151, 159
architectural history and modernism, 175; at the GSD, 65, 70, 95, 120–21, 218; Gropius and, 121, 214, 215–17; Hudnut and, 18, 39–40, 57, 70, 99, 121–22, 209–12
Architectural Record, 39, 44, 50, 97, 138, 214
Architectural Review, 94, 175
Armour Institute of Technology, 69
Aronovici, Carol, 44, 160

Barnes, Edward Larrabee, 1, 7, 110, 111, 180, 182

Barr, Alfred, 45, 144, 145, 149; hiring modernist for Harvard, 65–66
Basic Design (GSD course), 3, 15, 17, 80, 144–45, 201–8, 218–26, 230
Bauer, Catherine (Wurster), 149, 155, 157, 160, 164, 165–66, 180, 201
Bauhaus, 1, 2, 31, 39, 73, 105, 121, 203; Dessau, 80, 125, 126; pedagogy, 4, 17, 77, 44, 201, 220–21; students compared to GSD students, 78
Bauhaus Exhibition, Museum of Modern Art, 75
Bayer, Herbert, 105, 115, 215, 218
Bay Region Style, 6, 174–75
Beaux-Arts, 55, 67, 73, 75, 78; drawings in the manner of, *22, 23, 53;* Hudnut overthrows, 54–58; pedagogy, 1, 8, 18, 19, 20–21, 37, 40–44, 51, 105, 108, 202, 244n96
Belluschi, Pietro, 138, 149
Berlin-Britz Horseshoe, *87*
Black Mountain College, 80, 81, 111, 206
Blunt, Anthony, 72
Bogner, Walter, 116–17, 164, 170, 181; house (Lincoln, MA), *118*
Borie, C. L., 132
Boring, William, 37
Boston 1915 (Civic Improvement), 24–25
Breuer, Marcel, 1, 3, 5, 70, 82, *83,* 92, *111,* 116, 126, 149, 153, 166, *183,* 189; Aluminum City (New Kensington, PA),

Breuer, Marcel (*continued*)
112, *114;* Breuer House (Lincoln, MA), 181, 182, *183;* Chamberlain Cottage (Wayland, MA), 112, *113,* 182; feud with Gropius, 113–15, 192; Frank House (Pittsburgh, PA), 112, 176, *177,* 182; Garden City of the Future, 82, 83; Gropius House (Lincoln, MA), *181;* Hagerty House (Cohasset, MA), *112;* Harvard appointment, 81; 1938 exhibition at GSD, 83–84, 251n119; practice with Gropius, U.S., 82, 111–15, 176; students' opinion of, 110–12, 115; teaching at Harvard, 108, 110–11, *111*
Bruce, Edward (Ned), 131, 132, 135
Bush-Brown, Harold, 46
Butler, Nicholas Murray, 48, 246n132

Cambridge School of Domestic Architecture, 116
Carnegie Foundation, 82
Charlottesville, Virginia, 33–36
Chermayeff, Serge, 72, 98, 115, 147, 149, 218, 233, 237
Christ-Janer, Albert, 138
Church, Thomas, 93
CIAM (Congrés internationaux d'Architecture Moderne) 4, 6, 92 119, 120, 148, 188, 195; New York chapter, 145–47, 152
city planning, 24, 30, 60, 61, 146, 195–99; defined, 63, 189; education, 60, 61, 252n20; —, at Harvard, 61–62, 86–92, 116, 185–87, 190–91, 195–99, *196, 198,* 202, 220, 234
civic design, 2, 3, 9, 25–28, 30–31, 43–44, 48, 91, 123, 127, 151, 153, 208, 234–35; Hudnut's GSD courses in, 210, 235
Clarke, Gilmore, 77, 129, 135, 137
Coates, Wells, 70, 74
Cobb, Henry N., 1, 107
collaboration, 4, 42, 55, 56, 58, 59, 60, 64, 89, 102, 103, 104, 108, 117, 178, 189, 202
Columbia University, 2, 3, 8, 39, 43, 60; Institute of Urbanism, 44; School of Architecture, 19, 20, 37–45, 159; Teacher's College, 41–42; Town Planning Studio, 43–44
communism, 68, 180
Conant, James B., 5, 45–49, *47,* 77, 64, 85, 93, 104, 143, 151, 159, 201, 215, 222, 227, 233; agenda for Harvard, 45–49, 64, 108; German interest, 49, 65, 163, 229; hires Hudnut for Harvard, 45–49
Conant, Kenneth, 65, 120

Conference on Urbanism (1942), 188, 234
Congrés internationaux d'Architecture Moderne. *See* CIAM
Cornell University, 51, 60
Cram, Ralph Adams, 50
Cranbrook, 138
Currie, Leonard, 112, 133, 201

Dartmouth Eye Institute, 224–25
"Debunk: A Critical Review of Accepted Planning Principles," 234
decentralization, 158, 162, 164, 184, 185–86, 238
Delano, Frederic, 131, 133
democratic education, 43, 45, 46, 55, 56, 78, 79, 108, 128, 201. *See also* progressive education
Depression, the, 2, 40, 41, 51, 156
Design Fundamentals (GSD course), 218–26, 230, 235; course description, *219;* drawings/student exercises, *219, 220, 221, 222*
Design I (GSD course), 202, 206
Dewey, John, 2, 41–43, 46, 79, 124, 128, 130, 144, 145, 224
Dover, Massachusetts, 235
Dow, Arthur W., 15, 17, 241n17

Eckbo, Garrett, 93, 94–97, 100, 108, 180; drawings by, *98, 99*
Edgell, George, 2, 46, 50

FAECT (Federation of Architects, Engineers, Chemists, and Technicians), 148
FBI (Federal Bureau of Investigation), 153–54
Filipowski, Richard, 218–20, 221, 226, 228; drawings by, *219, 220*
flexibility in modern architecture, 133, 166–67, *167,* 195
formalism, 46, 125, 155, 172, 173, 201, 202, 208, 212
Friedrich, Carl, 192
Frost, Henry, 116, 166
Fry, Maxwell, 71–72, 74, 98; drawing by, *72*
functionalism, 39, 63, 72, 76, 98, 197
functional zoning, 188, 195, 197

Gabo, Naum, 218, 233
Gaus, John, 11, 189, *190;* ideas of city and regional planning, 190–91
general education. *See* "Objectives of a General Education in a Free Society"
General Panel Corporation, 167

Giedion, Sigfried, 6, 74, 117, 119–20, *119,* 123, 145, 149, 216, 233; *Space, Time, and Architecture,* 120; *Walter Gropius: Work and Teamwork,* 229

Goodwin, Philip, 45, 65, 66, 148

Gothic architecture, twentieth-century, 32, 38, 50, 140

Greenbelt Town Program, 157, 158, 185

Gropius, Ise, 14, 81, *83,* 182, 237

Gropius, Walter, 1, 2, 3, *13,* 45, *83, 107, 136, 159, 236,* 237; Aluminum City (New Kensington, PA), 112, *114;* architectural philosophy, 67, 104, 144, 214, 224–25, 230n81; architectural practice, U.S., 70, 74–75, 82, 111–15; arrival in U.S., 81, 85, 157; buildings and designs, 19, *20, 72, 112, 113,* 114, *162,* 176, *177, 181,* 212–15, *213, 214,* 237; Chamberlain Cottage (Wayland, MA), 112, *113,* 182; on the city, 155, 185–86, 188, 195–96; critics' view of, 76–77, 108, 109–10, 155, 186, 215–18, 237; on drawing, 19, 112; educational ideas, 79, 128, 143, 144, 201–8, 215–16, 218–20, 221, 223–25; Fagus Shoe Last Factory (Alfeld, Germany), 19, *20;* feud with Breuer, 113–15; feud with Hudnut, 4, 8, 17, 155–56, 188, 192, 198–99, 206–7, 210, 226–28; Frank House (Pittsburgh, PA), 112, 176, *177,* 182; Gropius House (Lincoln, MA), *181;* Hagerty House (Cohasset, MA), *112;* Harkness Graduate Center, 212–15, *213, 214;* Harvard appointment, 66–70, 74, 76, 78, 227; on landscape architecture, 95–96; in London, 70–74, 80; opinion of Hudnut, 4, 74, 81; Pan Am Building, 237; personality, 9, 13–14, 68–69, 110; practice with Breuer, 82, 111–15; as propagandist, 14, 56, 68, 71, 75, 129, 142–44, 161, 202, 214; students' opinion of, 77–78, 104–9, 110, 127, 176, 211, 215–18, 221, 226, 241n7; teaching style, 106, 108–9, 111. Writings: "Blueprint for an Architect's Education," 216; *The New Architecture and the Bauhaus,* 92. *See also* Basic Design (GSD course); housing: Gropius's ideas of

Gropius House (Lincoln, MA), 95, 106, 108, 110, 153, 181, *181*

Haffner, Jean-Jacques, 52, 75, 116; garden design, *53*

Hagerty House (Cohasset, MA), *112*

Halprin, Lawrence, 100

Harkness, Charles (Chip), 105, 201

Harrison, Wallace K., 133, 146, 147

Harvard Alumni Bulletin, 235

Harvard-Bauhaus, 1, 3, 75–80, 85

Harvard Crimson, 3, 77, 91, 221, 226, 227, 228, 233

Harvard Graduate School of Design (GSD): Architectural Sciences, 121, 220; curriculum, 80, 81, 85, 164, 202, 209, 210, 218–22; design problems, 51, 95, 100, 102, 104, 106, 108, 110, 157, 166, *167, 168, 169,* 170, *171, 172,* 184, 185–86, 190, 195, *196, 198,* 206, 224; founding of, 4, 54–60; Master Class, 104, 106, 107–8, 109, 201, 221

Harvard University: Faculty of Architecture, 48, 54, 59; Jewish quota, 68; Charles Eliot Norton Lectures, 118–19. Buildings: Harkness Graduate Center, 212–15, *213, 214;* Houghton Library, 213; Hunt Hall, 56, 124, 200; Lamont Library, 213; Littauer Center, 74; Paine Hall, 211, 212; Robinson Hall, 50, *51,* 54–57, *55, 56, 59,* 78, 124, 200, 220; Sever Hall, 215. *See also* Harvard Graduate School of Design (GSD)

Hegemann, Werner, 2, 24–31, *24,* 37, 42–43, 63, 91–92, 99, 151, 159, 160, 175, 188, 208; *American Vitruvius,* 27, 30, *31,* 243n65; city planning, 29–30, 65; Washington Highlands, 25; work with Joseph Hudnut, 25–28; writings, 28–30; Wyomissing Park (near Reading, PA), 25, *26, 27, 31*

Herdeg, Klaus, 7, 104, 170, 171, 186

Hilberseimer, Ludwig, 162

Hitchcock, Henry-Russell, 38, 40, 45, 83–84

Holabird, John, 133

housing: Gropius's ideas of, 159–63, *162,* 166–71, 186–87; Hudnut's ideas of, 163–65, 168, 187; U.S., 155–58, 159–78. *See also* postwar house

Howe, George, 45, 133, *149,* 230

Hubbard, Henry, 54, 60–62, 75, 78, 86, 93, 189; battle with Hudnut, 90–92, 104; *Introduction to the Study of Landscape Design,* 93

Hubbard, Theodora Kimball, 61, 93

Hudnut, Joseph, 2, 3, *12, 21, 136, 149, 190;* as architectural critic, 138–42; architectural philosophy, 4, 25–28, 30–32, 38–39, 43–44, 125–28, 135, 138, 151, 152, 155, 168, 172–73, 174, 191, 193–94, 207–8, 209–12, 230–33; architectural practice, 21, 31–35, 211,

Hudnut, Joseph (*continued*)
243n69; biography, 11–14, 17; buildings *18, 19, 33, 34, 35, 36,* 211, 242n27; city and planning ideas, 4, 28, 48, 54, 91–92, 151, 153, 155–56, 187–88, 189, 193–94, 196–99, 202, 234; at Columbia University, 19, 37–45; critics' view of, 35, 76–77, 125, 132, 152, 237; critique of modern architecture, 4, 6–7, 125–27, 168, 173–75, 191, 194, 195, 209–10; drawings, *16, 22, 23, 31,* 211; educational ideas, 4, 35, 37, 39–40, 41–43, 48, 58, 78, 128, 202, 207–8, 209–12; family, 14–15, 18; feud with Gropius, 8, 17, 155–56, 188, 192, 198–99, 206–7, 210, 226–28; hired for Harvard (1935), 45–49, 50, 51, 54; on landscape architecture, 96, 99, 103–4, 253n45; as propagandist, 14, 64, 75, 124, 128–31, 139–40, 141–42, 144, 153, 178; as public intellectual, 5, 14, 30, 43, 123–28, 144; relationship to Gropius, 85, 213, 236, 237; as student, 15, *16,* 17–18, 20, *21, 22, 23;* students' view of, 39, 54, 127–28, 211, 226–27; teaching, 3, 11, 18, 35, 39–40, 210–11, 227; work with Werner Hegemann, 25–28; Wyomissing Park (near Reading, PA), 25, *26, 27, 31.* Writings, 37, 38, 75, 124; "Architecture and the Individual," *232;* "Architecture and the Modern Mind," 126; *Architecture and the Spirit of Man,* 229; "Can Modern Architecture Build a Symbol?" 137; "La Casa Postmoderna," 217; foreword to *Can Our Cities Survive?* 146; "Housing and the Democratic Process," 163; "A 'Long-haired' Reply to Moses," 193; "The Political Art of Planning," 217; "The Post-Modern House," 6, 172, 173, 191, *231,* 237; "The Three Lamps of Modern Architecture," 230–33; "We Are No Longer Colonials," 212; "What a Planner Has to Know," 191. *See also* housing: Hudnut's ideas of
Hudnut, Richard, 113
Humphreys, John, 116, 200–201
Huxtable, Ada Louise, 8, 110, 155, 212, 215, 237

individuality in modern architecture, 171, *232,* 237
Institut d'Urbanisme (Paris), 44
Institute of Design, Chicago, 115, 145, 218, 259n84
interdisciplinarity, 37, 46, 48, 61, 93, 191, 234

Isaacs, Reginald, 228
Isokon, 70, 71

Jacobs, Jane, 163, 164, 237
Jefferson, Thomas, 33, 129–30
Jefferson Memorial, Washington, DC, 123, 128–31, *129,* 153
Johnson, Philip, 1, 7, 44, 106, 107, 108, 110, 117, 149, 213; "The Seven Crutches of Modern Architecture," 232–33

Kahn, Louis I., 149, 152, 228
Kelley, Earl, *Education for What is Real,* 224–25, *225*
Kennedy, Robert W., 133
Kepes, Gyorgy, 218, 223
Kiley, Dan, 93, 94, 97, 100
Killam, Charles, 75–76
Kimball, Fiske, 36, 129
Kocher, Lawrence, 44, 72, 78, 149
Krier, Leon, 30–31, 212

Landsberg, William, 112
landscape architecture, 61–63, 94, 103–4; at Harvard, 54, 61–64, 93–104. *See also under* Gropius, Walter; Hudnut, Joseph
Lawrence, Ellis, 47
Lawn Road Flats, London, 70, *71,* 98
Le Boutellier, George, 202, 205, 206, 235
Le Corbusier, 2, 6, 31, 32, 38, 39, 98, 108, 110, 160, 161, 237
legal realism, 46
L'Enfant Plan for Washington, DC, 130
Lescaze, William, 128, 133
library, Robinson Hall, Harvard University, 56–58, *56*
Lincoln, Massachusetts, 79, 106, 112, 181, 236
London: Bauhaus émigrés in, 70–71, 82; Gropius in, 70–74
Lorch, Emil, 15, 17–18
Lyman, William, 201, 224

Manning, Warren, 93
MARS (Modern Architectural Research Group), 71, 74, 105
McHarg, Ian, 228
McKim, Charles, 19, 38
Mies van der Rohe, Ludwig, 3, 44, 64, 65, 68, 69, 107, 110, 111, 125, 140; considered for Harvard professorship, 69, 78; Hudnut's opinion of, 67, 69, 141, 230
Minority Report of the Harvard Committee on Regional Planning, 90–91

MIT (Massachusetts Institute of Technology), 51, 60, 147, 175, 213, 228, 235
Mock, Elizabeth, 137, 149
Moholy-Nagy, Lázló, 70, 74, 78, 115, 145, 147, 218, 223
Moholy-Nagy, Sibyl, 115
monumentality, 133–34, 135
Moses, Robert, 192–94, 197
Mumford, Lewis, 6, 14, 36, 91, 94, 97, 119, 123, 124, 133, 149, 160, 164, 175, 189, 194
Museum of Modern Art, 3, 5, 44, 65, 75, 132, 137, 141, 144, 146, 148, 149, 159, 180

Nagel, Charles, 201
National Capital Park and Planning Commission, 131
National Commission of Fine Arts, 132, 135, 137, 141
National Gallery of Art, 131, 132
nature and modern architecture, 130, 161, 184, 185–86, 231–32
Nerdinger, Winfried, 20, 115
Neutra, Richard, 149, 161
New Deal, 46, 156, 158, 184
New Empiricism, 6, 175–76
New Republic, 128
New School for Social Research, 43
Newton, Norman, 185, 200, 206, 221
New Towns, 88, 195–96, 197
New Urbanism, 25
Noyes, Eliot, 133

"Objectives of a General Education in a Free Society," 222
Oechslin, Werner, 29
Olmsted, Frederick Law, Jr., 24, 62, 63–64, 128
"Opinion on Architecture, An," 176, 180, 182
organicism in modern architecture, 130, 139, 217, 232; Associazione per l'Architettura Organica, 217
Oud, J. J. P., 6, 44, 65, 105, 125

Parker, Stanley B., 212
Parsons, Talcott, 192
Pei, I. M., 1, 7, 180, 201; GSD student project, *168*
Peets, Elbert, 27, 31, 61, 63, 128
Pencil Points, 35, 76, 96, 97, 98, 99
People's Institute, 25, 38
perception, visual, 224–25
Perkins, G. Holmes, 13, 51, 70, 79, 89, 103,

116, 133, 149, 153, 166, 181, 192, 200, 202, 211, 227; house (Brookline, MA), *117*
Perry, William, 57
Pevsner, Nikolaus, 108, 123
Planning I (GSD course), 202, 208, 220
Pond, Bremer, 54, 60, 63, 78, 93, 100, 103, 104
Pope, John Russell, 129, 130; Jefferson Memorial, Washington, DC, *129*
postmodernism, 6, 173, 212
postwar house, 170, 172, 173, 181
prefabrication, 19, 167–68, 182–84
preliminary course. *See* Basic Design (GSD course)
Pritchard, Jack, 70, 71, 73, 74, 224
progressive education, 3, 41–42, 43, 55–56, 79, 85, 139, 144. *See also* democratic education
publicity and modern architecture, 68, 119, 124, 125, 129, 134, 137, 141. *See also* Gropius: as propagandist; Hudnut: as propagandist
pure design, 15, 16

Read, Herbert, 74; *Education through Art,* 223
regionalism, 6, 95, 174, 189
regional planning, 62, 189
Ring, Claire (Hudnut) 18, 235, 236
Rockefeller Foundation, 62, 87
Roosevelt, Franklin Delano, 132, 155, 156, 158
Rose, James, 93–96, 100; *Modern American Gardens,* 94
Ross, Denman W., 15, 17, 241n17
Rudolph, Paul, 1, 106, 108, 149
Ruhtenberg, Jan, 44

Saarinen, Eero, 133–34, *136,* 137–41, 149; Crow Island School (Winnetka, IL), *140;* Kleinhans Music Hall (Buffalo, NY), 138, *139*
Saarinen, Eliel, 13, 133–34, *136,* 137–41; Crow Island School (Winnetka, IL), *140;* Kleinhans Music Hall (Buffalo), 138, *139*
Sasaki, Hideo, 201
Saunders, Walter, 143
Scully, Vincent, 186
Seidler, Harry, 110, 181
Sert, José Luis, *119,* 120, 146, 149; *Can Our Cities Survive?,* 146, 233; as Harvard GSD Dean, 233–35; urban design at Harvard, 234–35
Shand, P. Morton, 70, 74

Shepley, Henry, 133
Simo, Melanie, 52, 103
Site and Shelter (GSD course), 88–89
Smithsonian Gallery of Art, 131, *136,*
    141, 152, 153; competition for, 132–38;
    Hudnut's ideas for, 134–35; jury, 133,
    134, 135
Stein, Richard, 106, *111,* 133, 180
Stern, Robert A. M., 32, 212
Stonorov, Oscar, 145, 147
Storrow, Helen O., 181
Stubbins, Hugh, 1, 108, 117–18, 133, 149,
    153, 166, 185, 200, 221, 222–23, 228
symbolism in modern architecture, 137,
    173, 237

Task, 147, 178–80, *178, 179*
teamwork. *See* collaboration
TAC. *See* Architects Collaborative, The
    (TAC)
Tugwell, Rexford, 157, 158, 193
Tunnard, Christopher, 5, 94, 95, *100,* 149,
    175, 185, 189, 200, 254n63; drawings/
    buildings, *101; Gardens in the Modern
    Landscape,* 96, 98, 99, *101;* at Harvard,
    97–104, 126, 180

United Nations building, 152, 153
University of Chicago, 90; architecture of,
    140; President Colwell, 140–41
University of Michigan architecture pro-
    gram, 15; Hudnut at, 17–18
University of Pennsylvania, 51, 149, 228
University of Virginia, 36–37
Unwin, Raymond, 92, 159–60, *160*
Urban Design Conferences (Harvard), 234

variety in modern architecture, 168,
    170–72, 195
Venturi, Robert, 228, 237
von Moltke, Willo, 180
Vorkurs. See Basic Design (GSD course)

Wachsmann, Konrad, 167
Wagner, Martin, 5, 29, 92, 116, 126, 157,
    159, 162, 165, 166, 182, 189; Berlin-Britz
    Horseshoe, *87;* city planning ideas,
    88–89, 185–86, 195–97; at Harvard,
    86–90, 184–86, 187, 189; on housing,
    162, 165–67, 173, 182–84, *184;* relation-
    ship to Gropius, 89, 173–74, 176
Washington (DC) Mall, 123, 131, 135
Weinberg, Robert, 235, 236
Wheaton, William, 166
Williamsburg, Virginia, Hudnut criticizes,
    212
women at the GSD, 200–201
Wood, Edith Elmer, 157
World War II, 92, 108, 158, 200; impact on
    universities and colleges, 103, 200–
    201; and modern architecture, 186
Wright, Frank Lloyd, 106, 217
Wright, Henry, 43, 159
Wurster, William, 5, 36, 133, 147, 149,
    175, 230

Yale University, 102, 103, 149
Yorke, F. R. S., 82

Zevi, Bruno, 6, 175–77; on Gropius,
    216–18; on Hudnut, 217–18; *Metron,*
    217
Zucker, Paul, 229–30